More Advance Praise for *Instant Appeal*

"I was truly blown away after reading Vicki Kunkel's new book. Not only does she supply strategies that almost any business can immediately use in its marketing efforts, she explains why they work in a deep, satisfying way. More importantly, the information in this book is evergreen and not based on some new marketing fad. This is the kind of book that ends up dog-eared with yellow highlights all over the place in a very short period of time!"

> —Michael Lovitch, CEO, The Hypnosis Network,
> www.hypnosisnetwork.com

"Reading Vicki Kunkel's *Instant Appeal* is a must. Whether you want to market yourself, your products, or your business, you have to read this book. She has mastered the understanding of what gets a person to act when it comes to making a purchase. If you want to increase your profits, you'll make this book your marketing bible!"

> —Kurek Ashley, international peak performance coach and best-selling
> author, *How Would Love Respond?*

"If your business is persuading people, changing minds, building brands, or creating consensus, this book will change your life. *Instant Appeal* reveals the scientifically proven secrets of human behavior that make your success in advertising, marketing, sales, and negotiation simple, predictable, and profitable."

> —Dave Lakhani, author, *Persuasion: The Art of Getting What You Want*
> and *Subliminal Persuasion: Influence and Marketing Secrets They Don't*
> *Want You to Know.*

"Spellbinding. This book includes strategy after strategy that you can immediately use to understand why people do what they do and apply it to develop your own persuasive power. An incredible read. You won't be able to put it down."

> —Kenrick Cleveland, persuasion coach

"Vicki Kunkel has done a great job with this book. It is fresh, insightful, and entertaining to read, but most of all it is practical with applicable information that will make a dramatic difference for you in your journey to success."

> —Douglas Vermeeren, achievement expert, film producer, and creator of
> the movie *The Opus*

"If you've been looking for ways to attract more business, more influence, or more kudos, you just found some exciting answers!"

—Rich Fettke, author, *Extreme Success*

"Clearly, Vicki Kunkel is a teacher at ease with her subject as she convincingly provides her readers with an entirely new way of looking at the root causes of human interaction. This is a must-read for any aspiring elected official."

—Michael D. Bishop, Senate Majority Leader, Michigan State Senate

"Amazing, outstanding, and exceptional. The information in this book totally blew me away. Vicki Kunkel not only understands primal appeal completely, but can also communicate it in such a way that the rest of us can understand and benefit from it. Everyone who sells a product, a service, an idea, or even just themselves (in other words, all of us) should own this book. Those who do will make more money, serve others more effectively, and have more friends and a lot more fun."

—Bob Burg, author, *Endless Referrals*, and coauthor, *The Go-Giver*

"Vicki Kunkel gives us the science, insights, and statistics behind what it takes to create instant appeal and make the factors of attraction work for you and your business. This brilliant book is interesting, informative, based on solid research, and a must-read for anyone wanting to gain influence and attract others to their offerings like a magnet."

—Dr. Joe Rubino, founder, CenterForPersonalReinvention.com, and creator, SelfEsteemSystem.com

"Instant Appeal is both brilliantly insightful and entertaining. It will show you how to use primal persuaders to make yourself stand out in a competitive marketplace and enhance your success. It's a must-read!"

—Debbie Allen, author, *Confessions of Shameless Self Promoters*

"This book teaches you about evolutionary psychology as it applies to business today. By cultivating the characteristics of instant appeal, you can pretty much guarantee that you'll never experience rejection again. Vicki's book is interesting, engaging, and, well . . . appealing. You owe it to yourself and your business to read it—and APPLY it—today."

—Rachna D. Jain, Psy.D., author, *Overcome Rejection: The SMART Way*

INSTANT APPEAL

The 8 Primal Factors
That Create Blockbuster Success

VICKI KUNKEL

AMACOM

American Management Association

New York • Atlanta • Brussels • Chicago • Mexico City • San Francisco
Shanghai • Tokyo • Toronto • Washington, D.C.

Special discounts on bulk quantities of AMACOM books are
available to corporations, professional associations, and other
organizations. For details, contact Special Sales Department,
AMACOM, a division of American Management Association,
1601 Broadway, New York, NY 10019.
Tel: 212-903-8316. Fax: 212-903-8083.
E-mail: specialsls@amanet.org
Website: www.amacombooks.org/go/specialsales
To view all AMACOM titles go to: www.amacombooks.org

This publication is designed to provide accurate and authoritative information in
regard to the subject matter covered. It is sold with the understanding that the
publisher is not engaged in rendering legal, accounting, or other professional service.
If legal advice or other expert assistance is required, the services of a competent
professional person should be sought.

Various names used by companies to distinguish their software and other products can
be claimed as trademarks. A list of trade and service marks in this book can be found
on page vi. AMACOM uses such names throughout this book for editorial purposes
only, with no intention of trademark violation. All such software or product names are
in initial capital letters or ALL CAPITAL letters. Individual companies should be
contacted for complete information regarding trademarks and registration.

Library of Congress Cataloging-in-Publication Data

Kunkel, Vicki.
    Instant appeal : the 8 primal factors that create blockbuster success /
Vicki Kunkel.
        p.   cm.
    Includes index.
    ISBN-13: 978-0-8144-0946-6 (hardcover)
    ISBN-10: 0-8144-0946-6 (hardcover)
    1. Success in business.   2. Success.   3. Consumer behavior.   4. Interpersonal
relations.   I. Title.
HF5386.K8794   2009
658.4'09—dc22

                                                                        2008033513

Printing number

10   9   8   7   6   5   4   3   2   1

TO MY PARENTS
Ralph and Darlene Kunkel

Trade and service marks found in *Instant Appeal*

1-800-COLLECT
Absolut Vodka
Amazon
America's Next Top Model
American Girl
American Idol
AMP Agency
AOL
Apple
Barbie
Barnes & Noble
Beauty and the Geek
Best Buy
Billboard
Borders
Budweiser
Burger King
Cabbage Patch Kids
Campbell Soup Kids
Cap Snaffler
Charmin
Chicago Cubs
Circuit City
Compete.com
Craigslist
Dancing with the Stars
Disney
Donald Trump
Dr. Phil
Dramamine
*E.T.: The Extra-
   Terrestrial*
Elle magazine

Epcot
Frys
Garfield
Google
*Harry Potter and the
   Deathly Hallows*
Heroes
iPod
Ixquick
James Bond
Jaws
Jericho
Jumbotron
KFC
Levi's
Long John Silver's
Lord of the Rings
M&M's
Magic Kingdom
Martha Stewart
Mattel
McDonald's
Michelin Man
Mickey Mouse
Microsoft
Monopoly
Mountain Dew
MSNBC
MySpace
New Balance
Nike
Oprah
Panera Bread

Pepsi
Pillsbury Doughboy
Pizza Hut
Playboy
PowerPoint
Pringles
PT Cruiser
Risk
Rocky
Scott
Scrabble
Showtime Rotisserie
Shrek
Snickers
Star Trek
Starbucks
Subway
Survivor
Taco Bell
TelePrompTer
The Apprentice
The Game of Life (Life)
The Tonight Show
Time
Top Chef
Trikke
Trivial Pursuit
Ugly Betty
Uglydolls
Wendy's
Whole Foods Market
YouTube
Yum! Brands

Contents

An Introduction to Instant Appeal

Judy was depressed. She recently left her six-figure C-suite executive job at a large downtown financial services company that she held for over 15 years to start a boutique furniture store. It boasted high-end, ultramodern couches, chairs, tables, end tables, nightstands, and art in a hip section of the city. As we sat eating lunch, she told me the reason for being so bummed: Six weeks after her grand opening, she hadn't sold a single piece of furniture.

"I don't know what's wrong!" Judy sighed. "I did my market research and the products and pricing should be right in line. The people who come into the store seem to be the right demographic. What's going on? I know the economy isn't the greatest right now, but my customers have a pretty healthy disposable income. I can't afford not to have this work out! I put everything I have into this."

As she talked on, she told me that customers would come into the store, walk around the entire space, even stop and, as she said, "look at something, pretending to be interested," then would ultimately leave without buying anything.

Because I had helped her former company successfully implement primal branding techniques—marketing strategies that align with our innate preferences and fixed primal triggers—she thought I may be able to offer some advice. But the first thing I needed to do was visit her store.

On a bright, sunny Saturday afternoon, I walked up the sidewalk to her storefront. The signage was fantastic, the curb appeal was great, and the window displays were well done. As I stepped across the threshold, a perky sales clerk bounded up to me. "Welcome! My name is Susan. Is there anything in particular you're looking for today?"

I explained that I hadn't been to the store before and was "just looking."

"Oh, okay. Well, if you need anything, my name is Susan. Just come and find me. Here's a brochure to look at in the meantime. And again, my name is Susan."

I hung out for a while near the front door to see how Susan greeted other store visitors. After about ten minutes of observation, I had a pretty good idea of what was causing Judy's customers not to buy. It had to do with lizards. That's right. Lizards.

When certain lizards encounter a foreboding predator, they have a peculiar way of fleeing. They don't just run and hide. Often, the lizard puts a lot of bravado into its escape. He actually lets the predator know where he is by thrashing around and making a lot of noise as he runs—often passing right by potential refuges before hiding.[1]

Why? To signal to the predator that there's no need to chase the lizard, because he has the ability to escape. The lizard is in effect saying to the predator: "Here I am. Catch me if you can, but because you can't, don't even bother."

That noisy and long escape dance is an innate response. The lizard didn't think about it and it's not a learned response; he instinctively knows that his best defense is to make the predator think it can't catch him. It's a primal trigger within the lizard that causes him to react the way he does to predators. That's not unlike the innate reactions customers had to Judy's sales reps.

Susan and her sales colleague, Bruce, did the same little welcoming ritual with each store visitor that Susan did with me. The customer reactions were fascinating—and universal. When Susan or Bruce simply said, "Welcome. Is there anything in particular you're looking for today?" customers would usually smile and pleasantly say, "No, just looking," or "No thank you." But something happened when the sales reps continued with the rest of the spiel ("If you need anything, my name is Susan/Bruce. Just come and find me. In the meantime, here's a brochure."). The customers would raise their voices slightly (making more noise), take on a more terse tone, and walk more quickly—*away* from the sales rep. But they didn't just turn and walk out of the store, they—as Judy had described—would make one round around the store first. As they were walking away from Susan or Bruce, they would usually curtly say something along the lines of, "I'll let you know if I want anything," or "Oh-KAY!" A few were terse with words as well as tone: "Let me guess; you're on commission." They were letting the sales associates know that they couldn't be "caught" and wouldn't put up with a pushy sales rep. In every case the customers' tone got terser, and they walked away from the sales associate as fast as they could. Only a handful took the brochure that was offered.

Judy's customers—and the lizard—all exhibited what ethologists call a fixed action pattern (FAP) response—an intricate sequence of behaviors set in motion by a trigger feature. A trigger can be specific words, sounds, colors, actions, visual patterns, gestures, or even the beauty or ugliness of a person or object. An example of a fixed action pattern response is yawning; when we see someone yawn, we almost always yawn, too. But it's not the yawner who makes us yawn; it's a yawning *trigger* within each of us that makes us yawn. This innate, genetically programmed trigger feature gets switched on every time we see someone yawn. The yawning trigger is not a learned behavior— just as the customers' reactions to Susan and Bruce were not learned behaviors—but instead part of a primal trigger response mechanism. A salesperson who is trying too hard is a predator to a customer. And, just like the lizard, customers run from the predator—in this case, the sales associate.

When I told Judy that her welcoming-committee-on-steroids was chasing away customers because of the negative fixed action pattern response that they triggered in store visitors, she was stunned. She told me that the main reason she wanted greeters at the door was to make sure every customer was personally handed a brochure that they would take with them. Fair enough. But rather than create a negative fixed response, why not create a positive fixed response in her customers? Judy wanted to know how to do that. To illustrate, I gave Judy a one-question multiple-choice quiz. I asked: Which of these statements would you most positively respond to if you were a customer coming into the store?

(a) "Please take a brochure. It has information about our store that we'd like you to have."

(b) "May I offer you this brochure because we'd like you to have more information about our new store?"

(c) "This brochure contains more information about our store. May I offer you one?"

"I liked the second one," Judy said.
"Why?"
"Uh, I'm not sure. It just sounds better for some reason."

The reason option (b) sounds better to Judy is because of another primal fixed response, this one in reaction to a specific trigger word—a word that instantly induces an innate and automatic response

In his book, *Influence: The Psychology of Persuasion*, Robert Cialdini, Ph.D., talks about a famous experiment conducted by Harvard social psychologist Ellen Langer. In her 1978 study, Langer set out to see under what conditions people would allow her to cut into a long line at a copy machine. She tested four different ways of asking permission.[2]

Here are the first two:

"Excuse me, I have five pages. May I use the Xerox machine?"

"Excuse me, I have five pages. May I use the Xerox machine because I'm in a rush?"

Only 60 percent of the people asked let her cut in line with the first request. But when she provided a reason as to why she wanted to cut in line, 94 percent allowed her to cut in.

Langer wanted to see if the *reason* or simply the word *because* was the trigger that caused people to grant her the favor. So she decided to try the experiment again, using the word *because* and citing a not-so-good reason for wanting to cut in line. Here's what she asked:

> *"Excuse me, I wonder if I could ask you a favor. May I skip ahead of you in line because I have to make some copies?"*

The reason was not a good one, because everyone in line had to make copies. Yet 93 percent of the people she asked let her skip ahead of them in the line. Even when the reason is bogus, the trigger word *because* elicits an automatic and innate response to grant the favor! The response mechanism to this trigger is so engrained that even a silly reason gets a positive response in many cases.

Judy had her sales associates offer customers a brochure and use the word *because* in the request. Store visitors seemed more receptive to the sales associates, and they browsed the store in a more leisurely manner.

But it wasn't enough just to have the sales associates use the trigger word *because* in their greeting as customers came in the door; they also had to make sure they used it in their sales pitches to customers. Simple phrases such as, "You'd really like this couch because it is made of Italian leather," or "This glass table would look great in your home because the design will go with any décor," resulted in a 39 percent increase in sales in just the first two weeks that these primal trigger words were used regularly with customers.

Trigger words are part of what I call the *instant appeal response*: positive, predictable actions that people take in response to a specific trigger. Cialdini talks at length in his book about the fixed action pattern response. But there's more to instant appeal than FAPs. And this book is not about FAPs at all. (Dr. Cialdini explains FAPs far better than anyone else could!) I bring up FAPs here only to illustrate that much of our response to things in our environment is the product of anthropological conditioning and is rooted deep in our DNA. Instant appeal taps into many other primal secrets—such as human universals—that have been previously unexplored in the context of mass appeal.

USING INSTANT APPEAL TO DRAW A CROWD

The instant appeal response is especially prevalent in a new type of product pitch that has been catching on in many parts of the country. The other day I was in the Sears store on State Street in Chicago. As I was walking through the store, I heard a bit of a commotion on the north side of the store. When I moseyed over, I saw a crowd of about 100 customers standing, mesmerized, all watching a slim Asian woman up on a stage with lighting and set design that could rival almost any professional theater setup. The audience buzzed with excitement and people pushed closer and closer to the stage as the show went on. I'd never seen anything quite like this in a store before. This woman had the audience completely eating out of her hand. Was this woman doing a comedic monologue? A one-woman play? No. She was pitching a microfiber dusting cloth. That's right: All the fuss and excitement was over something that you would use to do plain old boring, uninspiring housecleaning.

If you can imagine a live, in-store infomercial, then you can pretty much get the idea of the type of pitch she was doing—complete with cheesy jokes that no one laughed at. Yet people were buying. *Lots* of people were buying. Right there on the spot! About 60 percent of the people who were at the "show" that I watched walked away with a packet of two large dust cloths for $24.99. One well-dressed, middle-aged woman who seemed like the type who wouldn't be taken in by such cheesy sales pitches practically knocked over a teenage girl as the woman shoved and pushed her way to the stage to be the first to get her product.

Why would about 100 people take around 20 minutes out of their busy days, out of their shopping trips, to stand around and watch what amounts to a live infomercial for a product that isn't even all that inspiring? What made the saleswoman's spiel so appealing? It certainly wasn't the features and benefits of the product. I've seen nearly identical products at other stores for about the same price. Her secret: a cleverly orchestrated performance that included four specific anthropological triggers that make us buy. Yes, even those corny jokes that no one finds funny are one instant appeal factor that triggers us to buy.

Through her performance, this woman masterfully changed—albeit briefly—the biology of the people in the audience through the specific words she used, the exact body language movements she made at precise times, and even the carefully choreographed ways that she handled the product. Each audience member's neurons were firing in a different way when they watched her "show" than they would when watching a traditional sales pitch. And had she done any one thing differently in her presentation—such as not holding the product a certain way—her audience wouldn't have bought into her, or the product.

The woman was an actor working as an independent contractor for a company called US Jesco—a "retail-tainment" organization. What it does is set up stages in retail outlets throughout the country and put on shows that blend retail salesmanship and entertainment showmanship. But again, this isn't just an entertainment show: It's an appealing show with primal factors that not only engage and entertain people, but get them to whip out their wallets on the spot.

This company is very deliberate and exacting in how it trains the people who put on these shows. Every word is scripted. Every movement is carefully directed. Nothing is done by chance. A simple head turn when saying one word, a raise of the hand when saying the phrase "right now," or turning the product package in a certain way at just the right time activates that part of the brain that controls the trust response and urges us to happily open our wallets. Make no mistake: Infomercials—whether in person or on TV—are based on hard science in anthropology and biology. Those cheesy jokes that no one laughs at serve a primal purpose. Without those bad jokes, we wouldn't buy. You'll learn why in chapter 2. In chapter 8 you'll learn how activating "mirror neurons" through your movements during a presentation can trigger an instant and positive reaction. Most reality TV shows are successful because they have mastered the mirror neuron trigger.

Most of us think about how to become more appealing with our sales pitches, our product designs, or our speaking skills. But the biological and anthropological triggers that make us stick to products are the same ones that make us stick to ideologies—even buy into crises that aren't. For example, disease threats are especially susceptible to instant appeal.

THE ASIAN FLU "PANDEMIC"

In November 2005, Americans were worried about their Thanksgiving turkeys. The Centers for Disease Control and Prevention (CDC) couldn't field calls fast enough from people wondering if they should ditch the traditional holiday bird in favor of beef, fish, or vegetarian fare. Some callers also asked if they should take down their backyard bird feeders.[3] The level of concern over the avian flu reached bizarre proportions at times, such as when a Nashville woman asked science writer Wendy Orent why we "don't just kill off the domestic birds and poison the food on the migratory bird routes."[4]

The U.S. Senate jumped on the panic bandwagon with a $3.9 billion package to buy vaccines and antiviral medications, and the administration asked for an additional $6 billion to $10 billion to fight the bug.[5] Oprah dedicated a full show to the disease. Every major media outlet in the United States, as well as many in Canada and Great Britain, ran long feature stories about the massive threat this horrifying disease posed to humans.

But in reality, so far there have been only 383 cases of avian flu worldwide, and 241 deaths over the past five years.[6] That's an average of 48 deaths per year *throughout the entire world*! And not one single case or death was in the United States. Additionally, the current strain of H5N1 avian flu virus has rarely jumped from human to human (except in cases of lab handling), and not commonly from birds to humans either. Yet we're still convinced it's an important threat.

Certainly the avian flu isn't the only non-pandemic to become a believed pandemic by people across the globe. In early 2004 beef prices in the United States dropped, foreign nations refused to accept beef exports from the U.S., many people stopped eating beef, and there were widespread calls for the government to increase surveillance of cattle herds. The reason? Bovine spongiform encephalopathy (BSE)—otherwise known as mad cow disease. The sickness is caused by eating the tissue from the nervous systems of afflicted cows. So far, there have been only about 195 cases *worldwide*, with only two in the United States.

We bought into pandemics that weren't. We got stuck on the idea that mad cow disease and the avian flu would do us in. But why? Both of these diseases combined account for an average of fewer than 90 deaths per year worldwide over the past five years. While we're all in a tizzy about these manifested "pandemics," we have to be cajoled into getting flu shots (even though 36,000 people die each year in the United States from the common flu), we eat artery-clogging fast food (heart disease kills 700,000 Americans annually), and we continue to drink alcohol (there is a death from an alcohol-related car crash every 30 minutes in the United States).[7] Logic—and facts—tell us to be more concerned about these real threats. Yet we consistently disregard facts and are neurotic about minute threats to our health. What is it that makes us fear diseases that we have an almost impossible chance of contracting, yet we give real threats to our health a passing yawn? Why are some disease threats "stickier" to us than others?

Scientists tell us part of the reason is that we literally become physically addicted to news stories that have certain characteristics and that appeal to certain primal instincts. As the chapters of this book unfold, you'll be able to identify just what those factors are that make some pandemics—and some news stories—get such a strong reaction from us, while others make us yawn.

USING COUNTERINTUITIVE TRIGGERS TO GAIN RESULTS

As mentioned earlier, words and actions aren't the only primal triggers that elicit a specific and predictable response. In this book, you'll learn the eight main triggers of instant appeal and why they have such power over us. You'll discover myriad counterintuitive factors that influence our decision making and how you can use those to advance your own career, cause, or company. For example:

➤ Oprah is popular for the same reason that Mickey Mouse and Cabbage Patch Kids are adored by millions. (The "Kids" celebrated their 25th birthday with a big bash in Times Square in September 2008.) There is a strong link among the design of Mickey, "the Kids," and Oprah's packaging. If you incorporate this one primal instant appeal factor, you too can gain the allegiance of millions.

➤ British researchers followed national elections in the United Kingdom, United States, and Australia, and what they found is that they could accurately predict who would win those elections based on only two things: the face shapes of the candidates and whether the country was at war or peace during the election. They did this in the 2000 and 2004 U.S. presidential elections, as well as several elections in other countries. Apparently our primal programming has us hardwired to elect a specific type of face in war and another type of face in peacetime. What does your face say about *your* leadership abilities? And what can you do if your face shape isn't the shape that people expect from someone in your position? You'll find out in chapter 3.

➤ *Harry Potter* novels, Agatha Christie stories, Beatles songs, and Norah Jones's chart-topping album all contain the same addictive linguistic elements. (Interestingly, a study completed in February 2008 explains why so many people are having withdrawal symptoms after finishing *Harry Potter and the Deathly Hallows*.) Use these linguistic elements in your ad copy, and you could reap huge rewards.

➤ If you seat your audience in a semicircle, rather than the traditional "classroom rows," you'll get better reviews of your speech. It's because the semicircle corresponds to our anthropological preferences. What other innate preferences do you have that determine everything from the success of a restaurant to the reason we buy more hand sanitizer whenever the terrorist threat level is raised in the United States?

➤ Every time you choose a table in a restaurant, you are deciding where to sit based on a deep-seated (pun intended!) primal pull. This pull also affects the productivity of office workers in cubicles.

➤ Less attractive women are promoted faster than beautiful women in higher-status jobs, but the pretty women get preferential treatment over their less attractive counterparts in lower-paying jobs.

➤ Your company's name—and even your name—has a large impact on your potential for success. Researchers have found certain vowel-and-consonant combinations literally change our DNA and activate the part of the brain associated with pleasure and motivation. By changing even one letter in your company's name, you could change just how appealing your company becomes to customers.

CREATING ALLEGIANCE CAPITAL
The Importance of Appeal

Instant appeal is about the seemingly illogical hidden codes of attraction: the eight factors that can make one product, movie, song, or persona a hit—and another a flop. It's about the completely counterintuitive elements of attraction—such as why we believe in pandemics that aren't, why design flaws intentionally built into toys and certain products make them *more* appealing to the public than competitive products that have no such flaws, or why a bumbling speaker can be more bewitching in times of crisis than a silver-tongued orator.

Instant appeal helps us understand our seemingly contradictory reactions to scenarios that seem to be identical on the surface: why millions of people across the country have an unfortunate unbreakable allegiance to the ever-losing Chicago Cubs (winless at least at the time of this writing), while some winning teams can't fill their stadiums; why Americans fell in love with big houses and big SUVs and at the same time embraced pocket-sized electronics and tiny teacup dogs; why moderately talented (or in some cases *un*talented) reality stars are propelled to stardom, but classically trained artists with better voices can't find a following; or why we spend millions of dollars per year on weight control and beauty procedures, yet research shows that we prefer the average and plain over the pretty. It helps explain why we *say* we want experienced politicians and campaigns that don't sling mud but often elect candidates with the least political and international experience as president of the United States—and we nearly always elect the candidate who slings mud.

Instant appeal explains the popularity of icons and why some celebrities become media darlings and others media targets. It's part of what makes a movie a hit or a new product a must-have. It explains why the shape of the Absolut Vodka bottle triggers our primal pleasure response. It explains why Elvis remains popular even after his death, and why Judy Garland was able to have 42 successful comebacks in her career. Appealing personalities project hidden codes that produce instant, biological, and anthropological unconscious connections. Persuasive people and products literally produce chemical changes in our bodies that, in turn, change our biology and our reactions to a person or product.

THE FOUNDATIONS BEHIND THE EIGHT INSTANT APPEAL FACTORS

Contrary to popular belief, persuasion is not mostly psychological; it's anthropological and biological. Most of us aren't consciously aware that we are making choices based on thousands of years of evolutionary conditioning and our biological makeup. What makes us comfortable is embedded deep in our DNA.

Do you get irritated when people talk on cell phones in public? That reaction is caused by our evolutionary inclinations based in early tribal development. Why was the board game Scrabble a flop when it debuted in 1948, but just three years later when the exact same game was reintroduced, it became an instant hit? The answer is that the second product launch appealed to one of our primal motivators, while the first one appealed only to psychological factors. Why do Google, Apple, and Microsoft have little trouble attracting and retaining top-notch employees, while other companies struggle with keeping their best and brightest? That's because these three companies do one thing on their job application sites and in their employee programs that appeals to one specific human universal. What do the runaway success of *E.T.: The Extra-Terrestrial*, Oprah, and Cabbage Patch Kids have in common? You've guessed it: They all appeal to one specific primal preference. Throughout this book, I'll uncover the details behind each of these scenarios. But I bring them up now to illustrate the power and pull that primal motivators have on mass appeal.

To give you a quick example of how we make choices based in our anthropological conditioning every day, consider this scenario: Let's say you stop by a restaurant for lunch. It's not a particularly busy day at the restaurant, so when you walk in, the hostess says to feel free to sit where you want. Most of the seats in the restaurant are open. There are booths and some tables along the perimeter of the restaurant, and most of these seats are next to windows. Then there are tables in the center of the room. Where do you sit: in the center of the room, or in one of the seats around the perimeter? If you're like most people, you'd head for the booths. In all cultures across the globe, people would almost unanimously choose the seating areas around the perimeter of the room and near a window. This inclination to sit near a window or at a table located around the perimeter is what's called a "human universal": a preference that occurs in humans across all cultures. Anthropologists have identified over 200 of these human universal preferences, and they affect everything from where we want to sit, to what type of car we buy, to the face shape of people we choose for a president, and the type of person managers promote. When people, places, products, and pitches align with those human universals and primal preferences, we feel comfortable.

The second part of the instant appeal equation is *biological* persuaders. Biological influence is about activating the reward center of the brain. To put it simply, this reward center has two components: wanting and liking. When we see something we want, the dopamine center of the brain lights up. For instance, the dopamine receptors of morphine addicts became very active when the addicts were shown drug paraphernalia while undergoing functional magnetic resonance imaging (fMRI) brain scans. The same thing happened when scientists looked at the brain activity of gamblers when they were shown a deck of cards. Whenever we want something—whether it's a piece of pie, a person, or a *Harry Potter* novel—our dopamine receptors light up and trigger a craving response. Identifying what activates this craving response is a powerful part of *Instant Appeal*.

Attraction that creates unbreakable loyalty is the "liking" part of our internal reward system. When we enjoy something, the pleasure part of the brain—the opiate circuit—becomes active. This is what causes a release of chemicals that creates "runner's high," along with the same feeling of pleasure we get when we listen to our favorite music or watch our favorite TV shows. To create biological addiction to a product, person, or ideology, the key is to create a cycle of wanting and liking in the reward center of the brain.

To illustrate the biological pull, suppose it's mid-afternoon and you're having a bad day at the office. You decide to go for a healthy snack and eat a bag of bite-size carrots. But your body and brain still feel blah and your mood hasn't improved. You received no internal reward, no "high" from eating the carrots. So, you reach for a bag of potato chips. While you are eating the chips, you feel comforted. Your mood improves. You feel emotionally much better. And, as the popular saying goes, "you can't eat just one"; you keep reaching for more and more chips.

Neal Barnard is a nutrition researcher and president of the Physicians Committee for Responsible Medicine. He says sugar, chocolate, meat, and simple carbohydrates—like potato chips or French fries—all spark the release of opiate-like substances that trigger the brain's pleasure center and seduce us into eating them again and again.[8] People, products, and even literature can be just like potato chips: They create an opiate-like response in our brains and seduce us into wanting more. So this wanting-and-liking cycle continues and keeps us literally addicted to a product or person. We keep going back to it again and again.

Scientists have proved that Agatha Christie's novels triggered the release of endorphins—those feel-good chemicals—in the brains of her readers. We felt good when we read her novels, so we wanted more and purchased the next one. Five of the top Beatles songs and Norah Jones's #1-selling debut album *Come Away with Me* also activated the pleasure (the liking) part of the brain. Another study has shown that *Harry Potter* novels activated the dopamine centers of the brain—the craving or wanting part. Each of these addictive items used two specific techniques to create these biological changes in our bodies that made us feel as if we couldn't get enough of these artists. (You'll learn about these in chapter 7.) These biological codes of attraction transcend logic and communications and explain how our primal wiring decides if we either buy into an idea (or song or person or story) or dismiss it (or the person) out of hand.

Just about everything that we like and want is based deep in our DNA; it comes from our primal conditioning, which is why the anthropological and biological motivators are so closely linked. Instant appeal isn't about charisma or communication skills or mavens or connectors; it's about creating a powerful binding force at the primal and biological levels that results in unwavering allegiance to a person, a cause, or a product for the long haul. It's about a new approach to mass appeal that I've spent years researching and testing with my political, legal, corporate, and creative clients. These secret codes have the power to transform anyone into a celebrity or business icon with staying power. They have the power to propel a product to front-runner status. *Instant Appeal* lays out the specific stimuli that trigger our anthropological comfort filters and our biological addictive pathways and keep us hooked.

When we can decode our primal conditioning and our biological reactions to external stimuli—along with human universals that drive our behaviors—we can create what I call "allegiance capital": the ability to cement long-term loyalty. How much allegiance capital a company or person has is directly proportional to the effectiveness in using anthropological and biological triggers. When you understand that, you uncover the powerful codes that cause us to be enraptured by some people and things and disenchanted by others.

When you understand the codes outlined in *Instant Appeal*, you'll understand how to mobilize large groups of people—whether it's a nation, a company, or a community. You'll know how to get heard, how to get people to stick with you for the long term, and how to propel your career to new heights. You'll become a more persuasive person and know how to get the support of co-workers for a pet project or a promotion. Product-design engineers will be able to incorporate some of the *Instant Appeal* codes to create products that enjoy unparalleled popularity.

THE EIGHT INSTANT APPEAL FACTORS

So just what are these eight primal factors that will help you achieve instant appeal? They are:

1. The conspicuous flaw factor
2. The visual preprogramming factor
3. The reptilian comfort factor
4. The sacred cow factor
5. The jackass factor
6. The biology of language factor
7. The biotuning factor
8. The mental real estate factor

One chapter each is devoted to these eight instant appeal lures. The exception is chapter 5, which deals with two intertwined primal triggers.

In chapter 2 ("The Conspicuous Flaw Factor"), you'll discover why your flaws can be one of your best assets to achieve success, and why we are programmed to like failure. Chapter 3 ("The Visual Preprogramming Factor") explains the phenomenon of how we subconsciously cannot accept a person, place, or product that doesn't have a visual "look" that aligns with our primal programming.

Chapter 4 is a bit different: It deals not with one specific factor, but a *category* of instant appeal factors called human universals. Although I'll talk about specific universals throughout the book as "subfactors" to the main primal persuasion factors, chapter 4 is dedicated to the core universals, or the ones that are most commonly used by marketers, politicians, savvy speakers, and product manufacturers.

In chapter 5 ("The Sacred Cow and Jackass Factors"), you'll find out how to create instant and long-term loyalists by taking a firm and vocal stand on your most sacred ideologies. But perhaps more importantly, this chapter provides several examples of how political correctness robs companies of productivity and how—in at least two instances—it was downright deadly. The reason this chapter covers two instant appeal factors is that having a sacred cow without a jackass factor, and vice versa, results in no appeal or persuasive ability; to be effective, the sacred cow and jackass factors need to work together. You simply can't have one without the other.

Chapter 6 takes you on a journey through the biology of language factor and clearly demonstrates how certain words, phrases, stories, and plot lines trigger subconscious reactions that create an unbreakable bond in mass audiences. Then chapter 7, "The Biotuning Factor for Career Success," takes it a step further by talking not just about mesmerizing language, but also about spellbinding sounds and sound-wave patterns that are responsible for making some speakers and songs a hit, and others a flop. Finally, chapter 8 reveals the secrets behind the magnetic appeal of the mental real estate factor—or how you stage your personal brand.

These eight instant appeal factors are important because these techniques are the very ones that can make a difference in the big world events—and the events in our everyday lives. When you know the codes, *you* can create unwavering allegiance among the public; *you* can rally almost anyone to your cause, your case, your company, or your ideals—*you* can be "scandalproof." If you want to fast-forward your career, advance a cause, or avoid being duped into buying into someone else's dogmas, then *Instant Appeal* will be a fascinating exploration for you.

Most similar books on mass appeal and stickiness focus only on the psychological or communication aspects of persuasion, but *Instant Appeal* shows how our reactions to stimuli are embedded in our DNA and are more biological, primal, and anthropological than psychological. This book clearly demonstrates that there are universal codes of appeal that have worked from medieval times to modern times and can be applied to everything from politics to pop culture and consumer products.

Throughout this book I'll lead you on an intriguing journey through cutting-edge research in biology and anthropology to reveal the secrets to high-octane persuasiveness and mass appeal used by today's business icons, A-list entertainers, top-notch lawyers, major league sports teams, newscasters, and powerhouse politicians. *Instant Appeal* is about who gets heard, what gets our attention, who and what has staying power, and why. And it gives you a road map of how you can implement the eight primal factors to propel your career to new heights.

CHAPTER 2

Ducklings, Defects, and Devotion

⟶ THE CONSPICUOUS FLAW FACTOR

If you could change anything about your appearance, what would it be?

I often ask this question at my seminars, and most people respond with "lose a few pounds," "not be bald anymore," "have rhinoplasty to make my nose smaller," or "make my butt smaller."

But the thing these people don't know is that their flaws—a few extra pounds, a bigger-than-normal-nose, or baldness—may be *helping* their career advancement, not hurting it. Most people often try to hide or change the very qualities that research has proved could land them better jobs and help them climb the corporate ladder faster.

As contrary to conventional wisdom and logic as it may seem, physical flaws, it turns out, create an instant appeal to others. Now, I know you're probably having a hard time believing this. (I know I did when I first started researching what made people and products sticky, or appealing, with entire societies. That's why I wasn't satisfied with just one or two studies that touted the increased success potential of the average and even the somewhat ugly.) But stay with me awhile as we explore some case studies, some history, some current events, some scientific research, and some product failures and successes that bear this out.

We're duped into believing that the pretty, the pristine, and the perfect get all the perks, all the breaks, and all the glory. Just pick up any fashion magazine and you'll find beauties gracing the covers. The media certainly perpetuates the idea that beauty is good. We've all read the stories of how the pretty are treated better in social situations,[1] get jobs more often over equally qualified unattractive applicants,[2] and that, once hired, they get more raises and promotions[3] and receive better performance evaluations[4] than their physically "blah" co-workers.

But that's not quite the whole story. It depends upon what *type* of job you're going after, what *industry* you're in, and *just how far up the corporate ladder you want to go*. In short, if you're going after a nonmanagement or lower-paying job and you're a woman, good looks *will* get you the job over a less attractive candidate. But if you're a good-looking woman looking to land either a top management position or a job in a high-powered industry, your attractiveness is a proven *detriment* in getting hired.[5] In typical male-dominated occupations, the more attractive a woman is the less likely she is to be judged as qualified and, therefore, the less likely she is to be hired, according to one study.[6] (In chapter 3, I'll highlight several research studies that explain other biological reasons why the unattractive get hired more often for high-powered jobs than their pretty counterparts, and I will talk about unconscious *expectations* of physical appearance that we have for certain people and professional positions. But for now, just know that beauty can be a real beast for those hoping to climb the corporate ladder—whether you're a man or a woman.)

The career-climbing power of the not-so-pretty—whether you're a man or a woman—was highlighted in a decade-long study of CEOs, actors, musicians, and authors. Richard St. John wanted to find out if there were common factors that successful people shared. He found that average-looking and even "unattractive" people achieved a higher level of success in all fields than physically beautiful people. St. John interviewed more than 500 professionals in more than 20 occupations over a ten-year period for his book, *Stupid, Ugly, Unlucky and Rich: What Really Leads to Success—and It's Not Smarts, Looks or Luck*. He says we have it all wrong when we think of the typical super-successful person:

> *My production company had just finished casting auditions for a CEO part in a movie when I decided to attend a conference*

with the top 100 CEOs in the nation [United States]. As I looked around the auditorium, I said to myself, "I wouldn't cast any of these people as a CEO! They're all below-average looking and certainly don't fit my image of what high-powered, success- ful CEOs should look like!" That piqued my curiosity, so I started talking to these high-powered types. As I started inter- viewing these people, I learned that their less-than-attractive appearances were actually one part to their success.[7]

St. John found that having the look of an average or below-average Joe or Jane lowered the defenses of most people, which made others more likely to help these semiducklings in their quest for success. He interviewed people like Martha Stewart and Bill Gates to get some insight. He found that our image of the powerful, pretty, and preten- tious millionaire is about as far away from reality as you can get.

"AVERAGE" FACES ARE PREFERRED TO "BEAUTIFUL" FACES

Solid, scientific research also quashes conventional wisdom that beauties get all the breaks. In 1990, two University of Texas at Austin researchers found that people overwhelmingly rate "average" faces as more pleasing and attractive than "beautiful" faces.[8] The researchers took photos of 32 beautiful faces and 32 ugly faces, mathematically averaged them, then digitized them to create 32 "average" faces. His- panic, Asian, and Caucasian faces were used in the experiment. When 300 adults were asked to rank the attractiveness of the 96 male and 96 female faces (32 beautiful, 32 ugly, and 32 average), the average faces were overwhelmingly judged as more attractive. (All but three of the male average faces and all but four of the female average faces were judged as more attractive than the beautiful faces.) Two other studies, one done in 1970 and another in 1982, also found a prefer- ence for average faces over beautiful ones.[9]

Why do we prefer the average? The University of Texas scientists hypothesized that individuals with features close to the mean of the population are viewed as less likely to carry genetic mutations and, therefore, we unconsciously see them as being "normal" for our species. Beauty, in other words, is seen as a deviation from the norm and a genetic defect. It's interesting that these studies were done across cultures and over three decades, and all found the same preference for average over beautiful. Average as beauty is timeless, universal, and appealing.

There are many biological, historical, and anthropological reasons why we prefer the flawed to perfect beauties. But before I get into that, let's look at how we view handsome or beautiful politicians. It's not how you may have guessed!

BEAUTY AND POLITICS
The Look of Trust

Faces that most closely match the classical Greek idea of beauty—a symmetrical face where the features are in perfect mathematical proportion—are the ones that raise our defenses the most. This rare form of beauty is associated with oppression: In ancient civilizations only the privileged could have beautiful art and sculptures. And only the privileged could afford to look beautiful. The opposite of perfect symmetry is, by definition, asymmetry. So when people appear slightly out of proportion, slightly off in some way (having a degree of ugliness to them, if we are to consider only perfect symmetry as beautiful), we give them a mental thumbs-up and a nod of support. The average or not-so-pretty people elicit strong feelings of trust and comfort, which is why they have an easier time gaining the allegiance of multiple groups.

This was driven home in a 2004 experiment that my company conducted for a state-level political candidate who was running a tight race in the Midwest. His opponent was formidable in appearance: tall, lanky, with sort of a Tom Brokaw air about him. My candidate looked more like George Costanza on *Seinfeld*. Our goal with the experiment was to find out just how much of a handicap, if any, my client's less-than-dapper appearance would be in appealing to voters. (We'd all been brainwashed into believing the media hype that voters want a pretty-boy candidate.) Specifically, we wanted to identify who would have the upper hand among potential voters when it came to perceptions of trust, kindness, intelligence, and morality—a hunk or a slightly-below-average Joe. Because we work with a lot of different clients, we wanted to do a survey that could have applications outside of politics. So rather than simply doing a typical focus-group session where we would ask people how much they trusted, respected, or supported a specific candidate, we set out to do a more generalized test on the relationship between trust and general physical appearances.

Our first step was to define what type of person voters would universally consider handsome or beautiful. To do that, we looked at the research of Dr. Stephen Marquardt, a reconstructive surgeon in Southern California who believed that beauty could be quantified. Since the 1970s Marquardt has been compiling measurements of beautiful faces of movie stars and models. According to Marquardt, the "perfect" face isn't a creation of Hollywood or advertising agencies but is actually based on a simple mathematical formula known as the Golden Ratio. Beauty, it turns out, is not in the eye of the beholder but in a mathematical calculation.[10]

To picture the Golden Ratio, imagine two lines: The first one is one inch long, the second, 1.618 inches—or just over an inch and a half. The ratio of these two lines, 1 to 1.618, is the Golden Ratio. The face of perfect beauty is one where the distance between various facial features—such as from the tip of the nose to the chin, the top of the head to the pupil of the eye, and so on—fit the Golden Ratio.[11] Jessica Simpson has this so-called perfect beauty ratio. So do George Clooney and Paula Zahn.

Marquardt didn't invent the idea of the Golden Ratio, but what he did do was apply the formula to human faces and quantify the subjective quality of beauty. He developed a mask that represented the perfectly symmetrical face. What's interesting is that when Marquardt's mask was superimposed over the faces of hundreds of beauty models, it fit perfectly—even across cultures! As it turns out, what is considered beautiful is constant, even among different societies.

Because his research provided a clear-cut, quantifiable definition of beauty, we set out to apply the Golden Ratio to subjects in our experiment. We looked for 20 men and 20 women whose facial structure and features most closely conformed to the mathematical parameters of perfect beauty. To do this, we gathered over 100 headshots from local modeling agencies and began meticulously measuring the distances between a dozen key facial features. Then we did calculations on those measurements to see how closely the face of each model mirrored the perfectly symmetrical face. All of the headshots chosen were of models whose numbers either matched or almost matched the Golden Ratio. These became our "beauty" control group.

Once we had our "perfect beauties," we set out to find physically flawed folks to use as our comparison subjects. We went to the streets and solicited people to come into our studio for headshots. Because human beings don't fall neatly into only two physical categories—beautiful or ugly—we divided the photos from this group into four categories: attractive (but not meeting the Golden Ratio standard of beauty), average, unattractive, and very unattractive. For our experiment, we decided our comparison group would include candidates from only the "average" and "unattractive" categories. These people were categorized based upon how far away the ratio of their facial measurements fell from the Golden Ratio of perfection. In other words, the more asymmetrical the face, the further away it was from perfect beauty.

We went a step further than just facial asymmetry when forming our comparison group. We selected candidates who also had some sort of conspicuous physical flaw—a big nose, big ears, bug eyes, or some other type of clearly visible imperfection—so even the faces with average symmetry could be considered to have an "unattractive" conspicuous flaw. These people were by no means ugly, but they clearly weren't runway-model gorgeous, either.

Now it was time to set up the comparisons. We developed a series of 20 split-screen images—on one side we had our perfect beauties and on the other side our flawed average-or-below-average-looking folks. To avoid any gender bias, we only compared men with men and women with women. Various races were included as well: paired comparisons included African-Americans, Asian-Americans, Hispanic-Americans, and Caucasians. Even though we used headshots and not full-body photos, we also had each pair dressed nearly identically and placed in front of the same background to rule out any possible subjective impressions that may have been made based on attire or environment. All people in the photos had neutral expressions—they weren't smiling, smirking, or frowning. All models from both our Golden Ratio group and our flawed group were between 22 and 56 years old.

Finally, we brought in 423 survey participants between the ages of 18 and 64. These people came from varied backgrounds and held various positions, from receptionists and stay-at-home moms to retail sales professionals, CEOs, and even four medical doctors. We included all body and facial types in our survey group, too: the fat, the thin, the bald, the perfectly coiffed, the fashion conscious, and the fashion challenged. The group was almost equally split between men and women (207 women, 216 men).

The study participants were asked to write answers to four questions:

1. To which of these two individuals would you feel more comfortable giving the keys to your house?
2. Which of these two people do you think would be better at solving problems that required critical thinking?
3. Which of these two people do you think would be more likely to go out of his or her way to help a complete stranger?
4. If you loaned each of these people $50, which one do you feel would be more likely to pay you back?

Keep in mind the participants knew nothing else about the people on the screen; what they saw was all they had to go on. They had no idea of the jobs, education, or upbringing of the people in the pictures. The results? Sixty-seven percent of the survey participants trusted flawed folks more than beauties with the keys to the house (by a vote of 283 to 140) and 71 percent said unattractive types were more likely to help out a stranger (according to 299 of the 423 participants). But here's the really fascinating result: A whopping 82 percent, or 346 of our survey participants, considered those with conspicuous flaws to be a far safer bet to loan money to than the beautiful people! Apparently we trust the average-looking among us more than the swans to be moral, helpful, and honest.

Now, this was by no means a scientific survey and I realize there is a large gap between how people say they would react in a given situation and how they would actually react. (This is an inherent problem in focus-group studies.) Still, the results of our little experiment mirrored not only what happened in the state-level campaign that I was working on but also what occurred in the 2000 and 2004 presidential elections: Al Gore and John Kerry came across as too-handsome con men against the average-looking Bush. His comical-looking big ears were a conspicuous flaw often magnified in caricatures. Americans not only felt they could trust Bush to do the right thing, but they also felt a Darwinian-like need to rally behind and protect him—the unattractive (by classical standards) underdog—against the more aristocratic, handsome, and intelligent Gore and Kerry. (For other reasons George Bush had such strong mass appeal, especially in the 2004 election, see chapters 3, 5, 8, and 9.) It's also interesting to note that in the years after Gore's failed presidential bid, after he put on weight and became "less perfect," Americans and the world have embraced him. He is now more like one of us, and we are ready to accept him in a new role as world teacher on global warming.

In the 2008 presidential primaries, Mitt Romney's dapper good looks and smooth speaking style made it difficult for voters to believe what he was saying and trust him. (If you followed the primaries, you may remember that Mitt Romney consistently trailed in the polls.) Sure, the pundits will tell you it was Romney's policy positions that made Republicans uncomfortable. But, based on my extensive research on the impact that a candidate's face shape has on voters, there was also a very strong primal repulsion among voters to his near-perfect appearance and speaking style.

In a follow-up session we queried the survey participants about why so many of them thought the beautiful people were less likely than either average-looking or unattractive types to pay back the loan. The comments all ran along three themes: (1) participants thought the average to unattractive types looked like "salt of the earth people" who were "hard workers" and "wouldn't cheat anybody," (2) they felt the unattractive types would feel a stronger need to prove themselves trustworthy, and (3) the group thought the more gorgeous types looked as if they would try to "finagle their way out" of paying back the loan or "thought they could charm their way out of it."

As one average-looking woman told us, "People who are exceptionally pretty or handsome often think they're entitled to everything and have probably always had people giving them a break, so they just expect it. It's no big deal to them not to pay someone back a small amount like that." A very attractive man from the group—who was a dead ringer for Pierce Brosnan—added, "I think there's sort of a 'Garth syndrome,' you know, the 'I'm-not-worthy' thing. Unattractive people probably have a harder time getting things in life, getting people to do things for them. So when someone finally does give them a break, they're more likely to appreciate it and feel a stronger need to prove they were worthy of the kindness. That's why I ranked the unattractive people in the pictures as being maybe more honest."[12]

Clues to the amount of allegiance a political candidate may have with the public can also be found by studying caricatures. Because my company works with politicians, we're always scouring traditional and electronic media sources for political caricatures. These amusing drawings can tell a lot about how well a politician may be received by audiences. Depending upon which facial feature is exaggerated in the drawing, viewers will either feel more comfortable with the person, or less so. Usually candidates who are depicted with softer, rounded lines will trigger more positive emotions than those drawn with harsh, sharp lines. And if there isn't a prominent flaw emphasized, audience appeal will also be diminished.

It's interesting to note, too, how caricatures of Al Gore have changed with his post-election popularity. Sketches of him now emphasize his newly expanded girth; he is now human in both his appearance and his presentation style. We seem to like Al Gore much better now that he's not quite so perfect.

Caricatures of the two leading Democratic presidential candidates in 2008—Hillary Clinton and Barack Obama—both are reassuring to our reptilian brain. Drawings of Hillary are usually sketched with disproportionately round cheeks (a trait that makes us feel comfortable), and sketches of Obama typically overexaggerate his jutting chin; some of the caricatures show him with big ears (neither of these traits align with the Golden Ratio of perfect beauty, and this comforts the reptilian brain).

"HE'S TOO FAT TO BE GUILTY"

For a 43-year-old murder defendant in the Midwest, instant appeal—and specifically the conspicuous flaw factor—occurred with jurors the moment he stepped into the courtroom. Six years ago I was providing communication consulting on this case. The defendant was a five-foot-nine man who, roughly estimating, would have tipped the scales somewhere close to 210 pounds. He was accused of fatally shooting his wife after she was allegedly found cheating on him with two other men. His fingerprints were on the gun, he had no alibi, he was in the house the night of the shooting, and neighbors had testified the two were "having marital troubles." When the case went to the jury, it took only 47 minutes to return the verdict: not guilty.

The prosecution was, to say the least, flabbergasted. Although there is no such thing as an open and shut case, the evidence was clearly in the prosecution's favor. So what happened? Primal conditioning, that's what. One question we had written into a post-trial juror survey provided the insight into what went through the juror's minds as they watched the defendant during the trial: "We realize that you used evidence and the facts of the case to make your decision, but what other factors, if any, entered into your decision? Please list and explain your answer in detail."

Nine of the 12 regular jurors and two of the alternate jurors said the man wasn't capable of murder. Most of the explanations focused on his appearance and ranged from "he just seems too nice" and "I think this man is like a big teddy bear" to this one: "He's too fat to be guilty 'cause fat people are easygoing, at least more easygoing than skinny people." My client couldn't believe what he was reading! But I've personally seen this phenomenon while consulting on many court cases; jurors almost always believed an overweight defendant couldn't possibly be capable of committing a premeditated, violent crime (although juries do overwhelmingly think such a person could commit a crime of negligence). It's not just round physiques that make the reptilian brain feel secure. Our primal programming also makes us more comfortable around people with bigger-than-normal noses and chins, gapped teeth, or myriad other minor physical defects.[13] (I'm not talking grotesquely ugly here, but rather the little conspicuous physical imperfections.) In short, it is the "average" or somewhat plain person whom we want to rally behind—people who have flaws just like us. Contrary to what most of us believe on a conscious level, we really don't want to be around beautiful people, because we don't fully trust them. If a person has features that our historical experiences and primal conditioning deem threatening—like extreme beauty—we run away or, at the very least, keep our distance because we feel inferior and vulnerable in his or her presence. If he has comforting features—some sort of chink in the armor or vulnerability about him—then we want to hang out with, help, and support him. Physical perfection elicits a bow, imperfection a group hug.

THE COMMERCIAL APPEAL OF UGLY

Ugly reared its commercial head in 1982 and has hooked us ever since in everything from toys and dogs to pop culture. It was that year that a wrinkle-faced, hairless, bug-eyed alien waddled into the hearts and minds of millions. At the time of its release, *E.T.: The Extra-Terrestrial* was the highest-grossing film in history.[14] The fictional alien with an appearance that Steven Spielberg called "something only a mother could love"[15] was seemingly everywhere in pop culture—from commercials and public service announcements to books and songs.

The same biological and anthropological triggers, or primal codes, that made millions of us fall in love with E.T. also sent millions more into a worldwide frenzy just a few years later. At department stores across America, mobs trampled pregnant women, toppled display tables, and even caused "a minor earthquake" where "plate glass windows shook" as they tried to get their hands on the prize at one Vermont store.[16] Half a world away in Tokyo, the arrival of this same item "triggered a stampede," according to local newspapers. What was the precious gem these throngs were after? Chubby, dowdily dressed dolls described as "so ugly they're cute" by a leading toy-industry magazine. By 1984, sales of these Cabbage Patch Kids hit a record 20 million and a year later went to one billion.[17] And even today, after a late 2004 re-release of the doll, the Kids are still being made and still selling steadily to both children and adults.[18]

As shoppers made a physical stampede to stores in Vermont, Tokyo, and myriad other cities across the globe, television viewers made an electronic stampede to Channel 7 in Chicago every morning at 9:00 A.M. The lure? An overweight, coif-challenged, African-American woman who did what was unthinkable on a talk show in the 1980s: cry. At a time when stoic journalists with pretty faces and perfectly sculpted "helmet hair" graced news and talk shows, Oprah Winfrey's extra weight, nonconformist hair, and folksy style helped propel her show from last place to first in the Chicago ratings within just three short months of going on the air. (In its first month, the show was ranked even with *Donahue*, hosted by Phil Donahue. Three months later it had inched ahead.[19] Shortly thereafter, her show went national and she garnered the adoration of fans in all parts of the country and eventually the world.)

Scientists who study the evolution of "visual signaling" say we're hardwired to be attracted to anything that either appears itself to be physically vulnerable or makes us feel less vulnerable.[20] This code of attraction often manifests itself as a readily apparent conspicuous flaw, as it did in E.T.'s bug eyes and clumsy walk, the Cabbage Patch Kids' disproportionately large heads and pudgy limbs, and Oprah's weight. Of course, each of these mass-appeal icons has several other qualities that make them attractive to the general population. But visual vulnerability is the first code that our subconscious tries to detect in the initial seconds of meeting someone or something new; and it helps us decide if that person or thing threatens either our security or sense of identity, or makes us feel comfortable.

Throughout this book I refer to a field of anthropology called "human universals": things that people across cultures find universally appealing or comforting. Successful companies and people understand and use human universals in nearly everything they do. According to researchers, a preference for physical flaws is one of those human universals.[21] People who exhibit some sort of visual vulnerability—baldness, big ears, or big hips, for example—relax our defenses and get greater support for their causes and their companies.

If Oprah had been thin and runway-model gorgeous when her show first debuted, viewers most likely would not have had such an instant, deeply rooted connection to her. She didn't look like a typical TV star; she just looked like one of us and we welcomed her with open arms because of it. After more than twenty years on the air, viewers continue to stand by her because she intentionally perpetuates her own visual vulnerabilities through clever visual signaling.[22] The new, improved, slimmer, more glamorous Oprah is careful to perpetuate her "ugliness," lest we shun her because she's too threatening to our own confidence. She strategically "uglies herself up" from time to time—such as when she appeared in her bathrobe on international television wearing no makeup.[23] By doing so, she makes herself once again appear vulnerable to us—even though she is one of the wealthiest and most powerful people in the world. If she came off as too pretty or too polished, she'd tarnish her brand as representing "everywoman," and her wealth and power would be perceived as oppressing rather than admirable.

MAKING MICKEY AND TEDDY MORE LOVABLE

Another icon—Mickey Mouse—became less perfect (and more lovable) as he aged because Disney designers knew the power of a flawed figure. If you look back at the evolution of Mickey Mouse, you'll find a number of changes in his physical appearance.

When he first debuted in 1928, Mickey's face and limbs were in proportion to the rest of his body (a symmetrical appearance is considered unappealing to the mass consciousness, as I've already discussed). But along about 1947—just as the famous rodent's personality was evolving to become more adult and well mannered—his appearance became more juvenile. Artists enlarged Mickey's head, exaggerated his ears, and also lengthened his pants from above the knee to down to his shoes.[24] This had the effect of making his limbs look shorter and pudgier (much like the short, pudgy appendages of Coleco's Cabbage Patch Kids in the 1980s). Our psyches didn't like a Mickey who looked too good and acted too mature. And just since 1990, Mickey seems to have expanded a bit more in his belly and hips (just as our waistlines are expanding). Mickey's evolution has made him more infantlike in his appearance and, therefore, more vulnerable. What is vulnerable is lovable.

The teddy bear underwent a similar transformation. Early teddies had long snouts and low foreheads, and their eyes, noses, and ears were, if not anatomically exact, fairly close in size and shape to those of an actual bear cub.[25] But over time the teddy bear's features changed: The eyes got bigger, the foreheads higher, and the noses shorter. And the buyers preferred these less realistic, yet more vulnerable-looking bears.[26] Companies go to great lengths to incorporate "flaws" into the design of many of today's hottest toys.

Contrast the look of Mickey and the teddy with the Barbie doll. Barbie is goddesslike and glamorous. She had a long run as queen of doll land. But with her perfectly proportioned body, beautiful flowing hair, hunky boyfriend, and supercharged career, she's also been the target of aggression—by adults and children alike. According to historical chronicles that detail the doll's story, some moms refuse to let Barbie into their homes, and others scoff in disgust at her unrealistic beauty and perfect lifestyle.[27] Barbie even raises the ire of young girls. Researchers at the University of Bath found that of all of the toys they tested, Barbie provoked the most negative emotions from girls—including hatred, rejection, and violence.[28] They found that Barbiemaiming was a favorite activity among some children: Girls apparently found a sort of comfort in decapitating, burning, breaking, and even microwaving Barbie.

The Barbie beauty backlash created a market for one of the hottest new doll creations of all time: The American Girl doll collection. When Kirsten—the first doll in the collection—was unveiled in 1986, she was the anti-Barbie. Kirsten didn't have a hunky boyfriend, a flashy sports car, a high-profile job, or wear high-heels; she wore a prairie dress and was an 1854 Minnesota pioneer. Kirsten and her prairie gal pals were plain and stocky (with larger, rounder heads; thicker waists; and shorter, pudgier limbs), yet they struck a nerve with a society that was fed up with unrealistic beauty and perfection.

American Girls weren't about flaunting their looks; they had stories to tell—stories about courage, values, and determination. Mattel, the toy manufacturer that owns both the American Girl and Barbie doll lines, has been expanding the American Girl concept to offset losses from falling Barbie sales. In the first quarter of 2008, Barbie sales were flat, while American Girl doll sales were up by 10 percent. This downward spiral of Barbie has been evident since the first quarter of 2005, when the company reported a 25 percent increase in sales of American Girl products and at the same time showed a 15 percent decrease in sales of Barbie.[29] The unpretentious American Girls have shoved the beauty queen right off her throne, and at the start of 2008 accounted for 6.8 percent of the entire revenues of Mattel.[30] Barbie isn't a doll you hug; she's a doll you revere from a distance. She's too perfect for comfort.

So, if we like imperfect creatures so much, how did Barbie become popular in the first place? It has to do with timing. Barbie debuted in the 1950s—just as Americans were exuberant over a strong postwar economy. We were on a national happiness high: We liked Ike, Alaska and Hawaii joined the Union, and Detroit unveiled audacious new cars featuring big, bold tailfins. When we're collectively feeling bold, daring, and brash, beauty doesn't threaten us as much. Barbie and her beauty were palatable right up until the early 1990s when sales began to slow to a crawl. You'll remember that the American Girl collection debuted and became popular in 1986—a time when the signs of a world economic recession were just starting to emerge. Large companies had flat profits, which were linked to a weak economy.[31] When we're having a collective crisis of confidence, we always revert to the comforting allure of the less-than-perfect—whether in the form of a leader, a teddy bear, Mickey Mouse, or the American Girl dolls.

But we don't have to be in a crisis mode for imperfect body types to be popular; they always have been. Roly-poly, less-than-perfect physiques have been part of some of the most successful and lovable brand icons, including the Pillsbury Doughboy, the Michelin Man, and the Campbell Soup Kids. Marketers for the companies that these mascots represented understood that our allegiance to such characters isn't just a passing preference; it's programmed in us through evolution.

BEAUTY AND FEAR
The History Behind Our Disdain for the Pretty

"Beauty is only skin deep, but ugly goes all the way to the bone."

While this age-old adage normally elicits a philosophical comparison between the superficiality of appearances and the depth of a person's character, there's another dimension to this maxim: Our attraction to the flawed individual is literally in our DNA and is part of our biological makeup, historical experiences, and primal conditioning. That conditioning has caused us to have a built-in fear of beauty. Author Donna Tartt alludes to it in her 1992 novel *The Secret History*: "Beauty is terror. Whatever we call beautiful, we quiver before it."[32]

Tartt's declaration isn't just fodder for fiction. Beauty has historically been associated with oppression. During the Christian uprisings of the third century, mobs tore down the beautiful sculptures owned by the aristocracy. To those mobs, beauty was equated with injustice, because only the powerful (and many believed ruthless) had the resources to get the exquisite structures. Beauty seemed to be mysteriously aristocratic, and the common people were only too happy to knock the marble gods and goddesses right off their pedestals.

While historical oppression is one reason we fear physical resplendence, our primal survival instincts are another, and if you want to use your flaws to your advantage, then it's critical that you understand the biology behind the appeal of the less-than-perfect. If you understand what triggers the reaction, you can position your conspicuous flaw in a way that it will be most appealing to our primal instincts.

When our ancestors met wild beasts, the fight-or-flight response kicked in and they either kept their distance or went on the warpath. The same thing happens to us today. Although we don't face lions and tigers as our ancestors did, we face another foreboding predator: the beautiful people among us whom we feel have the power to undermine us in some way. And we begin looking for the beastly qualities of beauty the moment we first encounter someone or something new. In those first few seconds of a first meeting, our subconscious mind begins an immediate search for conspicuous flaws in that person. The absence of any flaws—perfect beauty, in other words—raises a red flag of distrust in our unconscious. Everything that person says or does is suspect, and we don't let him or her into our world as readily as we would someone who is less lovely.

You may have experienced this phenomenon if you've ever met someone and said, "I can't put my finger on it, but for some reason I don't like that person." Certainly, part of your reaction could be due to the person's behavior. But your initial recoiling from that person had a lot to do with your feeling of security, and that feeling of security is controlled by the reptilian brain, otherwise known as the primal brain. It is our most basic brain and controls most of our decision making. Most people believe our neocortex—the center of logic and reasoning—controls our decisions, but that's just not true. No matter how logically sound a decision may be, if it doesn't "feel right" to us, if it doesn't make us feel safe and comfortable, we won't buy into it. And history and anthropology show us that we don't feel comfortable around people who are too pretty or too perfect.

Those same instincts that cause us to fear or distrust someone are the same gut reactions that help us decide if we're willing to put our faith and trust in that person. Evolutionary scientists say we're drawn to and comforted by people who have round faces, big ears, are a bit on the chubby side, and have little or no hair[33]—qualities that historically have been considered physical flaws in adults (although these same qualities are considered "cute" in infants and some animals).

So why do we subconsciously like people with those attributes? As mentioned earlier, it turns out we associate these traits with vulnerability—and anything that is vulnerable, we reason, can't be a threat to us. Think about babies: They're roly-poly, have little or no hair, and need our protection because they're vulnerable. We're hardwired to protect and trust the vulnerable among us. When we see an adult with one or more of these vulnerable qualities, our Darwinian programming kicks in and we immediately trust and support that person—even when reason tells us we probably shouldn't.

Dr. Phil is a much-loved and trusted TV personality—despite some questionable past dealings that include a 1973 Texas attorney general investigation that linked him to a possible health club scam.[34] In 1989, the Texas State Board of Examiners of Psychologists imposed disciplinary sanctions (including license revocation) against Dr. Phil for hiring one of his clients (he denied claims of a sexual relationship).[35] As of early 2008, Mr. McGraw's license to practice psychology has not been reinstated, according to an MSN news article[36] and state licensing agencies.[37] Even with these highly publicized negative events, millions continue to place their trust in the TV host. That's partly because his baldness and large, round features make him seem vulnerable, lovable, and trustworthy to us—even when we're presented with information that seems to the contrary. Physical flaws—and the image of vulnerability they project—override reason in many cases.

BEAUTY GETS THE BOOT

It's no wonder why we want to protect our ducklings and punish the pretty. Our primal conditioning to equate beauty with oppression—

coupled with the documented pain and suffering that beauty can evoke—makes us want to knock the beautiful people right off their pedestal, much as the Christian commoners in the third century knocked statues representing "perfect beauty" off their marble pedestals.

Nowhere is the backlash against beauty more evident than in show business. We rally around *Ugly Betty*'s America Ferrara, who won the 2007 Golden Globe for Best Performance by an Actress in a Television Series (Musical or Comedy), yet we shun the near-perfect beauties.

Susan Lucci is the poster child for the backlash against beauty. She's the sultry daytime superstar who has a long list of acting credentials. In addition to portraying the larger-than-life Erica Kane on *All My Children* for nearly four decades, she's appeared on the popular *Dallas* primetime series as a regular guest and took over for Bernadette Peters in the Broadway revival of *Annie Get Your Gun*. Despite her acting credentials, it took Lucci 18 failed nominations before she won an Emmy award.[38] She's not alone: Beauty has proved to be a formidable barrier for many actresses hoping to win acting's top daytime award.

Tom O'Neil, host of the awards-predicting website Goldderby .latimes.com, was interviewed in 2005 by Catherine Donaldson-Evans for a story on FoxNews.com. In that interview, O'Neil said that the pretty often get shut out when it comes to handing out the Emmy awards. "We see beauty punished in show business all the time. These people who have everything else—beauty, fame, paycheck gold—are being denied the trophy from their peers because something has to be withheld."[39]

Donaldson-Evans outlines the long list of Emmy-less beauties. Sarah Michelle Gellar received rave reviews for her starring role on *Buffy the Vampire Slayer*, but she couldn't capture the Emmy. Eva Longoria of *Desperate Housewives*, Courteney Cox-Arquette of *Friends*, and Kristin Davis, who played Charlotte on *Sex in the City*, all have watched as their castmates walked away with Emmys and Golden Globes, yet they went home empty-handed.[40] Sure, the co-stars of these beauties are also sexy and pretty, but not in the classic

Golden-Ratio way as are Longoria, Cox-Arquette, and Davis. It's interesting that even in a group of beautiful people, we still unconsciously pick out the ones that most closely conform to the perfect mathematical proportions of beauty and unwittingly snub them.

Oscars have gone to big-screen swans, but only those who manage to turn themselves into ducklings for a role—as Nicole Kidman did as the big-nosed Virginia Woolf in *The Hours*; or Charlize Theron, the very unglamorous serial killer in *Monster*; and Hilary Swank, the transsexual in *Boys Don't Cry* and the boxer in *Million Dollar Baby*. It seems as if Hollywood beauties need to get ugly before they can get Oscars.

UGLY AS A WEB-DESIGN ELEMENT

Each year, roughly 25 million different people flock to one highly popular website.[41] In fact, it's the seventh most visited site on the Internet.[42] This crowd-pleasing, virtual third space isn't a pretty place. Lines of cramped black-and-white text in boring Arial font are surrounded by little white space and no graphics. Even so, some estimates have this visually ugly site raking in revenues in excess of $55 million.[43] Craigslist.com breaks all the rules of "pretty" website design—no video, no fancy graphics, no color, and no whiz-bang animation. Yet this little-site-that-could is the leader of classifieds service in any medium. So-called "ugly" websites have proved they pull in more revenue, are stickier, and build better brands than flashy, whiz-bang sites of large companies.

Google is another example. It's not flashy and it's not pretentious, but it's profitable. And it's the most-used search engine on the Web, with 65 percent of the market share.[44] Granted, user-friendly navigation plays a part in the success of these sites. But there are beautifully designed sites that are simple and easy to navigate but still can't pull in the profits.

Why are Web users drawn to sites that are mediocre in design? Two reasons. First is our resistance to oppression. Collectively we assume that big companies are behind the design of aesthetically pleasing sites, and big companies, we fear, are out for nothing more than to make a fast buck at the expense of the average consumer. We trust things more when they look like they were done for the love of it rather than the sheer commercial value of it. Just as we instinctively trust people who are ugly or below-average looking, we also trust ugly marketing design more than the oh-so-pretty high-end sites. Second, anthropologists have identified "valuation of ugly" as one of the universal social tendencies across all human cultures[45]; it seemingly doesn't matter if you're in India or America, humans are drawn to the plain and even the unattractive on a very innate, basic level.

Slick websites, it turns out, are just like slick talkers: They turn us off. Somewhat bumbling speakers, on the other hand, can be bewitching. It's not only flaws in our physical appearance that can endear people to us, but flaws in our presentation and performance.

THE POWER AND APPEAL OF PERFORMANCE FLAWS

In a Chicago courtroom, an aging attorney shuffles about as he argues a patent-infringement case. His tone is passionate and his body animated as he presents point by point the reasons why the jury should find for his client. Throughout the trial, he constantly reminds jurors of the "six reasons" why his client was harmed by the defendant. Nearly every time he gives those six reasons, jurors desperately try to stifle a laugh: Just as he says, "There are six reasons . . ." he emphatically holds up five fingers. This same lawyer, in the same case, continually refers to his client by the wrong name when speaking to the jury. One time he'll call him Bob, another time might call him Brian, and so on. By the end of the trial his client has about a half dozen different names, much to the amusement of those in the courtroom!

The jurors in this particular case voted in favor of his client and bought into just about everything the lawyer said. They weren't the only ones, as a plethora of other juries and judges have been enamored with this somewhat scattered litigator over the years. A business acquaintance of mine who worked with this attorney was confounded over how someone who made so many gaffes in his presentations could gain the trust and allegiance of jury after jury.

Just like the deceptively slow-witted, fictional TV detective Columbo—who often lulled criminals into a false sense of security to the point where they actually helped him solve the crime—people who lack polish often disarm and endear themselves to audiences because they make us feel less threatened. Subconsciously we think, "Someone this bumbling couldn't possibly con me." This was part of George W. Bush's persuasive appeal when he went on national television to convince the nation that going to war was the right thing to do: His verbal fumbles played into our collective unconscious and had us believing that he was really just trying to do the right thing and that dull-witted Dubya couldn't possibly have the capacity to dupe us.

Remember why we want to stick to people who have conspicuous visual flaws? We feel safe with them because they are vulnerable and, in the process, they make us feel less vulnerable ourselves. The same is true with presentation flaws. When you consider that *The Book of Lists* has rated public speaking the number-one fear among humans— greater even than the fear of death, which ranks seventh on the list of fears[46]—you can begin to understand the kind of kinship we feel with people who don't have silver tongues. If you really think about this statistic, more people would rather be in the casket than giving the eulogy at a funeral!

This explains why the eloquent Al Gore and John Kerry were no match for the often inarticulate Bush when it came to gaining voter allegiance. Gore and Kerry had the ability to speak about topics knowingly and eloquently, and because of that they were perceived as too slick, too smooth, too professorial, and too preachy. We couldn't relate to them because they are good at the very thing we fear the most.

In a February 2002 news story, the *New York Times* said on its editorial page that "it's a quirk of Mr. Gore's speaking style that the more right he is, the more he irritates people."[47] Gore's very clear, concise speaking style was too perfect for voters, and perfection is, in the era of candid and unpolished YouTube moments, an unacceptable quality for a modern politician. There was an inverse relationship between how well Gore spoke and how much voters liked him. We may have rated him highly on the issues because he spoke so eloquently, but we didn't like someone so silver-tongued to lead our country.[48] Kerry suffered the same problem in the 2004 election. Were Kerry and Gore like fast-talking salesmen out to sell us a cheap bill of goods by giving us a detailed data dump? Voters weren't sure, but they did feel a sure thing with George Bush because his presentation flaws made him appear more genuine, less suspect, and more like one of us.

The popularity of speakers with conspicuous presentation flaws has grown over the past 20 years as well. This is most evident in television news: Americans, at least, are loyal to the newspeople who are not such smooth talkers. Anderson Cooper is a good example. When he first began anchoring duties for CNN, he struggled with reading a TelePrompTer, often stumbling over words, and saying "um" almost incessantly—two distinct no-nos in the old days of TV news. But audiences were drawn to Anderson because, despite his good looks and privileged upbringing, he still seemed down-to-earth and just like one of us in the way he spoke and in the way he seemed to genuinely feel our pain. That was most apparent during his coverage of Hurricane Katrina, when Cooper had an on-air emotional breakdown as he almost tearfully chastised Louisiana Senator Mary Landrieu for her insensitivity in congratulating her government counterparts for their response to the hurricane. We liked Anderson before, but now we loved him. (In a poll of media types done by CBS Marketwatch's Jon Friedman, Cooper was voted the biggest media star of the Hurricane Katrina coverage.) If Cooper had been an always-composed, stoic, silver-tongued news reader, then we wouldn't have liked him as much, and wouldn't have accepted him as a trusted news source. In fact, we may even have rejected him during his debut. But his current style, with occasional vocal bumbles and nervously interjected "ums," lulls us into a sense of trust.

BEING "TOO PERFECT" CAN HOLD YOU BACK

In the professional arena it's not only important but necessary to have a conspicuous flaw to get ahead. And if you're interviewing for a job, being "too perfect" or too well prepared can backfire.

One of my corporate clients learned that early in her career. She tells the story of how she unintentionally raised the ire of a job interviewer at a high-end audio-components manufacturing company because her job interviewing skills were *too* good.

> *I was filled with excitement and optimism as I sat in the conference room at the corporate headquarters (of a high-end audio-components manufacturer), waiting for the director of human resources. This was my fourth call-back interview for a corporate-level trainer position. I was sure I had the job; why else would they invite me back for a fourth interview? Surely this was the meeting where they would make me an offer!*
>
> *The man who held the power to put me on the payroll then entered the room. As he sat down and opened his notebook, he took a deep breath. He looked only at the paper in front of him while he began asking questions at a rapid-fire pace. After I answered all of the questions, he slammed his notepad shut in frustration, looked up and glared across the table at me as he said, "You're either awfully good or an awfully good con, I don't know which! I've been trying to trip you up in several meetings now and you seem to have a good answer for everything, don't you? Have you been coached? You must have, because no one is this good! Everybody messes up on at least one answer!" He abruptly concluded the meeting by saying he would be in touch*

with me via phone within twenty-four hours. I sat in stunned silence. The next day I got a reluctant job offer, which I declined.

The conspicuous flaw factor caused a riff in Janelle's professional relationship before she even got her foot in the door. She was "too perfect" in her interview responses and that triggered a sense of uneasiness in the interviewer.

I had a similar experience at my first news anchor job right out of college. For the interview process, I meticulously prepared my appearance (complete with well-tailored suit and obligatory '80s news-anchor helmet hair, sufficiently glued in place so even a tornado wouldn't move it). Prior to the interview, I rehearsed and re-rehearsed what I planned to say in the interview and how I planned to say it. After the interviews were over and I was told a few days later that I had the job, I was elated. *Yes! I was part of the newsroom "club"! I was in!* The anticipation of the newsroom camaraderie to come was intoxicating.

Then came my first day on the job.

As I settled into the swivel chair at my desk and sat trying to adjust my chair, the station's bubbly, red-headed senior news producer, who bounced rather than walked, came up to me with a big smile and a warm handshake. I liked her. (She was, after all, a redhead like me. And we redheads have to stick together!)

This producer welcomed me to the station, said how glad she was that I was there, and then told me I almost didn't get the job because the news director thought I was too professional in the job interview and that made the boss nervous. (Apparently the news director thought that everyone needed a chink in the armor somewhere, and if they didn't have that, then they couldn't be believed or trusted.) Apparently I owe my first television news anchor job to the station's general manager and to the producer, who both liked my interview and audition and eventually convinced the news director to hire me, even though she thought I was "too professional" and, therefore, apparently, too much of a threat to work with.

The lessons of these two stories are: Be prepared for the interview questions, look your best, but also make sure you show at least some little flaw. Otherwise, you'll come off as too perfect to be believable.

UNATTRACTIVENESS OR "AVERAGE BEAUTY" STILL HAS UNIVERSAL APPEAL

The appeal of all things with conspicuous flaws continues in popular culture. Advertising campaigns like Dove's "Campaign for Real Beauty," which features full-figured, curvy women instead of reed-thin models, celebrates the physical imperfections of the average woman. Reality TV has survived and thrived partly because we can't help but relate to the starry-eyed singer who can't carry a tune in a bag, or the celebrity who tries to dance but has two left feet, or the aspiring apprentice who makes a mistake that someone in Business 101 would know better to avoid.

One of the hottest primetime TV shows of the past two seasons, *Ugly Betty*, has tens of millions of fans who tune in every week,[49] while smart shows like *Studio 60*, with pretty cast members, stumbled in the ratings and lasted only eight months.[50] (In alignment with the universal human tendency to "value ugly," *Ugly Betty* is also an international hit: It's a top-rated show in nine of the ten countries where it currently airs. Germany, which has its own localized version of *Ugly Betty* called *Verliebt in Berlin*, cancelled *Betty* after *Verliebt* received higher ratings in the same time slot.[51]) A new line of dolls, officially named "Uglydolls," won the 2006 Specialty Toy of the Year award for their looks-that-make-you-go-eew design.[52] The Deerfield Beach, Florida–based company that makes Cabbage Patch Kids says they're ugly as ever, and they're bringing the kids back in a big way in September 2008. The kids will be reintroduced at the New York Toy Fair before they go into toy stores in the fall, and the company is expecting $30 million in sales from the Cabbage Patch Kids promotion.[53]

Our heroes are no longer Golden-Ratio-perfect types but conspic-
uously flawed, everyday people like the fictional Hiro Nakamura of the
hit series *Heroes*, or the character Mayor Johnston Green of ratings-
winner *Jericho*. The perceived lust some women have for physiognom-
ically challenged men prompted Ross Quigley to pen a book called *01
Lesson: Beautiful Women Prefer Nerds!* and inspired shows like *Beauty
and the Geek*. Fashion has even embraced ugly with Ugg boots, named
for their less-than-stylish design. Millions continue to buy bad-news
tabloids that detail the physical and character flaws of celebrities such
as a failed marriage, scandalous behavior, or a mystery illness that has
caused the growth of a second nose, a third ear, or some other bizarre
physical appendage. Good news gets passed by, bad (ugly) news gets
read.

And then there's Sam, the purebred Chinese crested hairless dog
that was the three-time winner of the "ugliest dog contest."[54] This
pooch with the hairless body, crooked teeth, and knobby head was an
international sensation, appearing on TV in Japan, radio in New
Zealand, newspapers in Britain, and a talk show in the United States,
where he met Donald Trump. A profile feature about Sam was one
of CNN's most popular stories of all time.[55] The dog received royal
treatment, staying in luxury hotels and occasionally traveling in limos.
Sam died in 2005, but people still make posts on a blog dedicated to
his memory.[56]

CHINKS IN THE ARMOR
Character Flaws and Failures That Lure Us In

A conspicuous flaw doesn't have to be physical or performance-related
to have appeal; character flaws are also alluring. Why? Because we're
a country that doesn't trust anything that comes too easily. Notice
how just about every superstar, celebrity, and politician has a back-
story that either includes a troubled childhood or a character demon
that the person continues to battle. And for the rich and famous who

don't have conspicuous flaws, they will never quite achieve the allegiance of the population at large. Gail Sheehy, in a *New York Times* editorial titled "Flawless, But Never Quite Loved," said perfection was Gore's Achilles heel: ". . . he lacks glaring flaws: no dark past, no drunken parent or dubious paternity, no private demons, no cheating at Harvard, no bad-boy brother or left-wing wife; alas, not even a Gennifer. How is the poor man to compete in the Politics of Personal Biography!"[57]

Barack Obama, who enjoys rock-star status as a politician, cleverly disclosed in his book *Dreams from my Father: A Story of Race and Inheritance* that he used cocaine in his youth. Obama either consciously or unconsciously realized that he needed to portray some type of flaw, some type of mistake he had made, in order to be accepted by voters. He's intelligent, handsome, articulate, suave, and successful, and without some blemish he would seem too perfect for us to embrace. He wasn't about to repeat the "perfect appearances" mistakes of Gore and Kerry. He also didn't wait for someone else to uncover his youthful indiscretion: He brought it front and center himself. Unfortunately, that's a key lesson that most politicians continue to miss: If they would just fess up to their mistakes, we would actually like and trust them more.

Another part of the conspicuous flaw factor is suffering. *USA Today* ran a story listing the 25 people whom we admire most and why they inspire us. People like Princess Di, Lance Armstrong, Mother Theresa, and Oprah were on the list. The common denominator of everyone on that list was that he or she had endured hardship in the fight for goals, or suffered through a crisis, or encountered some other major encumbrance. But the bottom line is that each did in fact suffer, and that made each of them more like us. People resonate with a common vulnerability that we all share.

Our distrust for perfection or things that come too easily continues to permeate our manufacturing systems, too: Some experts, such as G. Clotaire Rapaille—a market researcher and cultural anthropologist who has consulted for the likes of Chrysler, Procter & Gamble, and Boeing—says we have the technology to produce cost-effective products with zero defects, but our own beliefs prevent us from buying into it.[58] Perfection, after all, is the domain of those who oppress. Hence, we have become a "throwaway society" of imperfect products that last only a short time. This contempt for perfection-on-the-first try is also a universal trait across cultures; according to Carleton Coon, a Harvard-educated physical anthropologist, "problem-solving by trial and error" is one quality all cultures have in common.[59] Because humans historically have had to make several tries to get something right, it "feels right" when there are initial failures. To be sure, programs such as Six Sigma, Zero Defects, and Total Quality Management (TQM) have a goal of perfection. But the best that such programs can ever hope to achieve is incremental quality improvement, not total perfection. Even Motorola—the company that started Six Sigma—hasn't reached a zero-defects goal.

PRACTICAL APPLICATION
Finding Your Own Flaw Factor for Success

Does this mean you should rush out to get cosmetic surgery to make you look less attractive? Does this mean you should intentionally stammer and stutter in presentations? Should companies intentionally create inferior products with ugly packaging? Should you air all of your dirty little secrets in public? Of course not.

It does mean, though, that we should take a new look at how we view ourselves and see the marketable value in our own flaws. But how do we do that? What if we're fat? Or bald? Or not all that bright? How could those things possibly help us in our careers when so many other people out there competing for the same jobs are thin, beautiful, and smart?

The first thing we can do is to remember just how people process appearances. We have a mental "comfort filter" that looks for people and products that reflect who we really are: imperfect creatures. They're not looking for how perfect we are; they're actually looking to see how *imperfect* we are at first glance. Dove knew the power of conspicuous imperfections when it launched its "Real Beauty" campaign—which featured full-figured, curvy women instead of reed-thin models and celebrated the physical imperfections of the average woman. The ads were an instant hit with women everywhere.

Remember the University of Texas study that showed most of us prefer average-looking people over the pretty? Keep in mind that what is "average" changes with time; as baby boomers (still the largest segment of the population) age, they get bald, put on a few more pounds, and get a few more wrinkles. That's the new average. That's the new beauty. Disney execs knew this when they fattened up Mickey.

As individuals, we should not fret so much about our little imperfections, because they are actually helping us. Those tiny, albeit clearly noticeable flaws enhance our trust quotient with acquaintances and strangers alike. One of the most overlooked (yet most important) attributes of a personal brand identity for professionals is highlighting and then properly exploiting a conspicuous flaw. That flaw can be a physical flaw, a character flaw, or a chink in your skill level (such as George W. Bush's poor speaking ability). Identify your own "conspicuous flaw," your own weakness, and then embrace it, promote it, and celebrate it; after all, it's good for your career!

Perhaps no one knows this better than Padma Lakshmi, the award-winning cookbook author and host of Bravo's *Top Chef*. A serious car accident when she was 14 left her with a seven-inch, very conspicuous scar on her arm. That scar propelled her to a lucrative career in an industry where perfection is usually a prerequisite: modeling. She got modeling jobs *because of* that scar! Designers and photographers were drawn to her scar and did commercial shoots that prominently *featured* the scar. It hasn't hurt her personal life either. As she said in an interview on MSN.com: "Guys seem to love it. It makes me seem fleshy and rugged and human to them. And women respond to it too: It shows that not everything is perfect."[60]

Examples abound of other successful people who have benefited from their flaws. We all remember another famous model who turned an imperfection into a very lucrative trademark: Cindy Crawford and her mole. While other actresses and models were covering up similar facial flaws, Crawford made it a prominent focus in her photo shoots. And then there is Madonna and David Letterman, whose gap-toothed smiles are part of their charm. Finally, let's not forget Geek-in-Chief Bill Gates, who has managed to do pretty well by perpetuating his dorky demeanor.

But remember: Flaws don't just have to be physical.

SHOW US YOUR DIRTY LAUNDRY

Another caveat about conspicuous flaws is summed up best by the lyrics in a Don Henley song: *We love dirty laundry!*

When I am hired by CEOs to write speeches, they often want to keep their dirty laundry in the background—or not bring it up at all. But strategically airing parts of your (or your company's) dirty laundry in a public presentation can be completely captivating. Not just mentioning, but also *highlighting* the negatives endears you to the audience and engenders a greater degree of trust. When you show your foibles, you become human, more real, more like the audience members, and more believable.

Audiences are suspicious of speeches that don't contain any dirty laundry about you or your company; it smacks of PR, spin, and lies (or at least the omission of part of the truth). Plus, the negatives are more emotionally stimulating. I spent many years in television news and I can tell you that, hands-down, the stories that generated the most interest had two elements in common: suffering and suspense. It seems as if people get more energy, and more emotional satisfaction, from stories about hardship and evil than from positive stories. That's because struggles and setbacks force us to really feel our lives and live more deeply. If life were rosy all the time, there would be no motivation; it's the downside of life that forces us to rise to the occasion and see what we're really made of. After all, you can't have a hero without some sort of trouble or antagonist. So go ahead: Show us your dirty laundry!

And that's the real message: We're most attractive when we're being ourselves—warts (or moles or scars or gapped teeth or dorkiness or oratorical clumsiness) and all. There is real power and panache in knowing and embracing our shortcomings, our flaws, and ourselves. As one of my male colleagues who owns a publishing business put it to me: "The most attractive women I know wouldn't be on the cover of a fashion magazine; they'd be the editor or publisher with the real power!"

CHAPTER 3

Does It Look Like a Duck?

— THE VISUAL PREPROGRAMMING FACTOR

Bob Bylak is a tall, lanky man with a thin, angular face, short curly hair, and large, round eyes set beneath thick, heavy eyebrows. He's worked at the same company; lived in the same small, close-knit Colorado town; and has had the same friends and business colleagues for the past eight years. Yet a couple of times each month—either while in a meeting with colleagues, or at a business networking event, or buying something from the local hardware store or the car dealer—someone will mistakenly call him by another name.

"It's not uncommon for me to be walking down the street and have one of my neighbors wave to me and say, 'Hey, Tom, er, I mean, uh . . . uh . . .' At this point they're stammering and I can tell they're desperately trying to remember my name. Then, it finally comes to them: '*Bob!* How's it going, Bob?' It just seems to happen all the time," Bob laments. And he finds that even people who are trained to remember names for a living—people like car dealers, insurance sales reps, and real estate agents—call him Tom instead of Bob.

"When I bought my first house, I'd be riding around in the car with this real estate guy, and he'd keep saying, 'You know, Tom, you'll probably have to adjust your expectations a little based on what you're willing to put down,' or 'What did you think of that last place, Tom?' I'd keep correcting him, but he still kept calling me Tom! He'd apologize profusely, but then the next time we'd meet to go looking at houses, he'd start calling me Tom all over again! It used to really irritate me because he's not the only one who does that. All my adult life people have mistakenly called me Tom. But I've just sort of gotten used to it now."

The problem is, Bob looks like a Tom.

Although looking like a Tom if you're a Bob may not seem like a big deal on the surface, it can have dramatic ramifications on a career. Scientists have demonstrated that if you don't "look the part"—if you don't look like your name, your job title, or the type of person who could be effective in a specific circumstance or position, then you are subtly sabotaging your professional success.

But just what does a "Bob" or a "Tom"—or for that matter a "Suzy" or "Samantha"—look like? How do you know if you look like your name or job title? And what can you do if you don't look the part you want to play? For the answer to those questions, we look to some scientific studies.

Dr. Robin Thomas of the University of Miami became intrigued with the idea that names carry visual stereotypes while she was teaching a group of 15 graduate students and kept confusing two women in the class.

"One (was) named Kristin and the other named Heather. They did not look at all alike; one was tall and blonde with long hair, whereas the other was shorter with dark brown hair. All semester, I struggled to learn who was who. Near the end of the term, I still could not call on them with certainty."[1]

As it turned out, Dr. Thomas wasn't the first—or only—one who couldn't keep Kristin and Heather straight; many of their friends and peers also had trouble recalling just who was who. That prompted Dr. Thomas to assemble a team to conduct research on exactly what types of visual images we associate with certain names.

Thomas and her team gave 150 students in an introductory psychology class an assignment: to sketch the facial features of an imaginary man with a specific first name. The fifteen male names chosen for the experiment were Bob, Bill, Mark, Joe, Tim, John, Josh, Rick, Brian, Tom, Matt, Dan, Jason, Andy, and Justin. The students used a computer software program to tweak a set of standard male facial features to create a face they thought best suited each of the names they were given. The drawings were not to include facial hair or eyeglasses.

After the first group finished their sketches, a second group of 139 other students, who were not part of the sketch experiment, were brought in. Their task was to try to correctly match the facial drawings to the names given to the sketches by the first group. The photos had been printed separately and shuffled so there could be no correlation based simply on the order of names and photos presented. Almost 70 percent of the time (10 out of 15 times), the students matched the faces of the imaginary men with the name given to the sketch in the first experiment. The University of Miami researchers had quantitatively proved that humans associate specific facial features with specific names. For example, they found that a "Bob" usually has a large, round face, and an "Andy" has a narrower, more angular face.

But how can this be? Dr. Thomas has several theories on why we think a "Bob" should have a round, large face and an "Andy," for example, should have a more narrow, angular face. The first theory is a linguistic phenomenon called onomatopoeia, often known as "sound symbolism," in which we expect objects to look the way they sound. (A smooth object will have a smooth-sounding label and jagged objects more jagged-sounding names, for example.) According to this theory, "Bob" simply sounds more round to most of us and "Andy" sounds more thin and angular. (In chapter 7, I thoroughly explore the role that sounds, auditory vibrations, beats, and tones have on our DNA, psyche, biases, and decision making.)

A second theory of why we expect certain names to be associated with certain physical traits, according to Dr. Thomas, is that people attach specific personality characteristics to specific names (for example, "Robert" is honest, whereas "Frank" is not) and we affiliate physical traits with character traits. So if we hear the name "Bob" or "Robert," we expect someone who is easygoing and honest and we associate an easygoing, honest personality with a round face.

Finally there is the theory that "Bobs" really are round and "Andys" really are thin. "That may seem implausible," concedes Dr. Thomas, "but consider that names tend to hang around in families.

For example, I'm named after my father, who was named after great grandpa, etc. As physical traits are clearly passed down through a family tree, there is some chance that this phenomenon may have some reality."

So what, specifically, is it that makes people call Bob Bylak "Tom" on a regular basis? According to the results of Thomas's study, most people think a Bob should have "a round, wide face with a larger nose," and a Tom should have "a thin, angular face and jaw with large, light eyes." Bob Bylak's angular features, coupled with his thin face shape, make him look more like a Tom than a Bob to most of us.

FIRST IMPRESSIONS
Does the Face Fit Our Preprogrammed Image?

In chapter 2 I discussed how, upon meeting someone for the first time, our brains immediately scan the face and features of that person, looking for signs of threat (beauty and symmetry being considered threatening). But when we first meet someone—and even on subsequent meetings with that person—our brain not only looks for a threat, but also for a fit between the face and the role that person plays. Does he look like a manager? Does she look like a senator? Does he look like a Bob?

If there is any disconnect at all between what the person looks like and what our subconscious minds believe a person of that name, title, or position should look like, then we are reluctant to accept him or her in that role. Two New York University scientists found in a 2000 study that these primordial, preprogrammed, visual stereotypes are based solely on face shapes (not things like clothing) and hold true across cultures.[2]

Bone structure, cranial shape, and the shape of various features such as the nose, mouth, and eyes, as well as the placement of those features, sends a signal to our brains to categorize the person. Things like the roundness of the head, the height of the cheekbones, the distance of the eyebrows from the eyelid, the curve of the mouth, how square the chin is, and so forth can be very accurate predictors of election outcomes, career prospects, reaction to public crises, and even jury decisions. It turns out that our subconscious conclusions about whether someone will make a good political leader, a good CEO, or a good "Bob" are biologically as well as socially and psychologically based.[3] Facial shapes and structures affect everything from whom we hire to whom we vote for.

PREDICTING A NATIONAL ELECTION
The Face of a President or Prime Minister

If you are reading this in a public place where you are surrounded by strangers—say, at an airport, in a coffee shop, or on a commuter train—before you read any further, look up and examine the faces of the first two strangers of the same gender that you see. Make sure the pair of men or women you choose to observe are complete strangers to you; you have never met nor spoken to them before. Don't pay attention to the clothes each person is wearing or to the expressions each person has on his or her face. Simply examine the differences in the faces of the pair. What is the shape of each one's face? Does one person have more angular features, such as high cheekbones or a square jaw line, and another more round features? Does one person have larger eyes than the other? What about the placement of the eyebrows of each? Is one person's forehead more pronounced? Don't spend too much time on this. (Staring too long and too intently at a stranger will put you smack in the middle of a completely different kind of social experiment!) Take a few seconds to study the strangers, then come back.

Now, after having briefly identified the primary differences in the faces of each pair, answer this question: If each were a candidate in a national election, which one would you vote for to lead your country? Never mind that you know nothing about the person's political affiliation, values, or experience. Based solely on the facial differences of the pair, which one would get your vote?

Scientists have pretty much proved that if the pair you were just observing were running for office, the person you just "voted" for would be the same "candidate" who would actually end up winning the election![4] And the face you favored to be the next president (or prime minister) would depend upon whether your country is at war or peace.[5]

Could it be that there really is such a thing as the face of a winning politician? It appears so. A quartet of UK-based researchers led by Anthony Little uncovered just how powerful facial features are in predicting voter preferences for a political candidate.

The group set out to stage a hypothetical election where the faces of the "candidates" would represent the faces of actual winners and losers from eight elections in four countries. Little and his team compared pairs of faces from two elections each in Britain (Tony Blair versus William Hague, Tony Blair versus John Major), Australia (John Howard versus Mark Latham, John Howard versus Kim Beazley), and the United States (George Bush versus John Kerry, George Bush versus Al Gore). They also included the 1999 New Zealand general election (Helen Clark versus Jenny Shipley) and one more from the UK (John Major versus Neil Kinnock).

You might be wondering just how researchers defined the "winners" in these elections, since presidents and prime ministers aren't chosen by popular vote alone, but also by the electoral college (in the case of the U.S. president) or seats won by each party (in the case of prime ministers for Australia and Great Britain). Little's group defined the "winner" as the person receiving the larger share of a two-way split between the popular vote in each election and the seats won or electoral college votes received. So under this definition, Al Gore won the 2000 U.S. election and Kim Beazley the 2001 Australian election even though they did not officially win their elections. (Gore, as you may recall, lost on the electoral college vote count, and Beazley similarly lost more seats to her competitor, Howard.)

Once they had settled on which elections to compare and how they defined the winners, the trick for researchers was to develop faces for "candidates" in the mock elections that represented the faces of winners and losers in the actual elections but couldn't be identified as the candidates. In other words, when you look at the mock candidate image of George Bush or Al Gore, you wouldn't be able to recognize Bush or Gore, but the face structure, facial features, and placement of features like the eyes, nose, and eyebrows would be the same as those of Bush and Gore.

The goal was to maintain the dominant elements of each face and, more importantly, to exaggerate the differences in facial features between the winning and losing candidates in each election. To achieve this, the researchers created a composite image for each candidate based on the prominent features of each person's face, as well as the main differences between the faces of the winner and loser in each election. So, a composite of George Bush in the Bush/Kerry election, for example, would look different from a composite of Bush in the election where he opposed Al Gore, because Gore and Kerry have very different facial features.

These composite images were then morphed with an image of an "average" face. Researchers warped together the faces of ten men—or ten women, in the case of the Clark/Shipley election—to create this average-face image. These final images represented a 50 percent exaggeration in the facial differences between each of the winning and losing candidates, which means that the composite of Bush would be, as the researchers called it, a "plus-Bush" face (with masculine features such as a broad face shape emphasized) and the composite of John Kerry would be a "plus-Kerry" face (with more feminine features like a narrow chin emphasized). Finally, the corners of the mouth were adjusted on each image so that the pictures wouldn't convey any positive or negative expressions. So the result was eight pairs of photos where the basic dominant facial features of each individual candidate were preserved, but the differences in features of the winners and losers in each pair were exaggerated.

It was time for the mock election. Researchers took each pair of composites that correlated to each pair of candidates from the actual elections and presented them to 110 "voters" (58 women and 52 men) in the hypothetical election. Participants were simply instructed to "please indicate which face you would vote for to run your country." The results were a bit surprising: 57 percent of the time, voters in the mock election chose the computer-generated composite that represented the winner in the actual elections.

But the researchers didn't stop there. They wanted to see if they could *predict* the outcome of an election based solely on face shapes. So they did the same experiment with composite images of Tony Blair and Michael Howard prior to the May 2005 British general election. The mock election took place two months before the actual election (March 2005) and again used composite, unrecognizable images so that voters in the hypothetical election wouldn't realize the images represented Blair or Howard. In this mock-election, Tony Blair won 53 percent of the popular vote and 57 percent of the seats in the house. What happened on the real election day two months later? Blair won 52 percent of the popular vote and 64 percent of the seats in the house. The researchers had not only predicted the outcome of the election, but had done so with impressive accuracy.

What does all of this mean? Two things. First, something that I call "face shape relevancy" (the degree to which a person's facial features fit the part or role) can trump incumbency in an election (because the composite images in the mock election weren't recognizable as representing the actual candidates, and therefore, the faces representing the incumbents had no advantage). Second, the degree of difference in face shapes and facial features between candidates seems to have a significant impact on voter decisions. (You'll remember that the composite images were not just based on each individual's appearance, but primarily on the *differences* between the facial features of the individual candidates.) The bottom line is that we decide whether someone is a good "fit" for a particular position—in this case a president or prime minister—based more on the person's face than we may like to believe: If he or she looks the part, then we can buy into that person in the role and vote him or her in.

BRAINS AND BRAWN IN WAR AND PEACE

When we see the face of a candidate, we look to see not only if the person's face fits the role, but also whether his or her face fits the political climate and circumstances. One research study shows that we choose leaders with very different facial features in times of war than we do in times of peace. Voters favor a more masculine face to lead us when we're at war and a more feminine face to lead us during peacetime.

Consider the experiment Little and his researchers did with the 2004 election between George W. Bush and John Kerry. They used the same method to create composite images of each candidate as they did in their previous experiments, but this time the researchers had a different objective: They wanted to find out if people would vote for a different type of face during wartime and peacetime.

A group of research participants was shown the pictures and asked to make seven personality judgments about the plus-Bush and plus-Kerry images. The plus-Bush face was seen as more masculine, more dominant, and more "leaderlike" than the plus-Kerry face, which was seen as more intelligent, more attractive, more likeable, and more forgiving.

An interesting thing happened when a different set of participants was asked to vote for the face that represented a person they would want to run their country in times of war or peace, as opposed to just a general "who-would-you-vote-for" question posed in the first experiment. The masculine, dominant, strong, "plus-Bush" face was preferred most in times of war, but the "plus-Kerry" face of someone who is intelligent, forgiving, attractive, and likable was the one voted to lead our country in peacetime. Apparently we prefer a bully to a brainiac in times of war.

And on the most basic, primal level, that makes sense. A 1996 study published in *Personality and Individual Differences* shows a strong, dominant, even obstinate leader is seen as more likely to stand up to aggressive competitors than someone with more prosocial attributes.[6] But in times of peace, we want just the opposite: a leader who exemplifies trust, altruism, and modesty, because we think those traits benefit society as a whole better than a domineering personality.[7] It all seems to get back to the self-preservation preoccupation of the reptilian brain—the oldest and smallest region in the human brain and the one that controls our fight-or-flight response. We're preprogrammed to protect ourselves and our society, and the primal brain tells us that the best way to do that in wartime is to choose a leader who is seen as a force to be reckoned with.

That preference for a face that fits the political climate helps to partially explain why Democrats were initially so divided in their support between Hillary Clinton and Barack Obama in the 2008 presidential primaries, but then switched to support Senator Obama in greater numbers. (Even though Obama lost six of the last nine primaries, he still had greater overall support.) At first, Democrats were schizophrenic in what they wanted in a president. Because America was still at war in Iraq, and Americans wanted the war to end, they were concerned about having a strong leader who could get the job done. Our primal brains said Hillary Clinton's strong, masculine facial characteristics were features of a strong leader who could stand up to foreign powers. Exit polls reinforced that sentiment, with voters saying they felt Senator Clinton would be a stronger leader and, therefore, a better president.[8] But the election wasn't about choosing a better president, it was mostly about unifying the country. The war became a background issue, and that's when the tide started to turn for Obama.

In a CBS Poll conducted in late February 2008, 67 percent of Democrats said uniting the country was more important to them than having a strong leader, and they thought Barack Obama would do a better job of compromising with Republicans.[9] We wanted to repair the political divide between the parties, make everyone feel warm and fuzzy, and have us all just play nice. Senator Obama's more delicate, feminine facial features made our reptilian brains believe that he was the best person to do that; a sentiment also reflected in exit poll results on Super Tuesday 2008.

So the dilemma was whom do we choose: a strong leader who can be tough when she needs to be, or someone who can rally support from various political groups within the country to achieve unity? The facial features of Senators Obama and Clinton came into play even more prominently in the 2008 Democratic primaries because there was little perceived difference between the two on what voters said were two issues of concern: health care and the economy.[10]

Little isn't the only one to make a connection between facial features and voting behavior. Another study conducted by researchers at Princeton University found that voters decide within *one second* of seeing a pair of candidate photos for U.S. Congressional races which one is more competent. In that study, researchers were able to use the actual photos of candidates (not composite images), because someone living in Iowa, for example, most likely would not recognize the face of a congressional candidate from Idaho. The results of this study not only mirrored the actual election results of the four U.S. Senate and three U.S. House races evaluated, but also accurately reflected the margin of victory for the candidate with the more competent-looking face![11] Separate studies in Italy and Hong Kong show that this mental shortcutting happens across cultures, too.[12]

So, is it that candidate policies, issues, and platforms don't come into play at all in elections and that we base our decision on who will run our country simply on a face? Not entirely, but as you saw from the two studies just discussed, it comes into play far more often than you might suspect. We do consider the policies of the candidates, but the structure of our current elections, coupled with candidate flip-flopping in the face of overnight polling, almost forces voters to use a shortcut to decision making.

In every election, there are large amounts of data available to voters—almost too much information. Each candidate has several pet issues with an accompanying set of solutions. Couple this with the barrage of back-and-forth accusations and counteraccusations between those running for office with myriad "expert" interpretations of the candidates in the media, and you end up with voters who are on information overload. To compensate, the brain uses a simplified cognitive strategy to decode the onslaught of information about politicians, their policies, their personalities, and the current environment, and that shortcut often involves unconscious impressions we form solely from the facial features of the candidates. This phenomenon is more prevalent if there aren't a whole lot of perceived policy differences between the candidates.

These shortcuts don't just apply to politicians. They also happen all the time in work environments and hiring situations.

THE FACE OF CORPORATE SUCCESS

Our ingrained expectations of who "looks the part" (not who is more beautiful or handsome, but who fits our *innate idea* of what someone in a certain position should look like) can unconsciously affect not only whom we vote for, but whom we hire and promote.

Imagine for a moment that you're vice president of human resources at a large health insurance company in a major metropolitan area. You have two positions open in the claims department: One is a level 8 (out of a 21-level hierarchy at the company) and the other is a level 16. The level 8 job is a nonmanagerial clerical job where the person will file, sort, and verify information, as well as keep records for the department and create letters using word processing programs. The salary range for this position is between $25,000 and $28,000. The level 16 position is a management post that requires someone who can make quick decisions, solve complex problems, review claims coverage, and meet aggressive cost-savings goals of the department. She will also manage 10 employees in a high-pressure environment and can expect a salary in the range of $64,000 to $68,000. Neither position requires public contact or a lot of interaction with customers.

The person who will supervise the level 8 clerical hire has just handed you resumés of the two women who are his top picks for the job. He tells you that both did superbly well in the interviews, and he thought both were equal when it came to traits such as work ethic and trustworthiness. The final decision is yours. As you read the resumés, you notice that both have nearly equal educational and work experience credentials, and both even live in the same suburb. On paper, it's a tough choice. But then you look at the photos, and you notice Candidate A is very attractive: She has delicate features and on an attractiveness scale of one to ten, you'd rate her an eight. Candidate B, on the other hand, you'd place at about a four, and her features are more "masculine" than those of Candidate A.

Whom do you hire for the clerical job: pretty Candidate A or somewhat unattractive Candidate B? And what salary, within the $25,000–$28,000 range, do you offer to her?

Now take the same scenario for the high-pressure management

position: You have two equally qualified women, both of whom did well in the interview, are the same age, have the same experience and educational credentials, and live in the same suburb. Once again, let's place Candidate A at an eight on the attractiveness scale and Candidate B at a four. Which woman do you hire this time? And what salary do you offer to her: Is it closer to $64,000 or $68,000?

If you chose the more attractive person for the clerical position and the less attractive woman for the management job, you just did what subjects in a Yale University research study did: You judged the less attractive person more suitable for the management job and the prettier woman to be a better fit for the clerical job. You also probably offered the attractive woman a salary closer to the lower end of the range and the less attractive woman a salary closer to the higher end of the range.[13]

How can this be? After all, if you ask most people, they'd tell you that they find the idea of hiring or not hiring someone based on physical attractiveness repugnant and adamantly proclaim that they would never do it. And they wouldn't—at least not consciously. But the Yale researchers say that we unconsciously prefer less attractive women for management jobs because we often think those higher-level positions require male characteristics, and the more attractive a woman is, the more feminine we perceive her to be. In short, there's a disconnect between the skills we traditionally associate with women and the talents we think are needed for a management job. This holds true whether the hiring person is a man or a woman. It also holds true across cultures; the propensity to prefer more masculine qualities for more prestigious jobs is another "human universal," or a mind-set that anthropologists say can be found in virtually all civilizations. (I discuss human universals more in depth in chapter 4.)

Four other independent studies have shown that unattractive women not only are perceived as more qualified for management positions, but they also get higher starting salaries than their attractive counterparts.[14] Attractive women have a job advantage only when the position is a lower-level spot where the duties don't require tough decision making and critical judgments.

Is this discrimination? Yes. Does this discrimination happen intentionally? As I've said, probably not. It happens because men have dominated power positions in the workplace for hundreds of years, and this has conditioned us to view masculine features as a prerequisite for power jobs. This, too, goes back to our "survival of the fittest" primal programming: We associate strength, power, and dominance as requisite qualities in competitive environments (such as managerial positions) and those traits are most often aligned with masculine features. So the woman who seems to have a more masculine face is seen as the best female candidate for a managerial job.

Attractiveness was not a detriment for men in the research studies: Good-looking guys got the job over their less attractive competitors. That's because masculine features—those associated with the skills necessary for a manager—are directly linked to male attractiveness.

So, is there a certain "look" that we expect in a leader? There seems to be, and that look includes facial structures that are more masculine than feminine. One study of West Point grads accurately predicted the final rank of cadets at the end of their careers based only on the facial features of individual cadets. You guessed it; the more manly the look of the man (the greater his "facial dominance," according to the researchers), the more success he had in rising through the military ranks to the top positions.[15] Facial dominance positively correlates to testosterone levels, suggesting a link to actual dominant behavior.[16] The downside to a leader having a masculine face in any occupation, as we talked about in the comparison of faces of political candidates, is that through evolution we have been programmed to think someone with such dominant features can't be trusted.[17]

Corporate communications managers would do well to pay attention to the facial features of the individuals they choose as spokespeople during a crisis. Here's a quick quiz: Let's say two top executives at your company have been accused of white collar crime. You have the choice of two spokespeople: one has a baby face, with large eyes, a small nose, and a small chin. The other has a more mature look, with angular facial features. Which person will get the more positive response from a mass audience?

Researchers from Hong Kong University and Columbia University in New York found that when trust is required, a baby-faced executive is the best choice for a spokesperson. But when the crisis involves questions of competency, a person with a more mature, angular (masculine) face is preferred.[18]

The researchers crafted news stories about fictitious corporate actions that violated either moral or legal codes, and then attached a photo or video of a CEO to each story. Then they gave the stories and pictures to a group of 500 people who took part in the study. The result? Baby-faced CEOs were seen as more honest, innocent, and less likely to intentionally deceive people.[19] But when the offense was more serious and raised questions of competency—such as a product defect—then a more mature, angular face was viewed more favorably. (This mirrors my study of portly courtroom defendants that I talked about earlier in this chapter. You may recall that people with more rounded features—although perceived as more honest—were also considered more likely to be negligent.)

This same look of facial dominance also affects how positively or negatively we view the actions of celebrities. Why is it, for example, that when Demi Moore and Sinead O'Connor shave their heads we see it as a sign of courage and strength, but when Britney Spears does it, we see her as a mental case on the verge of a breakdown? True, Britney had some issues prior to her head shave, and many more since then. And while all three women are beautiful, Britney has more delicate, feminine facial features than either Demi or Sinead, and her face conforms very closely to the Golden Ratio of perfect beauty that we discussed in chapter 2. We equate delicate, feminine features with delicate emotions. So when someone like Demi takes a razor to her scalp, we admire her strength (which our historical programming unconsciously links to masculine features). But when Britney does it, we see it as being an irrational act by an emotionally troubled woman.

Our faces can send signals (whether accurate or not) about our managerial skills and the strength of our personality, but what do they say about our intelligence? And what can we do if our faces send off signals that we're not the sharpest knives in the drawer?

STUPID IS AS STUPID LOOKS?
The Salutatorian Who Didn't Look Smart

Most of us would probably consider someone who graduated second in his or her law school class to be a smart cookie. But regardless of your class rank, if you don't have the face of an intelligentsia, then you may not get the full respect of your co-workers or clients. That was the case of a Midwest lawyer who was salutatorian of his class, was well respected by his professional peers, but couldn't get a jury behind him to save his neck. He had several published law articles to his credit, sat on the board of a couple of high-profile charities, and, according to his friends, had an engaging, outgoing personality. But he just couldn't win over a jury—despite compelling evidence and well-researched cases. When he argued a case in court, jurors were almost dismissive. Post-trial juror surveys that the firm had done showed most thought the lawyer's approach was unconvincing, even untruthful!

This lawyer was my client. We'll call him Jason, to preserve his privacy. The partners in Jason's law firm called me because they had heard of other work I had done to help lawyers improve their court-room presentation skills and juror strategies. They thought that if Jason could just improve his communication skills, he would improve his credibility. But after watching a few of his opening statements and closing arguments, I found his presentations credible. His tone, energy, body language, and eye contact with jurors were on target for his message, and the content of Jason's presentations was impressive, thoughtful, succinct, and veritable. So what was the problem?

As it turns out, Jason has a face that says "I'm stupid." And jurors had a hard time accepting "smart" information from someone who didn't look that bright.

I had read some interesting research about the intelligence judgments we make about people based only on someone's face and I wanted to see if those theories played out with Jason. So, I did two things. First, I took a headshot of him and recorded a 30-second video of Jason giving a brief factual account of a recent change in securities law. (I chose this topic because I wanted a subject that would be neutral and carry no emotional content.) The purpose of the headshot was to see how people would react to his face only. The video was used to see if people's perception of Jason would change when they heard him speak. I showed the headshot to one group of 53 people, ranging in age from 19 to 68. I showed the 30-second video to another group of 40 people, this time ranging in age from 18 to 55.

After showing each group either the picture or the video, I asked only two questions:

1. Using a traditional grading scale from school, what type of student do you think he was: A, B, C, D, or F?
2. On a scale of one to ten, with ten being the nicest, how warm and caring do you think this person is?

After the two questions, there was an area on the survey that simply stated: "Please add any other comments and impressions, either positive or negative, that you may have about this person. Be sure to include your initial gut feelings about this person, as well as assumptions you may have about his personality, temperament, intelligence, and demeanor."

How did our college salutatorian fare? Well over half (61 percent) of the people who saw only Jason's picture ranked him as a D student on the intelligence scale, and nearly a quarter (24 percent) put him only at a C. Folks who saw only the video thought Jason was slightly smarter, with 74 percent placing him at a C (or right at average), just under 19 percent giving him a D, and about 7 percent ranking him as a B student. Remember, this for a guy who was salutatorian at a prestigious college that has Nobel laureates among its alumni!

He did fare better, though, on the charisma question: More than 75 percent in both groups thought Jason was a nice guy. But this wasn't exactly good news, either, because if you have facial features that portray you as less intelligent than the average person, and you also have features that portray a nicer-than-average persona, the overall impression could be that you're naive and maybe even a little bit gullible.

One comment from a woman in the first group (the group that saw only a photo) really struck a nerve with Jason.

"That's the exact same shit I get from people around here!" Jason snorted as he slammed his fist on the table while he read the comment. What raised his ire? This commentary from a twenty-something woman: "He seems like a sweet person, but something about him also seems sort of like a dumb jock. I'd guess that he played football in high school, and probably got to college, if he went to college, on a sports scholarship. He's probably nice, but he's also probably not that bright, either." A male survey participant who saw only the video wrote: "I'd let him date my daughter. I'm not so sure I'd let him run my company."

This was by no means a scientific survey. But researchers Ran Hassin and Yaacov Trope of New York University have conducted scientifically valid experiments on this same issue, and they found that our idea of what makes someone look smart or stupid, mean or nice, is pretty universal and holds up across cultures.[20] Unfortunately, Jason has many of the universal traits that the researchers say most of us unconsciously associate with lower intelligence: a low forehead, straight, thick eyebrows, larger-than-average ears, and a prominently drooping mouth (where the corners turn down naturally even with a neutral expression). It seems, according to Hassin and Trope's research, that we think smart people should have rounded eyebrows, high foreheads, plunging eyes, and short ears.[21] And the corners of a smart person's mouth apparently turn upward, even when he or she isn't smiling.

It's important to note here that the researchers aren't saying someone with these facial features *is* stupid; they're merely stating that this is how people across cultures consistently *interpret* those facial constructs. But that interpretation can contribute to the success or demise of a political candidate, a celebrity, or a corporate manager. It's interesting to note, too, that Al Gore—who as I mentioned in chapter 2 was perceived as "too smart" for the presidency—used his look of intelligence and his real intellectual ability to propel himself to rock-star status through his global-warming educational efforts.

And that makes sense, because we expect our *teachers* to look smart, but not always our politicians.

So what features played into the inferences that our groups drew about Jason's personality (as opposed to his intelligence)? His thick, curly hair, low-set cheekbones, and short, round nose were some of the traits that made him seem like a nice guy to both groups. His wide face and wide, warm eyes were also traits that made him seem like a nice person.

But what can you do if, like Jason, you're in a profession where you're expected to be smart, but you have a look that says otherwise? You change your communication style to fit your face. By making a few simple changes in his style, Jason was able not only to gain the respect of his colleagues, but he also started winning more court cases. Although he had always been a good speaker, the problem was his speaking style didn't fit with what people expected from someone with his features. They didn't expect someone who looked like a "dumb jock" to give presentations that were so articulate, concise, and fact-laden. Because of that, jurors said in post-trial surveys that they didn't believe the claims he made during the proceedings. Unfortunately for Jason he had a face that triggered suspicions of incompetence and lack of intelligence.

So we tweaked his communication style to play into what jurors expected to hear from someone with his facial features. Certainly, we didn't "dumb down" his oratory. But we did have him speak in much more conversational and less lofty style. And we coached him to sprinkle into his presentations statements that would fit his look; phrases such as, "I may not be the smartest person who ever lived, and I may not know a lot about a lot of things, but I do know such-and-such about this case." By doing so, he played into the stereotype of the "dumb jock" a bit, and he eliminated the disconnect jurors had between how he said what he said and the type of speaking pattern someone might expect from a man who didn't have the professorial look. In doing so he became more believable and gained more credibility. Rather than trying to speak in a manner that he thought a persuasive lawyer should speak, he started playing into the hand he was given by nature. And he started winning cases. We also encouraged him to speak in a folksier manner and tell stories to reinforce his points—and not just to regurgitate facts.

It's interesting to note that many of the facial features that researchers Hassin and Trope found we associate with nice people—low cheekbones; a wide, round face; asymmetrical features; and round nostrils—are the opposite of the Golden Ratio qualities of beauty discussed in chapter 2. Once again it seems as if we find comfort in the people who are of only average attractiveness—not the pretty people.

PRACTICAL APPLICATION
Are We Trapped in Our Faces?

I was just a number to my college Communications Law professor. Number 17, to be specific. And that's the way Dr. Tom Jonas wanted it. Dr. Jonas insisted that the identities of his students remain cloaked for the full semester, so on the first day of class we all drew numbers, and they were to be our identities for the next 18 weeks. He went to great lengths to perpetuate the ambiguity: We were instructed to place only our numbers, never our names, on all of our assignments and exams. If Dr. Jonas found a student was off track in the course, he would simply announce during class something like, "Number 26 has had some trouble grasping the key concepts in the last two assignments. I'd like to explain that topic in more detail now. But, 26, if you need additional help, please make a note on your next assignment, telling me exactly where you're having trouble, and I'll try to help you with a detailed written response." If a student was doing particularly well, he'd highlight that, too: "Number 33 really got what this case was all about and had the best interpretation of it I've ever seen from a student. Keep up the good work, 33!"

This may seem like an impersonal way to run a class. And, to some degree, maybe it was. But Dr. Jonas wasn't there to make friends; his mission was to give grades that reflected only the true abilities of the students and not the personal judgments or biases he could have inferred from our faces, our names, or our previous interactions with him. So, even though outside of class he may have known that my name was Vicki and that I was in forensics, wrote stories for the college newspaper, and anchored the campus television newscast, in class he would never know what kind of assignments I turned in or how well I did on exams until the last day of the semester, when we matched our names with our numerical identities.

Dr. Jonas was so keenly aware of how perceptual biases can influence decision making that he went out of his way to try to eliminate those biases. And that's a good starting point for all of us: awareness. As managers, voters, and decision makers at all levels become more aware of how they are unwittingly influenced by appearances of workers and job candidates, they can consciously start to look beyond the face and into the substance of the person. We might not be able to give everyone a number to keep identities hidden, but we can invest the time required to truly get to know a person before we make snap judgments about his personality or her abilities.

But change like that happens slowly. In the meantime, what can be done? Are attractive women doomed to lower-level, low-paying jobs? Are "manly men" to be forever suspect as liars and cheats? Will politicians continue to be chosen based on whether they "look" like our primordially programmed ideas of what elected officials should look like? Can we blame Mother Nature for giving us a face that says stupid or a face that doesn't engender trust? If we don't "look" like our names, should we change them? Should women strive to become as unattractive as possible when they're seeking upper management positions?

Not so fast.

Although we may not be able to overcome our primal preference for masculine features in leaders, feminine features in people we trust, high foreheads and low-set cheeks in smart people, or angular features for an "Andy" and round features for a "Bob," we do have a fair amount of control over how people perceive us. That control comes into play when we align our verbal messages with the subliminal messages sent by our facial features, our names, and our current environment.

Let's take President George W. Bush as an example. His first name is often one that conjures up images of someone who is outgoing and charming but also scattered and slow-witted. (Many sitcom characters with these traits are named George. Think George Costanza of *Seinfeld*, or the unhandy handyman George Utley in the *Newhart* show of the 1980s.) His facial features are masculine with some elements of a "not-so-smart face": his eyebrows are thick and straight, he has larger-than-average ears, and the corners of his mouth turn down slightly when he is in a neutral expression.

If President Bush had tried to portray himself as an intelligent, thoughtful, polished politician who carefully measured his words, voters never would have bought into it because it would have been inconsistent with the nonverbal messages sent by his facial features. His often comically bumbling communication style, coupled with his "the-polls-and-dissenters-be-damned" attitude, meshed perfectly with the impressions made by his first name, his masculine yet not superintelligent appearance, and the chaotic environment we were in.

In the 2000 election, when the country was in a state of general prosperity, these characteristics did not play as large of a role because there were no pressing issues, despite the razor-thin margin of victory. But in the 2004 election, when America was at war, George Bush's often politically incorrect cowboy mentality was his ace in the hole, as voters saw him as an authentic, genuine man who had the tough-guy persona to help our nation win a war. His entire communicated message—both verbal and nonverbal—meshed perfectly with the war environment. His face, his delivery style, and his persona were perfect for his political purpose.

While other candidates in the 2004 election tried to use logic and facts to persuade a nation, Bush did a masterful job of aligning his messaging and communication style with the environment—war—and his masculine facial features. Voters used mental shortcuts and decided that Mr. Bush had the look (and sound) of a wartime leader. Remember: Voters prefer brawn to brains when the country is involved in international conflicts.

Just as political candidates can win votes by aligning their communication style with what audiences expect from someone with their facial features, so can we, too, become more persuasive by paying more attention to how we approach topics. One of my clients, Suzy F., is an intelligent and highly successful corporate vice president of marketing at a regional health care system. She doesn't look the part: Imagine someone stepping right out of Woodstock during the 1960s and walking straight into the corporate offices at this conservative company. That's Suzy. She dresses like a hippie, has very liberal political views, and is not afraid to let people know where she stands; yet she holds a high position at her organization. Her face is more "feminine" and her features suggest a "slightly less than average" intelligence.

So how did she land—and keep for over a decade—such a high-profile, high-powered job? Simple. She instinctively aligned her communication style with her look and her environment. Based on her appearance, people expected her to be a bit of a flake. And she played into that—even though she is very intelligent. She didn't "dumb herself down," but she did align her professional personality with who she really is as a person. Because she is in marketing, she passes her "flakiness" off as part of the creative persona needed to be successful in the job. She took the one part of her environment—marketing and creativity—and aligned her communication style with that.

But it's not an act; Suzy is one of the most authentic, genuine, intelligent, and comfortable-in-her-skin people I have ever met (especially in corporate America!). Most people would have donned an executive suit and changed their communication style to fit the *corporate*, not the *creative* environment of a marketing position in a big, conservative company. And that would have been career suicide for Suzy, because it wouldn't have meshed with her facial features (plus-feminine and minus-intelligence), her overall look, or her real personality; consequently she would have come off as not quite right for the company. Suzy chose the part that fit her (creative person) and capitalized on that rather than trying to fit a part (corporate department head).

We can also align our approach in other ways to suit our purposes. For example, I have a low forehead and high cheekbones—facial traits that typically send a message of not being all that bright. But I used that to my advantage when I was a reporter. When interviewing people who are usually tough to get to open up, I would adapt my questioning style to be softer than normal, and I would even use such phrases as, "I'm confused about this, can you help me understand?" in my questioning. The field photographers who taped the interviews often marveled at how I was able to get people to say things that they typically wouldn't. On more than one occasion legislators would call me after a taping and say, "You know, my advisor asked me why I disclosed such-and-such to you, and I really shouldn't have. Is there any way you can keep that out of the final piece? You just seemed so nice and I was so comfortable talking to you that I said more than I should have."

Had I played into another facial feature that I have—a square jaw line, which is considered masculine—and used a more forceful (masculine-like) communication style, I would have raised the defenses of those I interviewed and they would have not only considered me "not that bright" but also overly aggressive. The point is that few of us have one single message that is sent by the features of our face; the key is to play into the ones that suit your goals, your environment, and your personality.

Corporations can use this to their advantage, too. As we learned in the study about face shapes and public perception of newsmakers, matching the facial features of a spokesperson to the type of crisis can greatly increase the public trust and confidence in the corporate mouthpiece. Baby-faced features—large eyes, a small nose, a small chin, and a high forehead—are preferred for crises where the issue is one of dishonesty. On the other hand, if the issue is lack of vigilance, a spokesperson with more mature facial features will get a more positive reception from a mass audience. That's why it's good for corporations to have several well-trained spokespersons. Send the baby face when you want to portray honesty and the mature face when you want to portray competence. The face shape of a company spokesperson is not a trivial consideration.

One final message about the subconscious messages our face shapes send: Dr. Thomas, who did the study on faces that look like names, says that "hair trumps everything."[22] In other words, if you have a masculine, angular face and harsh features but have curly hair, the impression sent will be primarily that you are the guy-or-girl next door oozing with niceness. If you have a face shape that is round, soft, and pleasing, yet you have a harsh, angular hairstyle, the initial impression will be that your personality is a bit harsh.

The real opportunity to achieve success lies with each of us individually—regardless of how we look or the stereotypes that our appearance triggers. We're all responsible for our own personal "brand," and most of us unwittingly shoot ourselves in the foot by perpetuating negative stereotypes of ourselves and by not playing into our uniqueness. We have to stop trying to look, think, and act the way we think we're *supposed* to think and act in a particular situation, and instead play into our strengths—even if those strengths may seem counter to expectations.

Politicians lament that in the modern era, campaigns are all about the candidate who looks the part. But rather than trying to make politicians look the part, they need to choose the part that looks like them, just as George Bush did. The all-time best example of a politician who was successful at making the part fit him and being true to himself is Jesse Ventura—the professional wrestler turned Minnesota governor. His communication style was gruff and blunt, and his messages were often offensive, just like his "bad boy" image as "The Body" Ventura. His facial features, his bullyish body style, his bombastic speaking style, and his wrestler personality all fit his campaign slogan: No more politics as usual. (There were also the humorous *My Governor Can Beat Up Your Governor* bumper stickers.)

Of course, Ventura is an outrageous example of aligning appearances and linguistic style. But there are many other, perhaps more palatable examples: Ronald Reagan, John F. Kennedy, Oprah, and even Walter Cronkite. If you really want some fantastic examples of people who masterfully align their linguistic style to fit their facial features and physical appearances, just watch Comedy Central. Comedians almost without fail rely on some aspect of their physicality as a springboard for their schtick and style.

But sometimes to break the stereotype that people have of you, you have to play into it first; if you don't, people will mentally tune you out because something doesn't quite fit in their minds.

When we sit down and examine who we really are, how we want to be perceived, and how we are actually perceived based on the look Mother Nature gave us, we can each individually begin to create a persona that reflects who we truly are, yet do so in a way that aligns with the primal, often subconscious reactions people have to our physical appearances. Take a page from George W. Bush's playbook: By playing the hand we were dealt and accessorizing the look we got with an authentic communication style that aligns with our truest selves, as well as our environment, we achieve an instant appeal persona that can gain the allegiance of a mass audience.

CHAPTER 4

Small Dogs, Big SUVs, and the Failure of Epcot

— THE REPTILIAN COMFORT FACTOR IN CONSUMER CHOICES

Imagine that you own a restaurant and you're in need of an industrial food processor. Two commercial-kitchen sales representatives come in to pitch their competitive products. The price, quality, and functionality of both machines are identical. The only difference is in the sales pitch. Sales rep #1 tells you, "With this machine, you can chop, shred, slice, dice, and puree at practically the speed of light." Salesperson #2 has a similar, but slightly different pitch: "This machine chops, shreds, slices, dices, and purees at practically the speed of light."

From which representative do you buy: Salesperson #1 or salesperson #2?

If you're like most people, pitch #2 will prompt you to buy more often than pitch #1. It's because of something anthropologists and evolutionary psychologists call "human universals": behavioral and cognitive traits common to all neurologically normal humans in all cultures. In other words, just as all "normal" humans have ten fingers and ten toes, we also share common thoughts, rituals, reactions, and emotions in response to certain stimuli—including certain words and phrases. There are over 200 of these universal human traits, which influence everything from the profitability of a restaurant to which products, movies, songs, and politicians we prefer. Universals are potent in creating an instant bond with consumers because they reflect who we are at our deepest, primal level. It's virtually impossible for people to make any type of decision that is contrary to, or out of alignment with, these universals. Finding a way to tap into these universal preferences can help improve your image, your profits, and the appeal of your products.

Why are specific traits and preferences so prevalent across cultures? It's because they are preprogrammed into the reptilian brain—the part conditioned through centuries of evolution. When we like something or respond positively to a person or stimuli, it's not because we go through a logical analysis and arrive at a fact-based conclusion. Rather, it's because something just "feels right" to us or, more accurately, it feels right to the reptilian brain. Our preferences are primal and instinctive—not logical. These innate comfort factors are so strong because they are not even acknowledged by the conscious mind. Hundreds of these universal likes are at work every day in nearly every aspect of our lives. Because there are so many, it's impossible to discuss all of the universals in this chapter—or even in this book.

Although other human universals relate to the various factors of instant appeal, this chapter is dedicated to a specific *category* of human universals: those that trigger the primal comfort responses of the reptilian brain. You may not realize it, but we often make buying decisions based on how safe something makes us feel or how emotionally comfortable we are with the product, person, or idea.

I talked briefly about two other human universals in chapter 2 that support the conspicuous flaw factor: the "valuation of ugly" (which is one of the reasons physical flaws are often appealing to humans) and admiration for "failing on the first try" (which partly explains why we like a great comeback story or manufacturing systems that don't meet a zero-defects policy). Just as those universals support the flaw factor and other universals support other factors, the human universals presented in this chapter explain many of the consumer choices we make.

REPTILIAN COMFORT UNIVERSAL #1
The Principle of Least Effort

With the second sales pitch mentioned at the beginning of this chapter, there was another specific human universal at work—and it's among the most powerful motivators in marketing. It's called "the principle of least effort" or, as I like to call it, "The Garfield Rule" to completing a task.

When it comes to completing a task, we're really just like cats; we really don't want to do all that much work. Hard work, after all, isn't fun; it often doesn't bring us emotional (and sometimes not physical) comfort. Just like the cartoon character Garfield, whenever we humans take on a task, we'll look for the easiest, fastest, simplest way to complete it, and we'll stop the minute we get minimally acceptable results.[1] Highlighting Garfield's laziness was one reason for the success of the Garfield comic strip; our primal brains could relate to the slothful tabby cat. (This "Garfield Rule," coupled with our fetish for failing on a first try, also explains why we can't seem to implement a zero-defects manufacturing policy. We are primordially programmed to produce a product easily and quickly and stop as soon as we get bare-bones, acceptable results, rather than go after perfection on the first try.)

Today the principle of least effort has been applied to everything from technical writing, product ads, sales pitches, search engine functionality, GPS navigation systems, building design, and even reading a book. Public libraries were among the first to use the principle of least effort (Garfield Rule) to be more appealing to patrons. The biggest complaint of library users back in 1874 was the cumbersome process of trying to search through rows and rows of books and articles to find what they were looking for. Melvil Dewey had a solution: classify books into ten categories. Today we know that as the Dewey Decimal System.

But, as time went on, we Garfield-like creatures thought even that was too much work, and libraries saw a decline in users. Why go to the trouble of trudging to a library and sorting through the cumbersome card catalog when you can go to Barnes & Noble, where large signage clearly tells you at a glance where in the store you might find the book you're looking for? Plus, you can plunk down in a comfy chair and have a latte while you read. So, once again, the great minds in library science went to work to find another "Garfield" approach that would be appealing to book lovers. This time, they turned to the principles of Web 2.0 to lure customers back into public libraries.

"Webcats"—electronic catalog databases—now allow you to find the location of a book or journal article right from the comfort of your home. (Hmmm, is it any coincidence that they are called Web "cats"?) One of the most powerful of these Webcats is called World-cat (www.worldcat.org). Just type in your zip code, the title of the book or journal article you are looking for, and let the Internet do the searching. In just a blink of an eye you'll get a list of all of the public libraries in your area that have what you're looking for. Not only that, but Worldcat tells you the exact location within the library where you can find the book. (For example, "third floor social science" or "first floor reading room.") Public libraries, by being aware of the principle of least effort, were able once again to be a hit with patrons. To be sure, they also made other changes (such as creating comfy seating areas that align with our need for "high refuge"—which you'll also learn about in this chapter.)

This may simply seem like a logical thing to do: make life easier. But logic doesn't entirely drive our decisions or our behavior. If it did, we wouldn't be more afraid of giving a speech than we are of dying. The universal human preference to find the path of least effort is ingrained deep in our anthropological conditioning. This isn't just a product of our modern, overscheduled culture. The primal preference to expend the least amount of energy is found in ancient cultures, too.[2] Early cultures were concerned about conserving individual energy mainly because they never knew when they would have to fight off predators, go on especially challenging hunts, or walk long distances to seek shelter. Research shows that economy of effort and energy are evolutionary factors that are found in all biological mechanisms—not just animals and humans.[3] The tendency to conserve speech energy is so uniform over time that it has produced many "universals" in cross-cultural languages. We're all just lolling tabby cats at heart.

It's little wonder, then, why using this human universal in product marketing is so effective at making a *machine* that slices and dices stickier than one where *you* slice and dice. The preference lies in the structure of the two product pitches. It's a subtle difference—all that was done was to add an *s* to the verbs—but the meaning is obvious: In the first pitch, we will have to do the work, but in the second pitch, the machine does the work. Therefore the second pitch aligns with the desire to expend the least amount of energy.

The principle of least effort is so powerful that it's used in just about all appliance infomercials. Inventor Ron Popeil has used taglines that appeal to this human universal in many of his products. Remember the tagline for the Showtime Rotisserie: "Set it and forget it"? Or what about that for the Cap Snaffler: "It snaffles caps off any size jug, bottle, or jar"? Commercials for his smokeless ashtray showed the device literally drawing smoke from burning cigarettes back into the ashtray itself. The implication was that you don't even have to get a spray can out to cover up smoke smell anymore; the ashtray does all the work for you.

The *Secret*—a new age self-help book that has been on the *New York Times* bestseller list for well over a year—is based on the law of attraction: the idea that your thoughts alone cause a change in the physical world, that you can attract all the things and experiences you want into your life just by thinking about them and believing your wish will be fulfilled. (The formula promoted in the book is "Ask, Believe, Receive.") No action is required to bring health, wealth, or happiness into your life; just ask the universe for something, and then open yourself up to allow the physical manifestation of your thoughts, and you'll get everything you ever wanted.

The book—and its corresponding DVD movie—became a publishing phenomenon,[4] a self-help phenomenon,[5] and a cultural phenomenon[6] in part because many interpreted it as a method to get anything you want just by asking for it, visualizing that you have already received it, and then believing you'll get it. Action was an afterthought. You could, according to the theory, almost "set and forget" your path to success. This not only played right into the universal compulsion of people to seek a quick and easy path to success, but also into the universal desire for status and prestige—all of which bring emotional comfort through feelings of satisfaction. We could get recognition, success, and financial rewards just by thinking about it and believing we'd get it. What a concept; and how emotionally comforting to know that the good life was easy to attain! Our reptilian brains were in hog heaven!

Now, I'm not bashing nor condoning *The Secret*. The validity or fallacy of the law of attraction is not the issue here. Whether you believe in *The Secret* or not, your reptilian brain responds to the universal appeal of the principle of least effort. All of the coaches in *The Secret*—many of them successful millionaires—worked very hard (and took a lot of *action* over many, many years) to achieve their individual successes; but that little fact was cleverly omitted in the movie. The producers obviously knew about the principle of least effort as well as the law of attraction!

Simon & Schuster, publisher of *The Secret*, did a second printing of two million copies—"the biggest order for a second print in history."[7] For much of February and April of 2007, both the book and DVD remained at #1 or #2 at the three major book retailers: Amazon, Borders, and Barnes & Noble. To be sure, *The Secret* was also a huge phenomenon because of the ingenious viral marketing campaign. But make no mistake, the idea that you can just positively think and believe your way to success was an intoxicating lure for people because it tapped into our primal programming to expend the least amount of effort to get the results we want. It's been the subject of best-sellers for at least a century, and the Garfield principle worked its magic for *The Secret*.

Several years ago, the U.S. Army had a recruitment slogan that boasted, "We do more before 9 A.M. than most people do all day." New recruits weren't exactly signing up in record numbers. That's largely because the slogan repulsed the reptilian brain (and it's so un-Garfield-like!). The subconscious mind of each potential recruit was no doubt thinking, "Oh yeah, *that's* what I want to do; work my ass off!" The ad failed to point out the direct benefits of military service and appealed to no universal preference.

More recent recruitment efforts align fairly well with our anthropological preferences. They have portrayed an Army career as a way to serve our country, to get an advanced education, and to develop civilian career skills all at the same time. And the promotional video for its new recruitment campaign, *Army Strong*, positions the army as a one-stop shop to develop physical, emotional, and intellectual strength, as well as strength of character, purpose, and leadership. This approach directly aligns the human universal to seek out the most direct path to a goal. Army recruits don't need to bother with going to college, signing up for a health club, getting an internship, or pondering such things as who they are, whether they're making a difference in the world, or the meaning of life; the army, according to the new ads, will do all that for them.

While the video is compelling and hits the mark, the slogan "Army Strong" is ineffective. A better slogan would have captured in words the same human universal concepts that were clearly shown in the video. "Strength" isn't among the human universals (things that people of all cultures desire), but pride, conserving personal energy, kinship with fellow citizens, finding the path of least effort, and developing a positive self-image are among them.

REPTILIAN COMFORT UNIVERSAL #2
The Kinship Factor in Employee Retention and Consumer Spending

Consider a company where many workers are wealthy enough that they don't have to work another day in their lives, but they stay at the company solely because they love the place and can't bring themselves to leave. While other companies have a hard time finding top talent, this organization doesn't have to recruit: It gets thousands of unsolicited applications from highly talented and experienced people every week. This company also has an employee attrition rate of 4 percent, when the national average for other companies in its industry runs at 29.3 percent.[8] The few workers who do leave the company say they want to keep in touch with their bosses and other employees, and they want to regularly come back and visit the organization.[9] This request has been made so many times that the company created a corporate alumni association and regularly invites former employees back so that they can keep up with what's going on and maintain friendships within the company. Employees say the reason they stay isn't because of the benefits, the money, or the stock options; it's simply because they feel as if the company is home for them.

This isn't a fictitious company. It's Google.

Why is it that some companies like Google—and others such as Apple and Microsoft—rarely have to seek out highly qualified job candidates, while other companies struggle to attract even mediocre applicants? The first answer most people give to this question is that these companies offer fantastic benefits, and those benefits are a magnet for potential employees. But that assumption operates on economic theory, which assumes that people are motivated exclusively by self-interest.

That couldn't be further from the truth. If it were true, then charitable organizations would never see a dime in donations. In fact, the reason people give to charitable organizations is the same reason they flock to work at some companies and not others. It's not the salary or benefits offered that is the attraction in the workplace; rather, these companies have cleverly tapped into the powerful human universal of kinship. Kinship makes us feel all warm and fuzzy, all emotionally cozy.

Anthropologists define kinship in the strictest sense: people related by blood, marriage, adoption, or common descent. But in today's society of broken families and large geographic distances between many family members, we have taken to creating new kinships with those who may not be related by blood or descent, but who have a strong emotional bond. Kinship is one of the most basic principles for organizing individuals into social groups, roles, and categories. Yet it is the most overlooked when it comes to creating workplace communities.

However, you can't just throw a bunch of people who feel all warm and fuzzy toward one another into a group and call it kinship. Something else has to exist before the bond of kinship kicks in. That something else is kinship relevancy.

Kinship relevancy is how a group helps us to connect with how we see ourselves in the world at large. Companies that rarely have to recruit to get the top talent clearly address the kinship relevancy factor in all of their human resource activities—starting with the job-application pages on their websites.

Suppose for a moment we have two people who want to find a job in the computer industry. One is a former basketball player—let's name him Dave. Dave is a social butterfly and likes "big picture" ideas. The other job candidate we'll call Bill; he's a former high school chess champion and is more interested in minutiae and detail than the big picture. Dave is artistic, has a real talent in computer animation, doesn't like anything detail-oriented, and wants to find a computer-software developer position. Bill can't draw so much as a stick figure, but he lives to do complex calculations, to figure out how things work, and to troubleshoot computer hardware and software problems. He, too, wants a software developer position. Both decide to check out jobs at the two big computer giants, Apple and Microsoft. But when Bill gets to the Apple career page, he doesn't even bother applying; he can just tell from the page that this isn't the company for him. Dave is equally turned off by the Microsoft job site page and doesn't get any further than the registration page on the company's career site.

What was it that made each of these two so quickly decide that one company wasn't for them? The answer lies in kinship relevancy. After just a few minutes on the Microsoft career site it's easy to see that it reflects the mindset of the detail-oriented, analytical person. If you want to apply for a job through the site, you'd better enjoy detail and self-sufficiency. First you register, then you create your own personal Web page, then you upload your information, create a job search agent, and a job cart. Finally, you create a separate place to store your resumé so you can apply for multiple jobs at Microsoft.

The online application procedure is a multistep, complex undertaking—just the type of activity that folks who love facts, details, programming, and processes are drawn to. The page design also aligns with the mindset of those who prefer function to form: Lists and columns of monochromatic text greet the visitor, and there are few enticing graphics or colorful layouts. In short, it's a career application site that appeals to people who prefer to spend time in intellectual pursuits and complex activities. You have to read, think, reason, use logic, and already know a good deal about computers to figure out how to apply for a job on the Microsoft site. It's a site for applicants who love detail—exactly the type of corporate tribe you'll find at Microsoft. It's also a site that clearly shows a preference for independent self-starters. Although there is a FAQ section for the job applicant who may have a question, it is at the very bottom of the page, and it doesn't tell you how to create a shopping cart for your individual website; you already have to know how to do that. And the site has a fair amount of industry jargon.

Someone like Bill would take one look at the Microsoft site and see a culture that reflects exactly who he thinks he is, who he wants to be, what he wants to do, and with whom he wants to work. He has found kinship relevancy. Everything is in alignment with his worldview. The job application process is a reflection of the company's culture, and those who wouldn't fit in will know as early as the online job application process.

Contrast the Microsoft career site with that of Apple. The Apple site is more visually appealing; it has lots of white space, large fonts, colorful headlines, several interesting pictures and icons, clear and obvious navigation links, and common, everyday language. (Apple doesn't call its question-and-answer section "FAQs"; the company instead calls it "Common Questions." "FAQs" is a technical jargon term, something you won't find on the Apple job site.) The application process isn't really a process at all but rather a simple two-step activity: Create an account and complete an online application for one specific job. Done. The Apple site also offers help if you get stuck during the application. The Common Questions section answers such things as: "Do I need to be a lifetime Apple user to work for Apple?" (I'm not kidding! The last time I checked, that was an actual question on the job site!) and "The keywords I entered did not find any open jobs. How can I find the jobs I'm looking for?"

You won't find that kind of user-friendly help on Microsoft's application page, because people applying at Microsoft don't want that kind of help. They like to figure things out on their own. Even the job descriptions for technical positions at Apple clearly cater to the creative and "big dreamer" types with phrases such as "write code—or write the future?" and "change the specs—or change the world?" The Apple site is speaking the language of the creative, don't-bother-me-with-the-details tribe of folks like Dave. People here feel a kinship with co-workers because they are basically attracted to the same way of working and problem solving.

Companies like Google and AOL have found that kinship relevancy can be stickier with customers than their own value systems. For example, we say we loathe companies that use our personal information for advertising purposes. (In 2005, Pew Research did an Internet study where 54 percent of us said we think websites that track our browsing behavior are breaching our privacy.[10] Another study done by Annenberg Media in 2003 showed that 85 percent of us disapprove of websites that show us ads based on our Web browsing history.[11]) Yet we support en masse two companies that clearly violate those values: Google and AOL.

Every time you do a Web search on, say, Google, your IP address—the location of your computer—is stored on the company's search engine servers for up to a year and a half.[12] Every time a relevant advertiser signs up with Google, your computer is then sent an ad based on your browsing history. For example, if you visit a real estate website, you might end up getting e-mails and ads from home improvement stores. All kinds of information about you—your Web browsing habits and even your home address—can be gleaned from the IP address.

In August 2006, AOL angered users when it published the search histories of 650,000 of its users on its Web page—giving any interested marketer full view.[13] Media reports were quick to chastise AOL, pointing out that some very personal information—such as individual medical histories—could be published, too. Google caused a similar firestorm in 2002 when it was discovered that the company placed a cookie on each user's computer, which can be used to track that person's search history, and that the cookie wasn't set to expire until 2038. (Google's cookie now expires in two years but renews itself every time you use a Google service.) And in 2002, howls of protest were set off when Yahoo! granted itself the right to send ads to tens of millions of users who previously said they wanted to receive none.[14]

But for all of the hoopla, few of us have insisted on change. As it turns out, we won't even support a search engine that *guarantees* to protect our online surfing privacy. That's what a search engine called Ixquick offers. But it can't get customers.

In June 2006, Ixquick decided to make a radical move: to ditch a user's personal data the moment he or she leaves the site, and stop tracking users, period. Ixquick promoted itself as "the only search engine that deletes your personal data." But Ixquick can't catch on with Internet users. Web traffic research firm Hitwise shows that only 0.01 percent of U.S. searches are done with the privacy-protecting search engine. And the site doesn't even register on ComScore's search tracking stats, which means Ixquick—at the time of this writing—gets fewer than 50,000 users a month.[15] What's even more interesting is that the companies that have been shown to breach our privacy by collecting data about us continue to do well: Google posted record search numbers in January 2008 and AOL searches were also up from previous years, according to search analytics company Compete.[16]

Why won't we use a service that gives us exactly what we say we're looking for: complete privacy in our online searches? And why do we stick with companies that do the very thing we say we don't want them to do: collect and use our personal information to match us up with advertisers? It's because Google and AOL offer something that Ixquick doesn't: community and kinship. Kinship often trumps values when it comes to being sticky with customers.

The most successful companies and people do just what Apple,

Microsoft, and myriad others such as Google and Starbucks have done: They think about the type of person they want to attract (and also the type they want to repel) and then make every part of their brands reflect the kinship relevancy of the people they want to serve, to hire, and to engage; in doing so they align with the motives behind people's actions. This is often misunderstood: Consumer decisions and actions are based on the *whys*, not the *hows*. Many organizations focus on *how* we shop, *how* we vote, *how* we act and react to situations. But it's the *why* that has the most power to motivate, mobilize, and ultimately capture the long-term consumer, employee, voter, or charitable donor.

Think back to Dave and Bill for a moment. Both shopped for a job in the same way. But the *reasons* they were looking for a specific job were very different. Dave most likely wasn't interested in Apple just because the site was easy to navigate. The site layout and design was a clue as to what he was seeking most in a job: working at a company that valued creativity over detailed analysis. He considered himself a creative person and wanted to hang out with other creative people. Same thing with Bill. It was clear that Microsoft values complexity—where the applicant has to know how to do things like create a Web page and a shopping cart—which reflected Bill's desire to work for a company that valued detailed dissection of a process.

Had each site contained merely a bland, straightforward, cookie-cutter application form, the two companies would still attract candidates because candidates shop for jobs in much the same way; but the type of candidate each organization would attract wouldn't have the same qualities as the rest of the corporate tribe. Working is no longer about joining a good company; it's about joining a complementary culture, about finding kinship relevancy.

We subconsciously hold up the kinship relevancy mirror every time we encounter a movie, person, ideology, product, or piece of music to find out if it fits with our sense of our place in this world. If the reflection we get back looks like the place where we belong, then we're on board. This was brought out in a study of women shoppers conducted by a national brand-management agency. AMP Agency found that the way a woman shops has nothing to do with her age, where she lives, how much money she makes, or whether she has children. *Why* she shops solely determines whether the shopping experience is relevant to her. Some want to be the first to try new things—whether it's a new toy for their tot or a hot new fashion for themselves.

These are what AMP Agency calls the "cultural artists."[17] Most likely they would be hip and cool people who tend to be creative, impulsive, and on the adventurous side. They look at shopping as a fun adventure, and they see their role as one of a trendsetter. When they are "job shopping," they would like the visually stimulating page design of the Apple site, and they also like visually stimulating retail stores. Someone like Bill, on the other hand, would most likely be a "contact responsible" shopper: someone who isn't much of a spender and shops only out of necessity. The no-frills, straightforward Microsoft site suits this person well, as do no-frills stores. While being fashion-forward is important to the "cultural artist" shopper, being loyal and efficient is important to the "contact responsible."

So how do retailers appeal to groups of shoppers from such opposite ends of the spectrum? They don't. And they shouldn't. Successful retailers take the approach of Apple and Microsoft: Choose the tribe you want to appeal to the most, and design everything from advertising to store layout around the reasons why these folks shop. Most customer service training programs—which give unoriginal, scripted, step-by-step actions and phrases to use with every customer—fail because they don't take into account the differences in shopping preferences of most people. These programs usually encourage the salesperson to approach the customer, give a pat welcoming phrase, ask if the shopper needs assistance, and then either begin making recommendations for purchase or say, "If you need me my name is Kate and I'll be over there."

But a shopper who fits into the "content responsible" category is self-assured, knows what she wants, and doesn't need or want someone hovering around her and asking if she needs assistance. She wants to shop in her own way and on her own terms. She's smart enough to know that if she needs help with something, she can figure out how to find a sales clerk.

The cultural artist, on the other hand, or someone whom AMP Agency describes as "creative, impulsive, and adventurous," would probably welcome input from a sales associate because this type of social butterfly shopper wants to be in-the-know and up on the latest trends. She's a people person and likes to chat it up.

Shoppers from different "tribes" also prefer different store settings: A cultural artist would probably want a store with bright lights, bold colors, upbeat music, and a trendy in-store corner café and coffee shop where she could hang out and talk with her friends about the latest fashions. The content responsible would most likely prefer a basic, no-nonsense, clear-aisle store layout because it would reflect why he or she shops: out of necessity.

The kinship relevancy factor also creates allegiance for online customers. Google, AOL, Yahoo!, and MSN all remain popular search sites because they offer us more than just a search service; they offer us a community with like-minded people. Yahoo! has its "Yahoo! Groups" that allow users to search for communities of people with similar interests; Google has similar groups on its site; AOL has chat rooms, message boards, and blogs where members can communicate with one another; and MSN has its Instant Messenger, which allows people to chat in real time.

THE SHIFT TO KINSHIP-RELEVANCY MARKETING

The Internet has made kinship relevancy the new way to mass market. Online we can hang out in chat rooms with like-minded souls and join social networks that reflect our beliefs and interests, and even read news blogs that reflect our individual ideologies and views of the world. Groups are now formed less on shared activities and more on shared ideologies. We first identify our own values and preferences and then seek out communities that reflect those mores and inclinations.

This shift that started online has spilled over into retail, the arts, and business. It has changed the game in how successful products and services are marketed. Our collective mind-set has changed, and mass marketing no longer works. Now the way to get mass support is by microtargeting groups with strong kinship relevancy. Smaller tribes, where members have the same or very similar mind-set and a strong sense of kinship, have the power to create global success for a product.

The movie industry has taken great advantage of the kinship factor. The plethora of prequels, sequels, and remakes is no accident. Hollywood producers know that a movie franchise—a series of remakes or sequels of a previous hit movie—is an almost guaranteed box office success.[18] The most lucrative movie franchise of all time, *Star Wars*, created a cultlike following by tapping into the archetypes of the science fiction tribe and taking $3.5 billion to the bank in the process.[19] *James Bond, Jaws, Star Trek, Lord of the Rings, Rocky*, and more than 30 other movie franchises have enjoyed box office success in the billions.[20] These movies are successful because they attract a very specific type of person, and because they reflect the interests, fantasies, and beliefs of people who attend, audiences reward producers with their loyalty by attending sequels.

One of the most successful examples of a movie that took advantage of kinship relevancy to create a cultlike following was *The Secret*. It relied heavily on an Internet viral-marketing campaign to targeted groups that would be most open to the content: practitioners in self-help, metaphysics, astrology, numerology, and other related disciplines. The marketers for this movie didn't go after the mass audience. They went after the leaders of small tribes where people already believed in the concepts and ideology of the movie. Teasers for the movie were sent to these online tribal leaders, who then, in turn, passed on the information to their like-minded tribal kin, who in turn passed it on to their like-minded associates. It was only after *The Secret* had reached critical mass within these tribes that it then spilled over into mainstream America and reached mass market success.

The literary field is taking advantage of kinship marketing, too. Authors—whether they write fiction or nonfiction—are now undertaking similar kinship-relevant viral best-seller campaigns: They'll piggyback off the mailing lists of other authors, coaches, and business colleagues who target people with the same, single, narrow ideology and send a mass e-mail announcement about the release of the book to those targeted tribes. Authors who have used this approach have found their books on the best-seller lists of Amazon.com, Barnes andNoble.com, and even the *New York Times*! Kinship relevancy makes books sticky with specific audiences.

Amazon also uses the kinship factor every time you order a book. Have you ever noticed that when you place an order, the site offers up a list of related books for you to buy? It's the old "birds of a feather" theory that people who read one type of book will want more of that same type.

It's not just the best companies or movie producers or savvy authors that use kinship relevancy to persuade. The best speakers and personalities do, too, by creating tribes and the trust that goes along with being part of the group. To trust, you have to know how and where you fit into the system, whatever system that may be.

On April 4, 1968, our country got a fantastic example of how a speaker can unite an entire nation using the kinship relevancy factor. Speaking to the nation shortly after the assassination of Martin Luther King, Jr., Robert F. Kennedy drew the nation together at a time when the country could have easily been torn apart.

He spoke about how he, himself, had a family member murdered by a white man, referring to the assassination of his brother, President John F. Kennedy. By highlighting a tragic experience that both he and members of the black community had in common—the murder of a loved figure by a white person—Robert Kennedy helped create kinship relevancy by showing that we all really have the same goals and aspirations. He united a nation against a common enemy: not the white people responsible for Dr. King's death, but against the maladies of violence, lawlessness, and disorder, which affect us all. The kinship relevancy among the African-American community was changed from "a white man killed our leader" to "our country is bordering on disarray and we need to pull together with everyone else to do something about it." Kennedy gave our nation a common enemy and a single mind-set that allowed us to see ourselves as a microtribe polarized around one issue, rather than a large country of people with diverse social and political agendas.

Speakers in the $8-billion-a-year motivation industry rely heavily on the pull of the tribal connection and kinship relevancy. Self-help speakers are masters at helping you identify exactly where you fit in. Go to the program of almost any highly successful motivational speaker and you'll hear the presenter tell how he or she was once just like you: struggling, downtrodden, broke, overweight, or sick. He'll highlight the common experiences and common pains the two of you share. Then she'll say something like, "I found a way out of the trap I was in. And I can show, you, too! Just join my program."

The subtle message is: "Hey, we're part of the same tribe, so let's stick together and I'll help you out of the terrible mess you're in." Appealing to kinship relevancy is not only a powerful tool to get people *into* your circle; it's also powerful in *keeping* them there. In his book, SHAM: *How the Self-Help Movement Made America Helpless*, author Steve Salerno says that 80 percent of self-help and motivational customers are repeat customers and they keep coming back *whether the program worked for them or not.* The kinship relevancy factor is a powerful tool to develop a fidelity factor that is nearly impossible to fracture. Just as in high school, where at lunchtime tables were clearly divided up into different cliques, we're all still looking for the cliques where we fit in and are embraced and accepted. And once we find that group, we're reluctant to give up our seat at the table.

REPTILIAN COMFORT UNIVERSAL #3
An Overriding Concern for the Present

Now let's take a look at the primal preference that contributed to Ronald Reagan's success and the failure of Disney's Epcot Center.

"Are you better off now than you were four years ago?"

That was a very "instant-appeal-esque" statement. Ronald Reagan famously said those words during his 1980 presidential election bid. Reagan understood that humans are hardwired not to think about the future, but rather to have an overriding concern for the present. As Reagan knew, talking about the reality of the present moment is more appealing than making promises of a better future.

Although it may be true that the *conscious* mind is concerned with the future, the *unconscious* mind—which is the true driver of human behavior—is only concerned with the immediate present. Even though we are aware of the past and the future, the reptilian part of our brain—the part where most unconscious decisions are made—is programmed to worry only about the here and now. The unconscious mind just can't wrap itself around anything that's not happening in the moment. This, too, has anthropological roots: Our ancestors were constantly on the lookout for predators and immediate survival needs were top of mind.

That programming has remained in our current-day DNA, which is why it's so hard for us to stick to New Year's resolutions; they don't deal with the present, but rather the future. We may set long-term goals, but our primal programming has us in survival mode, and that keeps us focused on surviving day to day. Old habits and patterns are safe for us because we know what to expect. Change, on the other hand, is an unknown and counter to our internal programming. We shun the future in favor of the present. That's why when Ronald Reagan asked the "are-you-better-off-now" question, the collective unconscious mind answered a resounding "no," and therefore the *conscious* minds of citizens could immediately reject the current President (Carter) and give the command to vote for a new president. The reptilian brain, or the part concerned with our immediate safety and security, had to be convinced first that we were okay in the present, before the logical mind could give a thumbs-up to the future.

The 2008 Democratic presidential primary mobilized more voters than any election in recent memory not so much because of the *long-term* benefits our country might realize from the policies of the candidates, but rather because of the *immediate* prospect of having either a woman or an African-American as head of the free world. Unfortunately for Senator Clinton, there is also another powerful universal at work that has prevented many well-educated, financially successful women and many men from voting for her: the universal dominance of men—particularly in the public sphere.

Because men in our culture have historically held the top positions of power, and because women are socialized to be caretakers, both sexes—on a deep, reptilian-brain level—find it almost impossible to support a woman in a high-power position. We aren't even consciously aware of this bias in most cases, but it's there. It's part of our DNA.

This preference for male leaders extends beyond politics to the workplace. A January 2008 study on work and power conducted by *Elle* magazine and MSNBC.com found that stereotypes about sex and leadership are alive and well.[21] When asked whom they would rather work for—a man or a woman—three out of four women who expressed a preference said they'd rather have a male boss. California State sociology professor Janet Levor, who helped develop the work and power survey, said in a CareerBuilder.com story: "The enemy is omnipresent cultural messages, not women themselves."[22] Those cultural messages, perpetuated over thousands of years of conditioning, have sunk deep into our DNA. That makes it much more palatable to the reptilian brain for individuals to vote for a strong and intelligent African-American man than a strong and intelligent woman. But the appeal of both Hillary and Barack in the 2008 primaries was that they were seen as an immediate antidote to our current economic woes and international disputes—thereby instantly appealing to the reptilian brain's concern for the present.

Even self-improvement goals can be made "stickier" by making a slight change to the way they are positioned. If you want to stick to those New Year's resolutions, avoid saying, "I will work out five days per week," or "I will lose ten pounds." A better way to phrase it so that your goal will resonate with your subconscious mind is "I am making healthful choices." You can make choices right now: choosing the treadmill over the couch, a bag of carrots over a bag of potato chips, or health screenings over avoiding the doctor. But you can't lose ten pounds *right now*, so your subconscious mind doesn't accept the goal as valid.

Most self-improvement goals fail be
mal conditioning to focus on the imr
We say we *will* stop smoking or we
money. Business gurus often tell pec
cific, measurable, attainable, realis⁺
have a deadline). But remaining focuseu
not focused on the present, and that causes a stres
we're going against our natural intelligence, or our primai ̨ ̲ ̨di-
tioning.

Does that mean we shouldn't try to improve? Does that mean we shouldn't set goals? Of course not, because that would mean we stopped growing. But it does mean that we should have only a very *general* commitment to the *future* and an *intense* focus on the *present*. When you say, "I will lose ten pounds by June 30," you create stress ("What if I don't reach the goal?!"), and you are trying to create an emotional connection with a nonexistent abstract result. Most motivation is driven by emotions, not logic. The limbic brain—the center of emotions—can't get excited about an imaginary future outcome (and it is imaginary until it manifests).

A better way to self-improvement is to embrace what you have right *now*, where you are right *now*, and develop a theme of growth that will get you toward a *general* goal of losing weight. Don't focus on that end result—which is a milestone in the future and something your subconscious can't relate to; rather, focus on a theme of healthful living in the present.

Corporations would be more successful in having employees reach their goals if they would focus on "now" goals rather than future goals. An unappealing goal would be: "Develop your leadership qualities and take five leadership courses over the next year." An appealing goal would be: "Each day, do and document one concrete activity that will make you a better manager." Sure, that could include signing up for a class, but it can also be something as simple as reading a business article in a leading magazine today, then tomorrow implementing one thing you learned from that article.

Folk-rock singer-songwriter Jonathan Coulton used this power of the present to expand his fan base and boost sales of musical downloads of his songs. He implemented what he called a "forced march approach" to writing and recording, which he dubbed "Thing a Week."[23] It was his creative experiment, where he wrote and recorded one song each week for an entire year.

This primal propensity to focus on the present also explains why global warming just couldn't catch on as a hot issue for so long. It didn't become a sticky issue until it became an *immediate* threat with Hurricane Katrina and myriad other bizarre weather patterns that have been attributed to climate change. When we saw the devastation of Katrina, our reptilian need for protection kicked in. We knew we had to start to fight global warming for our own survival.

The most persuasive speakers, marketers, and leaders always frame their messages first in the present tense to get the "buy in" of the unconscious mind. Only after the immediate concerns of the unconscious have been satisfied can the conscious mind begin to be convinced of, or interested in, anything. Most politicians say, "I will do such-and-such if elected." But we can't think about that type of a hypothetical future; we can only process the "now."

The savvy politico combines the unconscious preoccupation with the present and the "principle of least effort" by saying something like, "Today we face such-and-such challenge, and my system of this-and-that automatically solves that problem." Notice she didn't say, "My system *will* solve these problems," because that's a future-tense phrase. Similarly, marketers have found the allure of phrases such as "get started today," "immediate delivery," and "instant rebate" to be almost irresistible with customers. Telling someone "It'll be ready in a month," or "It usually takes eight weeks for delivery," will make the sale much more difficult.

A classic example of how humans shun the future for the present was in Walt Disney's failed original concept for Epcot. Disney envisioned Epcot—the acronym stands for "Experimental Prototype Community of Tomorrow"—as "a futuristic community where people lived and worked in high-tech harmony."[24] It was to be home to twenty thousand residents, and the model city would be built in the shape of a circle—with businesses and commercial areas at its center, community buildings such as schools and recreational complexes around it, and residential neighborhoods along the perimeter. Automobile traffic would be all underground so that pedestrians could roam safely above ground. Above-ground transportation would take place via a *Jetsons*-like monorail.

Walt Disney said, "In EPCOT, there will be no slum areas because we won't let them develop.[25] There will be no landowners and therefore no voting control. People will rent houses instead of buying them, and at modest rentals. There will be no retirees. Everyone must be employed." But the public just couldn't buy into Disney's space-age version of the future, and it never became a reality. While they flocked to see Mickey Mouse and the Magic Kingdom of today, they shunned Disney's version of tomorrow. It became such a flop that Disney finally had to abandon his cherished pet project and change Epcot from an ahead-of-its-time town to a more present-day tourist attraction: an entertainment-based vacation resort with food, colorful characters, and interactive thrill-ride simulations. Present-day entertainment is sticky; futuristic communities apparently aren't with most people.

REPTILIAN COMFORT UNIVERSAL #4
Repetitive Motions That Make Us Whip out Our Wallets

Human universals also strongly influence the types of motions and activities that we find pleasurable and appealing, and they explain why we're so drawn to those amusement park rides at Disney World and Disneyland. Repetitive motions—particularly swaying motions—have a comforting effect on the psyche of humans.[26] This same principle explains why kids like merry-go-rounds, swings, teeter-totters, and whirring games, and why so many people find the cadenced up-and-down bouncing motion of horseback riding an emotionally soothing pleasure.[27] The appeal of repetitive movement is also partly what causes "runner's high"; the rhythmic running not only gets the feel-good endorphins going, but it also creates a semi-trancelike state that allows us to mentally escape reality for a brief while.

For this reason, many spas are now incorporating activities where patrons swing from ropes high above the ground. These retreats have seen an increase in visitors and income, and customers claim major emotional "breakthroughs" while swaying above the ground. These spas understand the opiate-like effect of the swaying motion on the human brain and, because of that, have a strong instant-appeal quotient to lure and retain customers.

Have you ever noticed how many pieces of workout equipment use swaying, swinging, or gliding motions? There's a reason for this beyond the aerobic benefits: People tend to work out longer on these machines because they are more fun. And they are more fun because they appeal to our primal preference for swaying motions, which can put us into a near-hypnotic state of pleasure. We're also more likely to buy workout equipment that has a swaying function built into it.

For example, Trikke hit the health market jackpot when it came out with its contraption that's a cross between a scooter and downhill skis. To make the machine work, you have to sway and rock back and forth. The product was an instant hit with workout enthusiasts and a media sensation: It even made the cover of *Time* magazine[28] and received a full editorial article in *Playboy*. Celebrity riders like Jennifer Aniston couldn't get enough of the Trikke, either! Our preference for swaying motions also helps explain the popularity of downhill skiing and rollerblading—and why rocking in a chair is pleasing to adults as well as babies.

Cults have always been masters of persuasion. Seemingly strong, intelligent people have literally been swayed to join—and remain with—their ranks. Many cults have rituals that involve swinging, swaying, and other repetitive movements that induce a hypnotic state, which makes our minds more open to suggestion. (This is especially powerful when prolonged rhythmic activities are combined with sleep deprivation.) Similarly, when you sway back and forth to the music at a concert, you are creating in your brain a feel-good chemical reaction that not only makes you feel good in the moment, but also makes you recall the event with warm feelings and positive emotions. This swaying universal is a powerful instant appeal factor in swaying (pun intended) opinion.

Some persuasive speakers have used motion tactics to improve allegiance capital (long-term loyalty) with their audiences, too. Because persuasive techniques used by successful speakers intrigues me, I often go to seminars given by highly profitable motivational speakers to find out what methods and approaches they are using.

A few years ago I attended one multiday motivational program where the speaker masterfully scheduled 12-hour programs for participants on top of several after-hours exercises (allowing for little sleep). This person also regularly engaged audience members in activities that involved swaying and other repetitive movements. He rarely spoke for more than 45 minutes without some type of exercise that involved rocking, swaying, swinging our arms or legs, or various other forms of repetitive movement—even if that movement was only for a minute or two. He claimed these were "stretch breaks" for participants. But there was more at work there.

We could have all done ten jumping jacks or simply stretched our arms and legs. But the "stretch break" movements he led all involved swinging, swaying, and rocking. At the end of the session, the speaker encouraged participants to sign up for a series of nine additional programs that he offered through his "motivational university," enticing them to register for the next one immediately. I took note of how many people signed up on the spot. They were running to the product table in the back of the room and frenetically whipping out their credit cards. I determined that about 40 percent of the audience members each doled out nearly $4,500 before leaving the seminar! There were roughly 300 people attending, so the speaker's take was over a half million.

Now, there's nothing immoral or wrong with the speaker choosing to incorporate activities that involved swaying, swinging, and rocking. But I doubt audience members were aware of what was happening to them on a primal level. Were they really making a logical choice for self-improvement by signing up for another $4,500 seminar, or were they unconsciously swayed by primordially pleasing techniques used throughout the program? This speaker was obviously well aware of the power that our primal preference for sustained repetitive movement has on emotional dedication and buy-in!

REPTILIAN COMFORT UNIVERSAL #5
Kinship Protection and Survival

Have you ever thought about why Americans simultaneously fell in love with small dogs and big SUVs?

If you have a dog in your house, then you are demonstrating another near-universal human trait. When anthropologists studied cultures all across the globe, they found nearly all had domesticated dogs, and most societies considered their four-legged friends to be a vital part of their family units.[29] But things get a little more interesting when you look at the type of dogs people prefer at different times in history.

Dog breed preference seems to reflect the mass consciousness and the societal pressures people face at a particular time. For example, if you look at the history of dog breed popularity in the United States, you'll see how the "hipness" of certain breeds coincides with social and political trends. In the 1950s and '60s—when there was great social and political unrest—small dogs were favored: The poodle was the pinnacle of popularity in 1967, with more than 250,000 AKC registrations.[30] They, and other small breeds, remained popular right up to about 1985, when the large Labrador retriever topped the list of preferred pooches.

The mid-1980s was just the time we started to feel rambunctious and almost giddy over the state of the economy; life was good as many of us landed good-paying jobs, moved to the suburbs, and built McMansions. The Lab was the perfect companion—in both temperament and size—for our new "larger" lifestyles and expanding optimism. This breed has remained atop the AKC list for over a dozen years, but the tide has again changed in recent years. According to the AKC, the toy group is making a comeback, and since 2000 four of the top ten most popular dog breeds have been small dogs. And it's not just *small* dogs that are gaining popularity, it's *tiny* dogs, often (unofficially) called "teacup" because they are so much smaller than even a typical toy dog. (Although, as an avid dog advocate, I have to mention that reputable breeders will not breed teacup dogs because of the health problems inherent in such "microbreeds." This is also why the American Kennel Club does not recognize teacup dogs.)

A small little underdog named "Uno" represented our need to believe that everything would be okay when he became the first beagle to win the Westminster Kennel Club dog show in 2008. After 132 years of being shunned, the beagle—which represents "everyman" and "everywoman"—won our hearts, and the hearts of the judges. He received a rousing standing ovation, the likes of which had never been seen before at the Top Dog competition. Why? He's cute, he represents the dog of the average person, and he represents our need to believe that despite a dismal housing market, a slowing economy, and increased layoffs, the little guy can still triumph. In short, because he's a little dog, he was instantly appealing for our time.

Why are our preferences apparently shifting back to smaller dogs, just as they did in the '50s and '60s? Two reasons:

1. *Small dogs—those in the toy group, in particular—were bred specifically as companions and for affection.* With terrorists, killer germs, economic recession, the housing slump, and global warming threatening our sense of safety and security, we once again feel the need to comfort and be comforted. Small dogs fulfill our psychological need to nurture and be nurtured; large dogs satisfy our universal human need for playfulness, or they serve as working dogs. During social unrest, political upheaval, or uncertain economic times, the nurture instinct is stronger than the play instinct and petite pooches fill that need.

2. *The changing family structure has made small dogs more practical.* According to the Census Bureau, for the first time in history single households outnumber married households.[31] Even in traditional families—with two parents and children still at home—we are interacting less and craving companionship. Our collective need as a nation for emotional closeness has led us to embrace the affection offered by pint-sized pooches. Dog breeders have taken note of the appeal that small dogs have in times of economic uncertainty.

The Power of the Protection Factor in Product Preferences

Tragedy can create a strong and instant bond between consumers and products. Post 9/11, antibacterial-soap sales skyrocketed, as they do after almost any major event that causes social anxiety.[32] Almost immediately after that fateful day in September 2001, sales of big SUVs also skyrocketed. What's the connection between antibacterial soaps and SUVs? Another human universal: the desire to protect our kin. This differs from the kinship relevancy factor (where we associate with like-minded people). This is about protecting those close to us.

Making a connection between increased sales of hand sanitizers and 9/11 may seem like a stretch—until you look at it from a primal protection perspective. Nancy Tomes, author of *The Gospel of Germs*, says when we're socially stressed, we turn to things we can control, such as fighting germs. She believes our use of antibacterials increases when we're concerned about issues such as terrorism or immigration. Tomes says our rationale goes something like, "I can't protect myself from bin Laden, but I can rid myself of germs."[33]

The desire to perpetuate the species and protect our close kin is one of the most, if not *the* most, powerful human motivators, and that is what was at work with the spike in sales of antibacterial soaps after the terrorist attacks on America. Marketers for many security products—whether it is antibacterial soap or home security systems—have found that stepping up marketing efforts after a major disaster (or even the threat of a disaster) reaps impressive profits. It's the same reason we flock to grocery stores and home improvement stores just before a major snowstorm. Many times we aren't in danger of running out of food, but our primal instincts kick in and we head to the grocery store to stock up—just in case—when weather forecasters tell us there's a storm on the way.

Several research studies show that SUVs are not safer than smaller vehicles, because their high center of gravity make them prone to rollovers; yet more than half of SUV buyers believe the monster vehicles are safer than typical passenger cars.[34] But what consumers latch onto is another statistic: that in a car-versus-SUV side-impact collision, the driver of the car is 30 times more likely to be killed than if he were hit by another car.[35]

Even high gas prices couldn't dampen SUV sales post 9/11. SUVs had two instant appeal factors at work: our primal hardwiring to protect our kin, and our unconscious impulse to act and react "in the now." Those kept people buying SUVs despite the increased threat of global warming and the claim that SUVs contribute to the planet's demise. Simply put, we are conditioned to protect our families and ourselves now, rather than the world later. This anthropologically grounded tendency is nearly impossible to override, which is why, despite a push to write an obituary for the SUVs, these big buggies remained popular until gas prices climbed to unprecedented levels. And that makes sense, because then our reptilian brains were telling us that our survival depended more on conserving financial resources than on providing sturdier shelter while on the road.

But SUVs remained popular for so long for another reason: They align with the type of living environment anthropologists tell us we instinctively seek out because we feel good in them. Geographer Jay Appleton tells us we prefer to be in places that are "high prospect" and "high refuge": That is, we want to be up where we can have a good view of the surrounding environment, and we want to be in a place where we feel safe and protected—especially from the back and overhead.[36]

The high profile and large frame of the SUV satisfy both of these primal needs. We get the same feeling sitting high up in our SUVs as our ancestors did sitting high on a hill underneath a large oak tree or in a hillside cave overlooking the land below. The high profile hooks our primal need to get a clear view of the landscape in front of us. If we can see the landscape, we can see what's coming, and that satisfies our primal protection need. On the other hand, someone sitting in a low-profile vehicle next to an SUV at a stoplight tends to feel—at least subconsciously—unprotected from above because the people in the SUV can literally look down into the car. And in cars it's nearly impossible to get a clear view of the surrounding area with all of those big boats blocking the view.

Two other subcategories of the kinship-protection universals should be briefly mentioned here: duality and the love of a common enemy to fight. We are programmed to prefer a construct that pits two opposites against each other: good versus evil, right versus wrong, cold versus warm, high versus low, black versus white, up versus down, heaven versus hell. As you'll find out in chapters 5 and 9, this preference for duality can have a powerful effect on political ideologies that we throw our support behind. Love of a common enemy closely fits into this, too: it's in our instinctual nature to want to gather with our friends to fight our foes.

Kinship Protection in Plants

Not only are we humans genetically programmed to protect our kin, but plants are, too. Take, for example, the Great Lakes sea rocket.

The sea rocket isn't just passive greenery that sits on sandy beaches. Scientists have found that it can identify whether nearby plants are family or not. If a next door neighbor is a part of the brood, then the sea rocket will politely restrain itself from sprouting roots that would eat up nutrients. But if the other plant isn't kin, the sea rocket will aggressively sprout roots and try to nab all nearly soil nutrients away from plants that are non-relatives.[37]

So it seems that just as an individual person has a built-in evolutionary propensity to protect his or her kin, plant organisms seem to compete with unrelated species to perpetuate their own gene pool, too. This finding underscores just how powerful kinship relevancy is, and why we go to such extensive lengths to protect our kin.

REPTILIAN COMFORT UNIVERSAL #6
Why High-Prospect/High-Refuge Preferences Drive Restaurant Profitability

The same primal instincts that make most people feel safer in an SUV than in a small car are the same ones that can cause a restaurant to be either profitable or struggle for customers. What makes a restaurant instantly appealing to our primal conditioning? A few things.

The next time you go into a restaurant that has both booths and tables, notice which tend to fill up first. In almost all cases, if a booth is available, patrons will request to be seated there rather than at tables. Many studies, including "The Impact of Restaurant Table Characteristics on Meal Duration and Spending," detailed in *Cornell Hotel and Restaurant Administration Quarterly*, found that people seated in booths spend more per person per meal than those seated at tables. This suggests that primordially pleasing environments make us more generous with our money.[38] This and other studies also show that anchored tables—those around the perimeter of the room—also tend to fill up faster than those in the center of the room because we prefer to be seated in a place where we are protected from at least one side and where we can look out to the vista to see what's coming. And finally, restaurants that offer us some type of overhead protection (other than just a roof) are most appealing. We like to sit under trees (whether fake or real) and canopies.

All of these restaurant seating preferences can be traced back to our primordial preference for what anthropologists call high-prospect and high-profile vistas. Booths, walls, and vegetation make the reptilian brain feel comfortable because they offer us a refuge and make us feel protected. There may not be any predators around, yet we instinctively feel more comfortable when we have some barrier of protection—especially behind us and above us.

I've noticed a lot of restaurants are getting very creative in how they provide high-refuge seating—and thereby increasing their profits. One example is a cozy little eatery on Catalina Island off the California coast. When I strolled into the restaurant, I noticed a very interesting seating pattern. The tables around the perimeter of the room all were next to little windows, and each window was covered with a little canopy that extended out over the table. But what was most clever was how this establishment soothed the reptilian brains of folks seated in those center-of-the-room seats. The restaurant owners cleverly put a large tree in the center of the room and constructed a large, octagon-shaped bench seat around the tree trunk. So patrons seated at those eight tables in the center of the room have their backs to the tree trunk, and the tree branches provided a natural overhead canopy. This is in perfect alignment with our innate preferences.

Recently I stopped in at a Panera Bread restaurant in a busy suburban Chicago shopping mall. Not one table was in an open or "unprotected" part of the room. All tables were placed around the perimeter of the room and most were booths. But what's really interesting is that the restaurant managed to increase its seating by placing several tables out in the busy mall hallway. Now, normally this would be an unpleasant and unnerving place to sit down for a meal. But Panera created a minirefuge center right there in the center of the mall by strategically placing flower boxes along a wall and installing a large canopy overhead. Patrons feel protected by the outside wall of the restaurant on one side, the flower boxes on the other side, and by the canopy overhead. Being able to look out and watch all the shoppers go by provides a "high prospect" view as well.

Window seats in general provide us with a high-prospect feel-good sense: We can look out and see anything that comes our way. Many studies have documented the decrease in stress and increase in productivity of people who have a window with a view to the outside.[39] Again, consciously we're not looking for predators, but subconsciously we feel the need to be able to get a full view of our surroundings. We'll also pay more for high-prospect restaurant locations—such as rooftop restaurants or those on the top of a bluff with a wide vista. Restaurants that have an interior design that feeds into our need for high-prospect and high-refuge seating tend to have higher profits than restaurants that don't.[40]

HIGH-PROSPECT, HIGH-REFUGE SPACES AND EMPLOYEE PRODUCTIVITY

Want to increase worker productivity? Then you may want to rethink a staple of most modern offices.

Office cubicles—which usually have high walls and an entryway that is to the back of the worker—are one of the most unnerving worker setups. Although we may like the refuge that the high walls provide, not being able to see what's coming makes us feel vulnerable, and subsequently, maybe even a little more sensitive and irritable than we would be in a different setting. I never could understand why these cubicles weren't designed with the desk facing the opening—so the back of the employee would be toward the wall—and the worker could at least have a limited view of the outside surroundings. This setup would be much more conducive to increased productivity because workers would feel more comfortable and more relaxed. Blame the current office cubicle setup for part of the stress in modern workplaces. Although these "worker boxes" may be ergonomically correct, they're anthropologically all wrong and put us on edge. And they most definitely do not adhere to primal factors of instant appeal.

REPTILIAN COMFORT UNIVERSALS AND CURRENT EVENTS

Current events—and how the reptilian brain responds to those events—guide many of our consumer choices. For example, anthropologists have found that all cultures use body adornment as a way of reflecting social, cultural, and political sentiments. In the United States, one of the best indicators of how this comfort universal for body adornment appears in current events can be found by examining the trends in men's ties.

In the late 1940s, four to four-and-a-half-inch ties were all the rage because they reflected our exuberance that war was finally over.[41] These ultrawide ties also can be found during the 1960s (liberal political passion ignited by the flower-power crowd) and 1990s (conservative political passion stirred by Rush Limbaugh). Wide ties reflect exuberance and political passion; narrow ties (like the one-and-half-inch nooses of the 1950s) mirror our conservative approach to bring about political change. And what about now—when the trend is for men to wear no ties? According to Gerald Anderson of the Men's Dress Association, it means that we are operating in a culture where we feel there are no rules.[42] It also means that clothing manufacturers who can identify and then respond to the reptilian responses we have to current events will always have high profits.

The lesson for businesses is that they, too, can use this same principle to gain a leg up in the marketplace by watching for cultural shifts and then identifying the reptilian comfort universals that match with that shift. For example, foods mirror our preferences and cultural shifts. The explosion of nutraceuticals—"functional foods" that prevent cancer, help us lose weight, reduce aging, protect our memory, and keep us heart-healthy—is no accident. It's a direct reflection of the Baby Boomers' obsession with staying young and their insistence upon high quality. We now want fresh, pesticide-free, chemical-free, hormone-free, and free-range foods. Politics, cultural leanings, and our innate inclination to perpetuate the species (kinship protection) determine which foods will be popular, and companies like Whole Foods Market that have tapped into all three of these "mirror motivators" have reaped the financial rewards.

Play is another human universal: Gaming boards dating back to 3000 B.C. have been found in ancient Egyptian archaeological sites.[43] But the types of games that we are drawn to and that become huge commercial successes are tied to what's going on in society.

There are basically two types of games: reality games that imitate what's going on in our culture and appeal to the reptilian, primal brain, and games that have no link to reality, which activate the neocortex. Reality games do best in times of major social upheavals, wars, or economic downturns because that's when the reptilian brain is working overtime in its concern for survival. If the game premise reflects a major issue society is mired in at the time of the game's launch, the game has a greater chance of being a hit. Why? Because it aligns with our primal need to have play that helps us deal, in a detached way, with what we are wrestling with in our day-to-day lives. That real-life connection to the game forms a deep emotional bond with the game, and that means it has the potential to become an all-time classic.

For example, Monopoly—a game about prosperity—was patented and first released to the public in 1935, in the midst of the Great Depression. That was a time when our reptilian brains were worried about financial survival. Risk, a game of war, was introduced in France in 1957, when the country was embroiled in the Algerian War. The Game of Life (also known simply as Life) debuted in 1860, just as Abe Lincoln was elected president, America's thirty-year moral conflict over slavery was coming to a head, and the primal part of the brain was preoccupied with the outcome. Life was a game about major life decisions and milestones—exactly what we were going through as a country. All of these games launched to great commercial success and also became classic games with long-term appeal.

Games of strategy, trivia, and logic, however, are more appealing during times of great technological advances and when there are no major pressing political, economic, or social issues. These include abstract strategy games like chess and checkers, and word games like Scrabble. This popular word game failed in its initial debut in 1949 because it was a non-reality-based game trying to find a footing when the country was preoccupied with economic woes. America was just coming off of a decade of war and a long economic depression. We were too involved in pressing real-life issues to be interested in a game that was based on intellect alone. Our reptilian brains wouldn't let us get excited about a game that couldn't help us cope with our reality.

But when Macy's re-launched Scrabble in 1952—a time more conducive to intellectual games that weren't tied to real-life challenges—it was a hit. The year 1952 was filled with great technological advances: The first contraceptive pill was developed; Dr. Jonas Salk developed the polio vaccine; the United States began construction of its first nuclear submarine, the *Nautilus*; and the United States detonated the world's first hydrogen bomb at Eniwetok Atoll in the Pacific Ocean. These conditions were perfectly suited to a game of intellect rather than a game of reality. The reptilian brain could take a rest and let the logical neocortex take over.

Trivial Pursuit is another example of an intellectual (non-reality-based) game that became popular in a year of technological advances. Its popularity peaked in 1984, just as the Apple Macintosh was released. That was also the year that Toshiba's Dr. Fujio Masuoka invented "Flash Memory": a nonvolatile computer memory that can be electronically erased and reprogrammed.

I've covered several human universals in this chapter. But there are literally hundreds more. In chapters 6, 7, and 8 I'll talk about a few others. But it's important to know that much of our behavior is driven by these universals, which have been programmed into our DNA through thousands of years of evolution. That doesn't mean, though, that we can't use our awareness of these universals to become more persuasive and more effective in our careers and our companies. Let's take a look at how we can apply the universals talked about in this chapter.

PRACTICAL APPLICATION
Using Human Universals in Your Day-to-Day Life

Certainly human universals have several applications. But the most obvious for the average person is in our day-to-day communications.

Does your audience have a primal connection to your products or promotions? When they look at your product, people have to experience two things: They have to see a reflection of their self-image and tribe (kinship relevancy), and they have to subconsciously feel that what you are asking them to do reflects their primal instincts. Do people see their "tribal" preferences in your product? Do they see their anthropological preferences for kinship mirrored in your message? If they do, you have mastered the power of the mirror factor of instant appeal.

Let's break down this application in more detail.

Applying the Kinship Relevancy Universal

First, align your communications with the preferences and tendencies of the specific groups you are targeting. If you're talking to a group of accountants, remember to engage the primal emotions of the accountant (someone who is detail-oriented). Notice that I did not say to play into the *cognitive* preferences of the accountant, which would be to include many facts and figures. I said play into the primal *emotions* of the accountant. No message will ever be effective unless you first activate the emotions of your audience. There are five primal emotions: love, happiness, anger, sadness, and fear. Several other emotions fit into these five main categories. For example, confidence would fall under the category of happiness, frustration is a form of anger, boredom is disguised sadness, and hopelessness and confusion fall under fear.

So what do you do with the accountant? How do you engage her emotions? Well, the biggest fear of almost any detail-oriented person such as an accountant is being wrong. The biggest feeling of happiness or confidence for a detail-oriented person, on the other hand, comes from having detailed knowledge. They like rules. They like facts and figures. They like complicated processes and procedures. Microsoft played into the confidence emotion of detail-oriented programmers by providing them with a job application site where they could feel good about showing off their programming knowledge in the application process.

Before giving any presentation, think about what keeps your audience up at night. If you're speaking to managers, usually their biggest fear is losing control—of profits, productivity, efficiency, or effectiveness. If performers, creative types, or socially gregarious "life-of-the-party" people make up your audience, incorporate the idea that their biggest fear is often losing prestige. Specialists in the helping professions are often motivated by avoiding one particular fear emotion: conflict. Once you know the type of "tribe" you'll be talking to, you can identify its members' preferred habits, emotions, and activities and tailor your message to them.

A final note about how to activate the power of kinship in your day-to-day activities: a few key words have been shown to immediately trigger the kinship bond and make someone part of your extended clan—even if you have never met the person before.

Suppose you subscribe to an online newsletter written by someone whom you admire. Now suppose that person sends you an e-mail saying "My good friend John Smith has just launched a new product, and I'd like you to support him in his efforts. Take a look at my pal's website now." Two phrases—"my good friend" and "my pal's"—

triggered your brain to activate the kinship bond, even though you know nothing about John Smith other than that he is a "good friend" of someone you admire. Because John is "in" with someone you have already accepted as part of your extended circle of friends and kin, you are more likely to take a look at his site and even to buy his products.

You can use this same concept to get more endorsements and support for your product or service. A client of mine wanted to get an endorsement from an international celebrity for her skin care product. She knew a big-time celebrity most likely would not just give her an endorsement. So she started out by getting endorsements from people who were not well known, but who were in the same industry as the celebrity. These people knew other celebrities who were slightly better known. These folks, in turn, knew others who were even more visible and well known. Each time she would get an endorsement from a celebrity, she would send a note to someone slightly more popular. Then, she researched celebrities who were endorsing other similar (but non-competing) products, and sent a note to those people. What happened is that once celebrities started seeing endorsements from other celebrities (people in their "tribe"), the endorsements flooded in. Not only did my client end up with *one* celebrity endorsement, but a *half-dozen*!

Applying Reptilian Comfort Universals

To tap into the human universals that motivate people in all cultures, you have to study and truly understand the hundreds of universals that directly impact our unconscious decision making. Craft your speech, letter, marketing campaign, or fund drive to align with these universals and you'll have a powerful message. Here are a few resources I have found helpful in the eleven years I've been studying human universals.

➤ Bidney, David. "Human Nature and the Cultural Process," *American Anthropologist* 49 (1947)

- Brown, Donald E. *Human Universals* (New York: McGraw-Hill, 1991)

- Connolly, Bob, and Robin Anderson. *First Contact: New Guinea Highlanders Encounter the Outside World* (New York: Penguin, 1987)

- Hyam, Ronald. *Britain's Imperial Century, 1815–1914: A Study of Empire and Expansion* (New York: Barnes & Noble Books, 1976)

- Linton, Ralph. *The Tree of Culture* (New York: Alfred A. Knopf, 1955)

- "Human Universals." *Encyclopedia of Cultural Anthropology* Vol. 2 (New York: Henry Holt, 1999)

- "Human Universals." *The MIT Encyclopedia of the Cognitive Sciences* (Cambridge, MA: MIT Press, 1999)

To improve your skill in using human universals in your communications, look at examples you encounter every day. Pay attention to the structure of advertising messages you hear. Look closely at book titles. For example, David Bach tapped into the human universal of "the principle of least effort" when he titled his book series *Automatic Millionaire*. So did Malcolm Gladwell with his book *Blink: The Power of Thinking Without Thinking*. The messages in these titles are simple: You don't have to work at becoming a millionaire, it can happen automatically; you can interpret your world without the work of having to think about your world and what it means.

Just as successful game manufacturers struck it big by producing reality games that reflected major economic and social upheavals (such as economic depression or war), when you are developing products and pitches, think about what's going on in society. If there is a major economic issue, have your ads or product more reality-based and more aligned with how the reptilian brain works. This part of the brain is preoccupied with surviving the current environment. If we're in a time of relative prosperity, then tap into the neocortex—the part of the brain involved in logic and strategy.

Human universals don't just work in marketing slogans or product development. They also work in persuasion of almost any type. So many times when a corporate manager is called upon to present his case for a new program or initiative, he will say something like, "This new program will allow our department to increase profits exponentially and help us all get higher bonuses. Let me show you the numbers." And then he launches into a dreaded PowerPoint show. Not only has this speaker just gone against a key human universal (principle of least effort), but he has also shut down our desire to listen. The audience is no doubt thinking, "Great! This program will add more work for me. Now I have to start doing things according to this new program. Yes, I want a bigger bonus, but how much harder am I going to have to work for it?!" The listener's mind has been closed before the speech even begins.

A better approach may be: "This program removes the guesswork from increasing our profits," or "This program can put us on autopilot to higher profits and bigger bonuses. Let me put this in real-life terms for you by walking you through one specific application." The example you walk them through is not some intellectual activity, but rather a real situation involving real people and real results. I'll talk more in chapter 6 about other power words and phrases. But for now, just remember to give the audience some human activity to mirror. And don't forget to turn off the data-laden PowerPoint slides!

CHAPTER 5

Gaining Power and Loyalty Through Attraction and Repulsion

― THE SACRED COW AND JACKASS FACTORS

In 1987, an impassioned Rush Limbaugh sat down at a Sacramento radio station, turned on the microphone, and began a tirade that's lasted more than two decades. He was—and is—brash, obnoxious, and in-your-face. He didn't care who he offended with his ideology and single-handedly defined conservative values in this country.

Rush Limbaugh created a lot of enemies. But at the same time, his approach breathed new life into AM radio at a time when it was losing serious ground to FM stations with better range and better sound fidelity. What was Limbaugh's big appeal? It was the very thing that made his detractors hate him: He was, quite simply, a pit bull stubbornly sticking to his ultraconservative ideology and spouting that viewpoint to anyone who would listen. That passion, that dedication to a belief, struck a nerve with listeners. AM stations across the country not only aired Limbaugh's show, but they built their entire programming around this single ideology—conservative values—and they were rewarded in the ratings.

Arbitron figures show *The Rush Limbaugh Show* has a minimum weekly audience of 13.5 million listeners, making it the largest radio talk show audience in the United States.[1] Both of Limbaugh's books have landed at #1 on the *New York Times* best-seller list.[2] *New York Times* writer Robin Toner even claimed Limbaugh was so powerful in his rhetoric that he was considered "a kind of national precinct captain for the Republican electoral revolution of 1994."[3] Rush Limbaugh's sacred cow—the ideology he would never waver on—made him a media superstar. Every person who had the same sacred cow as Limbaugh stuck to him like glue and vehemently defended him against his detractors.

On the Sirius Radio Network, Howard Stern—an ultraliberal radio talk show host—is literally and figuratively on a completely different wavelength. In 2004, Clear Channel Communications fired the controversial shock jock after he made a series of raunchy remarks that prompted the Federal Communications Commission (FCC) to impose some hefty fines on both Stern and Clear Channel. Many listeners—and even some of his detractors—weren't pleased. For example, Kate, author of a conservative blog called "The Original Musings," wrote in protest: "Howard Stern is a jackass. He's always been a jackass, he'll always remain a jackass. To suddenly yank him off the air because he said something offensive is almost equally offensive."[4] Arbitron data shows that all six Clear Channel stations saw ratings plummet and remain in the tank after the outspoken and controversial Stern left its airwaves, and subscriptions to Sirius soared when he arrived there.[5]

Stern—and his unapologetic style—have always enjoyed popularity: His 1993 autobiography, *Private Parts*, became the fastest selling best-seller in Simon & Schuster's history[6]; the 1997 biographical film by the same name, in which Stern starred, premiered at the top of the box office opening weekend[7] and raked in more than $41 million.[8] In 2006, Howard Stern was included on *Time* magazine's "Time 100: The People Who Shape Our World" list.[9] In the same year, Stern made *Forbes* magazine's "100 Most Powerful Celebrities" list.[10] Like Limbaugh, Stern isn't just popular, he's powerful.

We stand by our sacred cows and rally around our jackasses.

"Sacred cows" (protected ideologies that attract like-minded people) and the jackass factor (intentional repulsion of a portion of the audience by being unapologetically yourself) form the neural basis of much of our social behavior and constitute much of what we find appealing. They also are just two of several components that make up each person's linguistic fingerprint (a manner of speaking that is unique to us personally and no one else). We negotiate authority, respect, credibility, and acceptance every day through how we position ourselves linguistically in relation to others. This isn't about using power words or power phrases; rather, it's about the ideology you live by, the enemies you create through dogged promotion of that ideology, and the subsequent factions of loyal followers you create by remaining true and vocal to those ideals. Successfully orchestrating those elements of your personal brand will give you instant appeal and nearly unbreakable allegiance with the many loyalists you'll create.

People who combine their sacred cows with a strong, polarizing message and deliver that message with a clearly identifiable manner of speaking will get a ferocious loyalty from their intended audience— and brutal verbal attacks from their opponents. And that's a good thing. The result is a leader with clout, mass appeal, and a strong instant appeal factor. This explains why mega church pastor Joel Osteen (whose non-denominational Christian ministry attracts 47,000 to weekly services and reaches 10 million more faithful through Sunday television broadcasts of the services[11] can attract a stadium full of followers each week, but Catholic leaders often can't fill the pews of an average-size church. Osteen often preaches that wealth is a spiritual right, and nearly all of his sermons include that theme— which mainstream religious leaders attack on a regular basis.

Blame the lack of a sacred cow theme for the Democrats being unable to mobilize Americans in the 2000 and 2004 presidential elections. Credit the jackass factor for the success of people like Glenn Beck, Nancy Grace, Madonna, George W. Bush, Howard Stern, and Rush Limbaugh. If at least some people don't think you're an idiot, then you aren't promoting thought-provoking, cutting-edge ideas; you're merely regurgitating politically correct sentiments that don't require a lot of thought.

Though you may think the jackass factor has to do only with being outspoken, obnoxious, or uncompromising, it doesn't. I grew up in rural Wisconsin and had the opportunity to meet some real jackasses (the four-legged kind). The jackass is really a misunderstood animal. Most people think they are stubborn (and they can be!). But they're stubborn for good reason. Their stubbornness doesn't come from some narcissistic arrogance; it comes only from a highly developed sense of self-preservation. It's nearly impossible to force, frighten, or cajole a jackass into doing something it sees as contrary to its own best interest. (*"Niiiiice donkey. I know it's heart-attack weather with it being ninety degrees and all today, but how about I hook you up to this little cart to you so you can pull it to . . ."* EEEEEE—HAAAWWWW. Kick. Stomp. *"C'mon, it won't be all that bad, just . . ."* EEEE—AAAAAAWWWWWRRRRR. Kick. Bite.)

When a jackass thinks something doesn't suit him, he'll belt out a bray that can literally be heard up to two miles away! He's not afraid to stand his ground. He's not easily swayed. He's not a pushover. But he's also not pigheaded for no reason. What lies at the heart of the jackass factor is being unapologetically yourself, standing up for what you think is in your own best interest—and not conforming to what you think you should be or say or do based on your position or status.

ATTRACTION AND REPULSION
The Radical Principles of Power, Authority, and Trust

The thing with Stern, Limbaugh, Bush, or Beck is that they polarize people: You either love them or hate them; there is no in between. They each have a linguistic fingerprint that is not only unique to their individual personalities, but also to their ideologies. They are bold, brash, and, because of that, controversial. And they don't kowtow to anyone; they aren't afraid to take a stand and stick by it. That is why they are so popular and powerful. That's why people stick to them for the long haul. Repulsion creates loyalists.

To gain supporters, you have to create enemies because when you do that you at the same time energize your base of loyalists and give them an external force to combat. Attraction and repulsion aren't just universal laws of physics; they are also principles used universally by all people who achieve status, power, and authority. If you don't have critics or opponents, then you won't have strong loyalists either. You won't have instant appeal.

Contrast the linguistic fingerprints of powerful people with how most of us are conditioned to communicate: Our bosses tell us to minimize offense to cultural or religious groups, and communications consultants tell politicians to be constrained and conventional. Don't rock the boat. Don't offend anyone. Keep your emotions out of it. We are conditioned to be a nation of namby-pamby people who pussyfoot around the issue at hand. We're also taught to soften statements that may be perceived as too assertive or that may challenge authority. But being politically correct in our speech patterns is counter to our natural instincts and our primal programming. It causes us to lose prestige and power in the workplace. It causes miscommunication. And it can be downright deadly.

LINGUISTIC SABOTAGE AND THE CRASH OF AIR FLORIDA FLIGHT 90

January 13, 1982, was a particularly nasty winter day in Washington, D.C.: Bitterly cold daytime temps were in the low- to midtwenties, and snow fell at moderate to heavy rates throughout much of the afternoon.[12] A particularly rare meteorological phenomenon known as thundersnow—where thunder, lightning, and heavy precipitation occur (except snow falls instead of rain)—sent many kids home from school early and closed down nearly all offices in the D.C. metro area.

At Washington National Airport, Air Florida flight 90 was getting ready for its nonstop trip to Fort Lauderdale when the snowstorm temporarily shut down the airport. After the airport reopened, seventy-nine passengers sat on board the Boeing 737 as it remained idle on the taxiway for roughly forty-nine minutes waiting to be cleared for takeoff. At 3:59:24 P.M. local time, flight 90 got that clearance and the pilot took off. The flight remained airborne for only 30 seconds and flew less than one mile before it slammed into the commuter-packed

14th Street Bridge—killing all but five of the passengers on board the plane and another four people in cars on the bridge.[13]

A review of the cockpit black-box recording reveals that the copilot had tried to warn the pilot several times about the long wait between de-icings and some instrument readings that seemed out of whack. The National Transportation Safety Board (NTSB) named pilot error as one of the official causes of the crash, specifically stating: ". . . (T)he captain did not react to the first officer's repeated comments that something was not right during the takeoff roll."[14]

Think about that: Why would a pilot endanger his own life and the lives of the passengers and crew when he was told not only once, but many times, that instrument readings were abnormal and ice was building up on the wings? Why wouldn't he act on that information? It's because of who told him and how he was told. And it's the same reason why so many bad decisions get made every day in corporate America, in politics, and in life. It's what I call linguistic sabotage: the practice of making ourselves seem less capable, less competent, less confident, and therefore less believable by the words we choose and the wishy-washy speaking style we use. Through our speaking patterns we often voluntarily hand over our credibility and expertise to others, thereby positioning ourselves as inferior. This often happens when we talk "up the chain": such as when a department manager addresses a CEO, a copilot talks to a pilot, a young nurse makes a suggestion to a seasoned doctor, or a junior law associate interacts with a firm partner. But it occurs between colleagues of equal stature as well (especially, though not entirely, between men and women).

Charlotte Linde is an expert in anthropological linguistics and a senior research scientist at NASA's Ames Research Center in California (her official title is socio-RocketScientist!). She has used her training in sociolinguistics and anthropology to study the use of language in a variety of settings, including the conversations that go on between bosses and subordinates in the workplace. An area of specialty for Linde has been analyzing the cockpit conversations of many doomed flights, as well as myriad flight simulation chitchats. She reviewed the black-box conversation between the pilot and copilot of flight 90.

What she found was that although the copilot did try to warn the pilot of the impending doom, he never directly suggested they abort takeoff; he only indirectly alluded to it, and because of that the first officer's concerns about an imminent danger didn't stick with the pilot.[15] The black-box flight recordings revealed a clear case of linguistic subordination by the first officer and linguistic superiority by the captain. Let's take a look at parts of that conversation, as taken directly from the NTSB accident report, and why the copilot's statements were so ineffective.

3:47:53 P.M.; **Copilot:** Look how the ice is just hanging on his, ah, back, back there, see that? Side there.

Filler words such as *ah* or *um* make us appear less confident in what we are saying. They are also often used as an attempt to soften the impact of what we're about to say. The use of a question also diminishes the importance of the copilot's observation. Rather than firmly stating, "There's ice hanging on the wing," he asked if the pilot saw the icicles. When the copilot didn't get a response to his first comment, he yet again indirectly expressed his concern by asking another question rather than making a statement about aborting takeoff.

3:48:24 P.M.; **Copilot:** See all those icicles on the back there and everything?

Captain: Yeah.

If you ask a question, you'll get an answer but not always an action response. This would have been a perfect time for the copilot to say something such as, "Those icicles need to be removed before takeoff. We need to call for another de-icing."

After about five minutes had gone by without the captain acknowledging the first officer's uneasiness over the time that had elapsed between de-icings, the copilot again *hinted*, but didn't directly *state*, his concern. He also did not call to abort the flight. This is another clear example of the first officer's pattern of linguistic subordination.

> 3:53:21 P.M.; **Copilot:** Boy, this is a, this is a losing battle here on trying to de-ice those things, it [gives] you a false feeling of security, that's all that does.

> **Captain:** That, ah, satisfies the Feds.

It's obvious that the copilot didn't feel comfortable making a direct request of the pilot. Notice how the captain picked up on this and used linguistic superiority to let the copilot know that he didn't have the last say-so and he shouldn't be concerned about the de-icing. He was basically saying, "Hey, the Feds are happy, so why should a lowly first officer worry?"

A little more than three and a half minutes later, after they were given clearance to take off, the copilot wanted to do another safety measure.

> 3:57:50 P.M.; **Copilot:** Let's check those tops again, since we been sitting here awhile.

> 3:57:55 P.M.; **Captain:** I think we get to go here in a minute.

This was the first, and only, direct comment from the first officer throughout this entire conversation. But the pilot once again used linguistic superiority to let the copilot know they weren't about to do another safety check: The ultimate decision about whether to go or not rests with the pilot, and he wasn't about to extend an already long takeoff delay. Then, two minutes later, just as they were about to take off, the first officer noticed an anomaly in the engine instrument reading.

> 3:59:58 P.M.; **Copilot:** God, look at that thing!

> 4:00:02 P.M.; **Copilot:** That doesn't seem right, does it?

Here he used a question combined with a qualifier—*seem*—which is a double slam against his certainty and credibility. Someone with the copilot's experience definitely knows when an instrument reading is not right. Yet, he chose to ask a question and throw in a qualifier. His initial reaction to the reading ("God, look at that thing!") is clear evidence that he knew what he knew: that there was a clear problem and a real danger. A few seconds later, the copilot made another attempt to express his concerns, albeit in a submissive manner.

4:00:05 P.M.; **Copilot:** Ah, that's not right . . .

4:00:09 P.M.; **Captain:** Yes, it is, there's eighty.

4:00:10 P.M.; **Copilot:** Naw, I don't think that's right.

The first officer reverts back to using a qualifier—*I don't think*—rather than directly and firmly stating the reading is wrong. After getting no response from the pilot, the copilot decides to back off and not challenge the authority of the pilot.

4:00:19 P.M.; **Copilot:** Ah, maybe it is.

4:00:21 P.M.; **Captain:** Hundred and twenty.

The copilot went from astonishment at how far off the reading was ("God! Look at that thing!") to "maybe" believing it was right. The pilot's authoritative and declarative "Hundred and twenty" further discouraged the first officer from sticking to his guns. Giving up the verbal challenge entirely, the copilot goes into complete linguistic subordination and withdraws from the conversation with an indifferent verbal shrug. In doing so, he sabotaged not only his credibility, but also the flight.

4:00:23 P.M.; **Copilot:** I don't know.

Thirty-seven seconds later, the pilot and copilot exchanged their last words:

4:01:00 P.M.; **Copilot:** Larry, we're going down, Larry.

4:01:01 P.M.; **Captain:** I know.

4:01:01 P.M.: Sound of impact.[16]

After a June 1979 crash where a copilot had demonstrated a similar lack of communication confidence, the NTSB issued a safety recommendation for assertiveness training for cockpit crewmembers.[17] In its final report on the Air Florida disaster, NTSB investigators reiterated their concern about copilots kowtowing to captains: "While (the first officer) clearly expressed his views that something was not right during the takeoff roll, his comments were not assertive. Had he been more assertive in stating his opinion that the takeoff should be rejected, the captain might have been prompted to take positive action."[18]

If you—like the copilot of flight 90—are in the habit of using qualifier phrases such as *I think, I feel, I believe,* or *it seems* before a statement, then you are voluntarily making yourself subordinate, regardless of your title or expertise. For example, statements such as "*I think* my suggestion is on the mark," or "*I believe* the facts support what I am saying," and "It *seems* as if this is the right approach" send a subliminal message that you don't believe in your own credibility. And other people won't believe you, either. In working with lawyers to coach expert witnesses for court trials, I've found that jurors believe the testimony of the expert witness far more when he or she avoids the use of qualifiers. Other methods of linguistic subordination, which were also found in the Air Florida incident, include asking questions or giving indirect *hints* of what we know to be true, rather than making direct, clear, confident (and yes, sometimes even controversial or authority-challenging) statements.

Unfortunately I hear people diminish their own credibility every day with the words they use and the way they say those words. Linguistic sabotage takes on several forms—not just using qualifiers or questions. It also occurs when we demonstrate a lack of confidence with our tone and our inflection. The Valley Girl syndrome of ending every statement with an up tone as if you are asking a question is the credibility-smashing technique that I hear most often in women. Beyond tone and inflection, your voice quality sends subliminal messages about your credibility. In chapter 7 I talk about how slight variations in your breathing patterns, nasality, vocal resonance, and articulation influence your credibility factor—and the likelihood that people will or won't buy into your ideas.

GENDER-NEUTRAL PRONOUNS AND THE LOSS OF CREDIBILITY

Authors, news anchors, reporters, and public speakers are routinely told not to use masculine pronouns (*his, he, him, himself*) to refer to both men and women in an effort to be more gender neutral in their communication. *The Chicago Manual of Style*, as well as style guides for most major publishing houses, recommends instead that writers either alternate between masculine and feminine pronouns (using *his* in one scenario and *her* in another) or by pairing masculine and feminine pronouns together (saying *his or her*). They also recommend using gender-neutral nouns (*chairperson* instead of *chairman*, for example).

The conventional wisdom is that gender-neutral language won't offend readers, viewers, or listeners. But two researchers from the University of New Mexico found that such politically correct communication turns people off and diminishes the perceived quality of the article, book, news story, or speech. "Readers perceive alternating pronouns to be biased in favor of women—even if the use of masculine and feminine pronouns are equally distributed throughout a piece," says Dr. Laura Madson, one of the authors of a detailed study on the use of pronouns and reader perceptions.[19]

Authors who use alternating pronouns also run the risk of negative content reviews: "It didn't matter whether the topic related to men, such as how to change oil in your car, or women, such as how to weave, or a neutral topic like how to improve your grades," according to Dr. Madson. "Whenever alternating pronouns were used, the test subjects rated the quality of the work much lower than text with generic masculine pronouns. Readers said the works were 'poorly written' and 'biased.'"[20]

uncaring, and nasty? No. The goal is to help the other person improve and to produce a better end-product. Giving constructive criticism with kid gloves doesn't accomplish that goal. The "sandwich style" of giving criticism can lead to confusion and loss of credibility for you. If you gently ease into criticism with supportive comments first, you are sub-consciously downplaying your certainty about the suggestions you are giving. And that means you run the risk of not having your criticisms and suggestions taken seriously. Worse yet, you may not get the results you want, because the other person may think, "Gee, this wasn't so bad; he just mentioned one little negative thing but he had two really posi-tive comments. I really don't have to change it after all."

That's not to say you have to be downright mean and nasty. You don't. Go ahead and be nice, but don't be a sappy chump in the proc-ess. Don't confuse assertiveness with meanness. Be direct and to the point, and also include a benefit to the person if he or she takes your advice. In the example with the sales forecast report, you could have simply stated, "The writing in the report is too technical and unclear for the audience, and that prevents your message from getting across. Eliminating the jargon and writing in a more active voice will help read-ers understand the implications of your research and insights, which you worked so hard to develop. Unforunately, the way it's written now, all of your hard work will fall on deaf ears." Notice there was no, "Gosh, you did such-and-such so well, but . . ." statement. No sapless sugges-tions. It's to the point, clear, yet congenial. You can be nice when giving criticism by including a benefit to the person for changing his or her ways—not by giving a compliment. Save the praise for the improved finished product. Then feel free to load it on.

THE JACKASS FACTOR IN COMMUNICATIONS
Attraction Through Repulsion

Imagine a political candidate in the conservative Midwest who sup-ports the medical use of marijuana, believes prostitution should be legalized, and thinks organized religion is "a sham and a crutch for weak-minded people who need strength in numbers."[24] He takes on just about every established institution and every respected politician. He doesn't filter what he says; his style is bombastic and unapologetic. This person is a third-party candidate, has few funds, and spends considerably less than his Democratic and Republican opponents on the campaign. The media hates him, his opponents loathe him, and even a large contingent of his own party staunchly opposes him. Oh, and in political debates, he admits that he hasn't formed an opinion on some policy questions. But he does have a strong opinion on two issues: taxes and education. Specifically, he supports eliminating the income tax and implementing a so-called retail fair tax: a national retail sales tax levied at the point of purchase on all new goods and services. Although he generously supports education in general, he opposes teachers' unions and doesn't believe in funding higher-educational institutions.

What chance do you think such a person would have of winning an election? As it turns out, a good one.

Former pro wrestler Jesse Ventura won the governorship of Minnesota despite a barrage of criticism aimed at his often-inflammatory remarks. But his upfront honesty about controversial subjects was a breath of fresh air for voters. And voters said they had the most confidence in him to deal with his two most controversial campaign issues: taxes and education.[25] Ventura went on to gain the highest public approval ratings of any governor in Minnesota history, with some polls showing 73 percent of the populace giving him a nod of approval, despite his controversial comments.[26] Even if some didn't agree with his political stand, they admired his pit-bull-like adherence to his sacred-cow issues and his jackass-style (direct and not politically correct) of communicating. Many called him an idiot mainly because he didn't fall in line with political correctness.

Jesse remained popular until he strayed from his original ideological sacred cows, began calling for $2 billion in tax increases to close a budget gap, and confused voters by trying to be both "Jesse the Governor" and "Jesse the World Wresting Federation commentator." Trying to perpetuate two competing personal brands is what ultimately led to his downfall. Voters were no longer sure what he stood for. But even today, Ventura enjoys a cultlike following. Just read the over-whelmingly pro-Ventura blog posts when *The Huffington Post* ran a January 2008 article about his new book. *Post* readers called him "brave," "honest," and a "Patriot." Many called for him to run for President.[27] And when Jesse Ventura appeared on Larry King live in April 2008, the host posed this question to viewers: "Should Jesse Ventura run for president?" Before the show was over, 85 percent cast a "yes" vote.[28]

Why were voters initially drawn to this bad boy? Some media commentators have suggested it has to do with the intellect of Minne-sotans. But that wasn't the issue at all. What Ventura's victory and ongoing popularity really has to do with is our primal conditioning to crave controversy and to have enemies. Conflict, it turns out, is another of the human universals; and Ventura certainly knew how to stir things up.

Humans need duality and opposition to make sense of things. We are programmed to think in terms of black or white, right or wrong, left or right, up or down, friends and enemies. When we don't get a clear sense of a line being drawn in the sand, we become apathetic. It's not just that we get an emotional charge out of controversy, but controversy helps us sort out issues and ideas. When things become too comfortable, too routine, or too pleasant, we mentally tune out. Conflict forces us to take sides. People who are brash, outspoken, or even considered by some to be obnoxious jackasses, polarize people: We are forced to side either with them or against them. They become friend or foe. And we'll invest a lot of energy to protect our friends and ward off attacks from anyone who opposes them. Just as there are human universals that support the other instant appeal factors, there is also a human universal that supports the jackass factor: the need to have duality—good versus evil, right versus wrong, black versus white, friend versus foe, or a "for or against" mentality.

Each campaign season we hear voters say they want candidates who don't sling mud. We say we just want the politicians to play nice: don't argue, don't attack one another, be buddies. But we really don't want that at all. It sounds like the right thing to do and the right thing to want, but cordial, chummy verbal contests aren't in our makeup. Most

Americans expect a ritual linguistic fight. We want ideas to be presented in absolute form (not PC speak) and we want them to be challenged—even attacked—because if the ideas aren't boldly attacked, they can't be put to the test. And if ideas aren't tested, we end up with untested policies and even untested laws. Untested policy decisions lead to economic and social problems with shaky solutions.

This same thing applies in companies. We're so worried about hurting other people's feelings that we often don't challenge their suggestions, and we end up implementing policies out of politeness rather than practicality. Even though we may say we want peace and harmony, when it comes to communications, we would rather have a linguistic fight between two people who throw verbal barbs than two goodie-two-shoes exchanging pleasantries. (Back to folks like Rush Limbaugh and Howard Stern; their appeal would have been far less had they diplomatically expressed their views.) Even people who truly do despise conflict in communications give their loyalty—and the power—to the folks who have a more brazen linguistic fingerprint.

Almost all successful people from politics to business achieved success partly because they had enemies. Just do a Google search for "I hate ———" and fill in the blank with the name of a person who has achieved a high level of success. Try Steve Jobs. Or Bill Gates or Bill Clinton. Or Dr. Phil. Or even Oprah. (Yes, even internationally beloved Oprah has an equally vocal group of vehement detractors!)

When George W. Bush unapologetically led the country into war, he experienced that same kind of unyielding support in part because of the "linguistic repulsion" factor (which is part of the jackass factor). You may recall a news conference statement by President Bush that raised the ire of a lot of people: "When it comes to our security, we really don't need anybody's permission."[29] He had an "I'll-do-it-my-way" attitude, and it was clear we were going to war one way or the other.

His detractors criticized him for being a cocky and crass cowboy, but his champions were maniacal in their loyalty and were quick to pounce on anyone who uttered a word of discouragement against him or his policies. When Natalie Maines of the band Dixie Chicks said the band was "ashamed that the President of the United States is from [their home state of] Texas," program managers at country music stations pulled their Dixie Chicks CDs and many fans boy-cotted their music.[30] When talk show host Bill Maher disagreed with President Bush's characterization of the 9/11 terrorists as "cowards," advertisers withdrew from Maher's show, *Politically Incorrect*, and it was eventually cancelled.[31] By stating his ideas so brazenly and so unabashedly, Bush had created a throng of loyal followers.

You may be wondering why the jackass factor didn't work for Bill Maher and the Dixie Chicks when they denounced conventional wis-dom. Maher, especially, has never wavered from his political stance nor his outspoken approach. And he has legions of staunch support-ers. So why did he get the boot? Why did the Dixie Chicks get kicked off radio airplay? It's because just one instant appeal factor alone won't guarantee mass allegiance. You can't have *just* the conspicuous flaw factor, or you can't *just* look the part, or you can't *just* have the jackass factor, or promote a sacred cow, or use human universals. At least four of those primal triggers, or instant appeal factors, need to be simultaneously at play.

George Bush had several going on at the same time: His facial features supported what we subconsciously expect from a leader in wartime, he had several apparent conspicuous flaws, he had the jack-ass factor, and he had the sacred cow factor. He also had a more powerful element in his ability to rally a mass audience: moral entre-preneurship, or the ability to tap into human morality universals. This was George W. Bush's real talent. (I'll talk about George Bush's moral entrepreneurship as it relates to the war in Iraq in chapter 9.)

Bill Maher certainly had the jackass and sacred cow factors work-ing for him. But—just after 9/11—our primal programming and human universal to protect our kin and fight back was too powerful for Maher's typically appealing jackass-factor rants to overcome. With the Dixie Chicks, the Bush-bash came out of the blue: They were known as singers, not political commentators. Plus, lead singer Natalie Maines didn't have the look of someone who challenges the leader of the free world. Her beautiful, pleasingly proportioned facial features didn't mesh with someone from whom we expect to hear tough or insightful political commentary. More important, the timing was all wrong. Just as Bill Maher couldn't overcome our human universal for self-preservation that was put into overdrive with 9/11, Ms. Maines didn't stand a chance against our primordial programming either.

The real appeal of a strong—even a Ventura-like loose cannon—leader boils down to one thing: confidence. We are drawn to people who know who they are, know what they want and go after it, and are so independent and self-assured that they don't need or want the approval of anyone. They are comfortable in their own skin. They have found their own voices. Their strong and assertive nature is intoxicating and makes us feel safe in their company because we get the feeling that they can overcome anything.

Several people trigger safety and security feelings in the primal brain because of their in-your-face, bold style. Motivational speakers have mastered the power of the sacred cow and jackass factors. Take, for example, James Arthur Ray. When you watch him on the speaking platform, his delivery can, at times, border on arrogance, and his ideas are on the radical side. He's not namby-pamby in responding to audience members who may disagree with him. He believes in his ideas, he believes in his mission to help other people, and those are the only things that matter. Political correctness is not part of his consciousness. He's the only expert from *The Secret* who boldly came out in support of tenets of the book that some psychologists, classically trained scientists, and religious leaders called pseudoscience. Yet *Fortune* magazine has touted Ray as the next Tony Robbins, Stephen Covey, or Deepak Chopra—all sell-out-event megastars in motivation.[32] Gauging by the attendance at one of his recent seminars that I attended, it's clear Ray is a hit with the self-help crowd. That's due largely to his belief in his message, his brashness, as well as his subtle yet powerful use of hypnotic words and phrases that make people so quick to align with him—and to buy from him. (I'll talk about primordially appealing words in Chapter 7.)

We often equate polished, politically correct people with privilege; they just don't seem to be real people with real emotions and real problems. People like Ventura, George W. Bush, and the late Governor Ann Richards of Texas, on the other hand, came off as real people just like us who had strong beliefs and even stronger voices.

SACRED COWS AND THE "SURE THING" MENTALITY

Watching gamblers in Vegas is an interesting activity. Some gamblers stay at one table; others flit from table to table. The decision-making process that drives a gambler to a new table is not unlike the process of deciding whether to elect an incumbent or a challenger, whether to buy Charmin or Scott toilet paper, or whether to eat at McDonald's or Subway.

Nathaniel Daw and John O'Doherty of University College London used slot machines and functional magnetic resonance imaging (fMRI) to see how gamblers decide whether to stay at a slot machine that reaps steady profits or test the payout potential of a new machine. Researchers called staying with a known entity "exploitation" and switching to an unknown "exploration."

It turns out we seem to prefer exploitation to exploration; we feel safer with what is known—even if something new may be superior. Daw and O'Doherty found that a specific region of the brain is responsible for whether we stick with the old or try something new: The frontopolar cortex and sulcus are particularly active when we choose to explore.[33] But these regions only become active if we perceive the status quo to be marginal or that the benefits of trying something new will exceed the risks.

As an example of how these regions of the brain can be influenced to change behavior, consider the most common lunch item in the United States: the hamburger—offered by McDonald's, Burger King, Wendy's, and similar vendors. How is a competitor to overcome the entrenched burger behavior? The answer is to highlight the inadequacy of the hamburger habit. Although Subway sandwich shops have been around since 1965, it wasn't until the chain attacked the status-quo hamburger habit head-on by minimizing the risk of exploring a new lunchtime habit that its sales really took off. Through spokesperson Jared Fogle the chain clearly showed the healthful benefits of eating Subway sandwiches. Taco Bell took the same approach of minimizing the risk of switching when it attacked the hamburger habit as boring. Currently, Subway is the third largest fast-food franchise in the world in sales, behind Yum! Brands (KFC, Taco Bell, Pizza Hut, Long John Silver's) and the long-time king of fast food, McDonalds.[34] Subway may have changed the lunchtime habits of a lot of people through exploration, but the primal brain still seems more comfortable with the old standby.

George W. Bush hit on the same neurological triggers that make us favor exploitation over exploration in one critical campaign trail interaction in his re-election bid. Political reporter and *Time* pundit Joe Klein, in his book, *Politics Lost*, says the 2004 presidential election came down to two sentences:

KERRY: I actually voted for the $87 billion [to fund Iraq] before I voted against it.

BUSH: You may not always agree with me, but you'll always know where I stand.[35]

With his one-line statement, Bush created the same type of unbreakable brand allegiance that causes us still to prefer hamburgers to tacos or subs (even if it is by a smaller margin than before). Candidate Bush, in typical instant-appeal manner, activated the frontopolar cortex and sulcus when he so strongly held to his sacred cows. By reminding us that his opinions and stands were unwavering, many Americans felt Bush was a safer bet than Kerry—even if we didn't like Bush's ideas. At least with Bush, voters knew what they were getting, and that made us feel more at ease in choosing to stay with him rather than go with what Republicans called a flip-flopping Kerry. Our memories went back to another leader who firmly stood his ground: Ronald Reagan, who was viewed by many as a man who made decisions without consulting the polls first.

This same idea of going with "the sure thing" even when the alternate could yield better—although not guaranteed—results is also reflected in many studies on gaming theory.[36] Most people simply want to place their money (or their vote) with a *guaranteed* (even undesirable) outcome rather than the *potential* for a better outcome.

British politician Tony Benn—Labour's longest-serving member of parliament who served for 51 years—tapped into this "sure thing" mentality. Benn was much beloved by his constituents for his firm stand against formal authority and war. Once again, people knew what they were getting with Benn, and they re-elected him to parliament for a half-century. Electing him was a comfortable habit.

A lot of politicians fail to gain mass allegiance because they rely too heavily on polls. Voters hunger for authenticity in candidates, but candidates can't be authentic when their opinions change with the poll results. In his book, Klein brilliantly outlines the downfall of Al Gore and John Kerry, detailing how they just couldn't find their sacred cows and stick to them. Gore is a passionate environmentalist and wanted to speak out on those themes during the 2000 election, but his consultants wouldn't let him do it. Why? The polls said to stick to Social Security.[37] John Kerry wanted to talk about his anti-Vietnam activism. But his consultants said it was too risky, so Kerry kept quiet. Unfortunately, that allowed Swift Vets and POWs for Truth to launch a smear campaign that stuck: He was subsequently portrayed as a traitor instead of a passionate activist.[38]

Perhaps the most successful example of a politician who ruled solely by her sacred cow ideology was Margaret Thatcher, who served as British prime minister from 1979 to 1990. Thatcher was one of the most powerful and longest-serving politicians in the UK. She is the first and to date only woman to hold posts as prime minister and leader of the Conservative Party. Her tenure as prime minister was the longest since that of Lord Salisbury, who lead the country for thirteen years.

Obviously, this woman had some serious political clout. What was her instant appeal? She had two sacred cows—reversing the UK's economic decline and reducing the role of the state in the economy—and every decision she made supported one of those two ideologies. What Thatcher knew is that the sacred cow factor is so powerful because philosophy trumps policy when it comes to long-term loyalty: Even if a politician doesn't get her policies implemented, she can still change the mind-set of the nation and leave a lasting legacy. Leaders who focus on a scorecard of victories rather than larger societal themes often have short-term popularity and short-term loyalty. That's why inexperienced politicians can often unseat long-term incumbents: Pitching a new philosophy resonates more with voters than a tally sheet of laws passed.

SACRED COWS IN TV NEWS
Why We Prefer Biased Coverage

A report by *Broadcasting and Cable* shows that Americans trust Fox News and CNN far more than any other media.[39] In a national survey, Fox and CNN each got 11 percent of the confidence vote, while the big three networks, major newspapers, and news magazines all received 4 percent or less each of audience trust.[40] How can this be when Fox and CNN both have anchors who unabashedly bellow their biases with the fervor of a braying jackass? Fox's feisty überconservative Bill O'Reilly has had the highest-rated cable news program for seven years.[41] Sean Hannity is another provocative, outspoken, and free-wheeling commentator who cohosts the #2 cable news program[42] with hard-hitting (and equally outspoken) liberal Alan Colmes. CNN has opinionated Lou Dobbs, who vehemently promotes his anti-immigration platform and what he calls the "excesses of capitalism"; Glenn Beck, who sarcastically screams his slanted orthodoxy; and Nancy Grace, who takes on crime and criminals with the vengeance of a pit bull.

It's interesting to look at the link between biased coverage and ratings. According to a 2006 report by The Project for Excellence in Journalism, 68 percent of Fox cable stories contain personal opinions.[43] A 2005 "content analysis" report showed that "Fox was measurably more one-sided than the other networks, and Fox journalists were more opinionated on the air."[44] And where does Fox stand in the cable news ratings? Number one. What was once an upstart news organization (Fox News launched in 1996, compared to CNN, which first aired in 1980) now has eight of the ten top programs on cable.[45]

Much of Fox's success in winning the ratings war for total audience share—and in the process becoming the dominant player in the cable news category—comes from its headstrong anchors and hosts who, depending upon your point of view, are irritating, ossified, or refreshingly frank. CNN also is a ratings winner with its outspoken anchors. In terms of cumulative Nielsen ratings or "unique viewers," CNN rates as America's number-one cable news source; but it's ranked number two behind Fox News in total audience share.[46] Liberals hate Fox News. But conservatives stick to the news network like glue. Its audience is loyal and supportive. CNN enjoys the same allegiance from its viewers who are looking for news from like-minded personalities.

Local news stations are—either consciously or not—becoming more and more biased in an attempt to follow the successes of Fox News and CNN. Stations will put on only what viewers will watch, and sacred cows and jackasses seem to be ratings winners. A 2004 study on the state of local television news conducted by Journalism.-org showed the trend toward more bias in local news coverage.

> The study consistently found a distinct one-sidedness to controversial stories. Indeed, in stories that involved some controversy, 60 percent of the stories told mostly or only one side. Another 40 percent contained a clear mix of opinions. This was true every year of the study, and though there were differences each year, no pattern emerged to suggest that this was an issue of resources or people being increasingly pressed for time.[47]

Why the preponderance of bias in local TV news? Why are the biased and opinionated anchors on CNN and Fox so popular? It is precisely *because* they are so blatantly biased in promoting their political sacred cows that these two networks have received the highest trust ratings of news consumers. Yelling your bias (being a jackass about your sacred cow) from the rooftop sells. If you've ever heard the phrase "birds of a feather," you'll begin to understand the dynamic behind why we want to watch news stations that align with our personal beliefs. Conservatives flock to Fox News because they know when they tune into the network they will get a news viewpoint that aligns with their own personal political leanings. Same thing over at

CNN when people tune into Lou Dobbs, Glenn Beck, or Nancy Grace: Viewers know what these people stand for and that's comforting.

Several independent social science research studies clearly concluded that we run to the brand we know as a mental shortcut.[48] Sifting through unbiased news accounts takes up too much mental energy for most of us; we would rather have the news of the day "interpreted" through an organization that shares our own views. We don't have to think then; we can just nod our heads in agreement. In addition to being a sacred cow factor, this also aligns with the "principle of least effort" that was discussed in chapter 4.

CNN and Fox intentionally create opposition and conflict through their bias because they know that having strong detractors will also make their core audiences more loyal. Local stations are getting that message, too, and are becoming blatantly biased in many cases. And even though we *say* we don't like biased coverage, our actions tell a different story, as evidenced by the ratings. Our preference for bias— for ideas that we are comfortable with—is one reason for the success of many blogs and websites: People with similar viewpoints want to read ramblings by people with other similar viewpoints. Don't rock our mental boats; just give us more of what we already believe so that we can continue to feel good about our viewpoints, and give us something to rally behind and someone to cheer for. It's ironic that leaders in corporate America go to great pains to avoid opposition to their ideas, for fear of alienating any segment of the general population that might someday be a customer. But bias is profitable. Just ask news executives.

THE BOLD AND THE BASHFUL
Who Gets Promoted

I do a lot of corporate communication consulting, and so many times I see watered-down messages that are "safe" and "nonthreatening." They're also ineffective.

For example, about a year ago I did a session with two managers at a large pharmaceutical company as they were preparing a company-wide presentation to announce the rollout of a new national marketing plan for one of their new products. One manager, Tina (not her real name), would conduct the part of the presentation that explained the creative concept behind the plan, since she came up with the entire idea; the other manager, Bill (again, not his real name, since I want to protect the identities of my clients), would talk about the unconventional and unproven strategy for execution. The new marketing approach they were going to introduce was a radical departure from previous, conservative, "in-the-box" tactics. But when I looked at the content of the speeches, I noticed that neither contained any of those countercultural components.

The presentations were rather generic and vanilla, not giving any specifics of the plan, which is where the real genius of the program hid. I was surprised that these truly brilliant ideas weren't included in either speech. I suggested that they add some of those more forward-thinking specifics to the presentation, but Tina would have no part of it. Her response was: "I'd be opening myself up to some questions and we don't want anyone to question anything in the speech. You see, our corporate culture doesn't like anyone to rock the boat. The goal is to have no one challenge the proposal, so we need to keep it vague. My boss says to just make sure not to make any waves so we can push this thing through pretty much unnoticed until after it's rolled out. We want to make sure everyone is on board with this and no one raises any concerns."

I asked her how people could be "on board" with it if they didn't really understand it and weren't given all the specifics.

"It's not important that they fully understand it," she said, "just that no one opposes it. If we don't give them any meat, there'll be nothing for them to jump on or attack."

Huh?

This approach—to avoid attack or confrontation—is completely counter to our primal programming. Sadly, I hear this all the time in organizations (good ideas getting buried for fear of a little challenge). Unfortunately what Tina (and her boss) didn't realize is that by avoiding opposition, she would come off as insecure in her ideas and, although she may avoid challenges and questions in the short run, she will also never have enthusiastic, long-term buy-in; she'll get a ho-hum sign-off on the proposal, but there will be no real passion behind that sign-off. What happens when you "get everyone on board" is that, at the first sign of trouble, everyone will also jump ship. When you state your ideas boldly and create opponents in the process, what you do is also create a ferociously loyal base of supporters who will stick with you through good times and bad.

After hearing my arguments for why it would be more effective to face opposition head on, Bill decided to be bold and include some of the more controversial elements of the proposal in his speech. (It's interesting that Bill and Tina had the same boss.) He even started his comments with, "This program isn't going to be for people who like business as usual at (our company). If you're comfortable with the way you're doing things, then you're about to get very uncomfortable. And that's okay. You're either going to be with this program or against it. I hope you'll be with it after hearing the details. But if you're not, let's find out now."

The result? As he expected, some people were staunchly opposed to his ideas and were very vocal in their opposition; others were strongly in favor of it. No one was neutral. The verbal salvos flew in his Q-and-A session. Yet Bill got a lot of respect for "telling it like it is," and his supporters were so enthusiastic and so excited to finally have a new direction that they immediately began working "fast and furious," as the saying goes, to implement the plan components. His boss took notice of the faster-than-usual progress and within three months Bill got a big promotion.

What about Tina, who played it safe in her speech? Her presentation got exactly the response she hoped it would: a pleasantly neutral reception. No one asked a single question after her talk. And because she is still afraid to take a stand and voice confidence in her ideas, that's exactly where her career remains: in neutral. She was left with the mistaken impression that her speech was a success because no one asked any questions and many people went up to her after her talk and said, "Nice job." Yes, it was all very nice. Yes, she did do a "good" job. But she didn't knock it out of the ballpark. She created no opponents and, therefore, also created no loyalists. It just wasn't very motivating or mobilizing, and it certainly didn't do much to promote her as a champion of her own ideas. Ironically, Tina thought the corporate culture wouldn't accept a bolder approach. But by shaking things up a bit, Bill got a promotion while Tina remained stuck—even though most of the ideas in the marketing plans were *hers*, not Bill's!

Too many professionals today give speeches that all sound the same: They adhere to a formula of safe content that doesn't ruffle any feathers; abides by a cookie-cutter format of slides, graphs, and charts; and is often delivered with mind-numbing mediocrity that puts their audiences to sleep. Those who boldly and unapologetically put forth their ideas are seen as real leaders, because, as I mentioned earlier, conflict is a universal human need; without it we lose interest.

Operating in a politically correct (PC) manner also costs companies a fair amount of money. Not just from the lost productivity and inefficiency that PC communications cause, but in consultant fees. So many times employees lament, "I can say something and it falls on deaf ears, but if a consultant comes in and says it, then it's gospel." Oftentimes consultants don't offer any earth-shattering new perspectives. What they do is present information and make observations in blunt, direct, often feather-ruffling form—something employees typically aren't allowed to do at a lot of companies. Consultants don't have to worry about going against a corporate culture or upsetting co-workers or the boss. They can speak freely and openly without "sugar coating."

When you are politically correct, the core message often gets missed. "Blunt-speak" gets heard—and acted upon. Tell-it-like-it-is consultants get paid big bucks; verbally placating employees are tied into salaries that are oftentimes less than their experience and skill warrant.

LINGUISTIC SHOCK AND AWE
Monikers to Reflect Our Mind-Set and Reinforce Support

Cubbie's diner in Beaufort, North Carolina, seems like any other restaurant in small-town America. That is, until you look at the menu.

If you want french fries to go with your hamburger, you won't find them. But you can get "freedom fries." For a buck sixty-nine.

Neal Rowland decided to rename the starchy treat after French officials started to back away from support for the war in Iraq. Soon afterward, official legislation was introduced—and passed—to replace french fries and french toast in all restaurants and snack bars run by the House of Representatives. "Freedom toast" and "freedom fries" became standard fare on the menu instead.

You might call this the "moniker" jackass factor: names that brazenly promote a belief system. And retaliatory nomenclature is nothing new. During World War I sauerkraut became "liberty cabbage," hamburger was called "Salisbury steak," and Germania Life Insurance was renamed to Guardian Life. Even dogs couldn't escape the linguistic retaliation against the Germans: dachshunds were called "liberty pups." We did, however, continue to refer to rubella infection as German measles. These labels have an instant appeal power all their own: They rally people to causes, against adversaries, and pump up our patriotism.

Wars are fought on linguistic battlegrounds as well as physical battlefields. In a National Defense University report titled *Shock and Awe: Achieving Rapid Dominance*, authors Harlan Ullman and James Wade explored the impact of war rhetoric in creating a sense of doom in the enemy.[49] They found that the most psychologically powerful rhetoric is a combination of what comes from official sources (such as phrases describing military operations as "a campaign of shock and awe" with "overwhelming force") as well as from civilians, such as Neal Rowland and his freedom fries. Once a retaliatory phrase against a political rival is adopted by the average Joes and Janes of the country, it has added power; our opponents know the mind-set of the country is united behind the leaders.

This was another instant appeal tactic used by the Bush administration to gain widespread support for going to war. Giving a label to the enemy and then using that label repeatedly to make an association between the enemy and morality is a powerful subconscious persuader. Following the terrorist attacks of September 11, the Bush administration repeatedly used the word *evil* and the phrase *evil empire* to describe Osama bin Laden and gain support for a war. Here are just three of many excerpts from President George W. Bush's speeches that were clearly designed to incite a sense of moral obligation to fight bin Laden. Notice how many times he uses the word *evil* and how he clearly paints a picture that it's our moral obligation to go to war.

NOVEMBER 2, 2001:

I don't accept the excuse that poverty promotes evil. *That's like saying poor people are* evil *people. I disagree with that. Osama bin Laden is an* evil *man. His heart has been so corrupted that he's willing to take innocent life. And we are fighting* evil, *and we will continue to fight* evil, *and we will not stop until we defeat* evil.

NOVEMBER 10, 2001:

In a second world war, we learned there is no isolation from evil. *We affirmed that some critics are so terrible they offend humanity itself. And we resolved that the aggressions and ambitions of the wicked must be opposed early, decisively, and collectively, before they threaten all of us. That* evil *has returned, and that cause is renewed.*

NOVEMBER 11, 2001:

It is also a reminder of the great purpose of our land, and that is to rid this world of evil *and terror. The* evil *ones have roused a mighty nation, a mighty land. And for however long it takes, I am determined that we will prevail.*

Retaliatory monikers make us more loyal and have the power to mobilize people to support a cause. President Bush's speech writers knew this.

I've mentioned that we need enemies. But having enemies isn't enough; we also have to have a retaliatory language unique to our enemies (or our corporate competitors). Just listen to popular media celebrities such as Maher, Beck, and Limbaugh; they all have labels that they place on the people and things they see as "the enemy."

Savvy companies incorporate "enemy phrases" into their marketing slogans, too. Chicago station AM 560 (WIND) has on its billboards: *Liberals Hate Us*. This simple phrase has the effect of drawing a philosophical line in the sand and, as a result, gets tremendous loyalty from its conservative listeners.

Leaders who want to clearly state their sacred cow beliefs would do well to create powerful "shock-and-awe" monikers and slogans reflecting their values, and they should use those linguistic phrases frequently in their communications.

PRACTICAL APPLICATION
Who Ya Gonna Turn Off?

If you want to be appealing, you have to be ready to stand by something that you really believe, and you have to be willing to express your opinion boldly and unapologetically. Of course, being a jackass about your sacred cow is going to turn people off—ironically, the more you turn some people off, the greater you will turn other people on. That's why when I coach leaders on how to be more appealing I start many discussions with a counterintuitive question: Whom do you want to repel?

After a long silence and a perplexed look from the client, I usually have to repeat: "What type of person do you want to turn off with your communications?" (They seem to have a hard time getting past the conventional wisdom, which says not to rock any boats.)

I invariably get the question, "Why would I want to turn anyone off? Isn't the purpose of building a strong personal brand and personal communication style to build a large base of followers? You want me to turn people off?"

Yes, I do. To expand your base of support, you have to reduce your appeal. Identifying exactly who you *don't* want to align with you is just as important, if not more important, than identifying whom you *do* want to support you.

To build strong, successful companies, it's imperative that all of the managers within that company—not just the CEO—have strong sacred cows and jackass (passionate) linguistic fingerprints. Some people have challenged me, saying that if all of the managers develop their own style and values, then the corporate brand will be diluted.

Not so.

Apple is a great example of how the corporate personality and leadership personas can be successfully aligned. Apple built its reputation on being a rebel, the "anti-Microsoft." Its co-founder, Steve Jobs, is like that personally. And in every communication about him—whether in a *Time* magazine cover story, a blog he's written, or a podcast—he sends off that same rebel, free-thinking vibe.

Apple is the anticompany. It's run by the antileader. It produces out-of-the-box products and often hires unconventional employees. Because of this consistent corporate personality, it consistently attracts a particular type of customer and a particular type of employee. It has a cultlike following; a customer base whose loyalty is the envy of many a wannabe competitor.

I'm not saying your corporate personality has to be unconventional to gain customer allegiance. It doesn't. But it does need to be clear, strong, and distinctive. It needs to have a point of view, a sacred cow. Other industries—not just the media, as I've already discussed—can harness the power of the sacred cow, too. Many companies point to their mission statements as their sacred cows. In most cases, the mission statement is so watered down and convoluted that it carries no clear message or ideology. If your mission statement isn't strong, clear, concise, and at least mildly controversial, your employees (and your customers) will have a hard time rallying behind it.

But a sacred cow—even a controversial one—without the jackass factor will have little impact. To gain a large loyal audience, you need detractors.[50] Much of Fox's success in winning the ratings war for total audience share—and in the process becoming the dominant player in the cable news category—is because of its opinionated anchors and hosts who force us to side with them or against them. For example, over at CNN, Nancy Grace is the pushy prosecutor who presents cases from the alleged victims' point of view; her opponents accuse her of sensationalizing complex legal cases,[51] yet her supporters see her as a dedicated victims' rights advocate. Her style is bold and even bombastic all the way around—from the way she speaks, to the way she dresses, to the way she attacks people on her show with contrasting viewpoints. Some viewers love her, others can't stand her. Regardless, her program is immensely popular.

The message is clear: For a corporate personality to be believable, individual leadership personalities within that organization must be believable, too. You can't have the "corporate clone" approach—even in conservative industries such as banking or law. If all of the news anchors on CNN or Fox looked and sounded the same, it would be a turnoff.

We're in the creative economy now where the focus is on participation. Seemingly everyone has a blog, a MySpace page, or a YouTube video where he or she gives an opinion. There's so much information out there and myriad viewpoints that if your leaders and your company *don't* have a strong point of view on critical issues then it seems odd. Consumers now crave diversity, creativity, originality, and especially straight talk in their corporate leaders and corporate personalities. They want companies—and leaders—to take a solid stand on important topics and promote that stand with fervor.

What does your company stand for? What are its values? What is your personal sacred cow and how can you bring that into your corporate culture? What is the "larger purpose" for your career existence? Is that message communicated in everything you say and do?

And, perhaps the most important question of all to answer if you are going to create an authentic brand and an effective linguistic fingerprint is this: What's your jackass factor? (Who ya gonna turn off?) Identify people who won't align with your style and sacred cow and don't worry about not having their support. Their deference will make your supporters rally around you even more.

Had the copilot of Air Florida flight 90 stuck to his guns, he and the rest of the passengers on that ill-fated flight might be alive today. Had Al Gore been stauncher in articulating his belief in global warming during his political career and not relied so much on the advice of consultants to stay away from the hot-potato issue, maybe he would have won his presidential bid and altered the course of history. If Tina had been more secure in her ideas, she might now be the regional division head instead of Bill. The success of your career depends largely upon your willingness to stand firmly by your beliefs and to communicate those beliefs unabashedly and unapologetically. Sacred cows and jackasses create an instant appeal bond that can withstand almost any adversity, overcome almost any adversary, and survive nearly any misstep with aplomb.

CHAPTER 6

Words, Names, and Story Lines with Addictive Appeal

➤ THE BIOLOGY OF LANGUAGE FACTOR
(Or Why Agatha Christie Novels, *Green Eggs and Ham*, and *The Young and the Restless* Get Under Our Skin)

Here's a quick quiz: What do an Agatha Christie novel, the Beatles hit *She Loves You*, and Dr. Seuss's *The Cat in the Hat* all have in common? The answer: They all have specific words or word combinations that change our biology and produce an opiate-like high in our brains.

The next time you need a pick-me-up, rather than reach for a bag of potato chips or a chocolate bar, you might want to read Dr. Seuss or listen to the Beatles or Norah Jones. (It certainly will be friendlier to your waistline!) You may not realize it, but when you read novels that contain certain words and phrases, watch TV shows with a specific story formula, or listen to songs with specific lyrics, your brain goes through a biological transformation that is not unlike what happens when you eat chocolate, potato chips, or other addictive "comfort foods." Just as comfort foods produce a chemical reaction in our bodies, "comfort art" and "comfort literature" also have opiate-like powers because of the words and phrases they contain.

But not all words or stories or phrases are pleasure-inducing; only those that adhere to our biological processes or change our brain waves have that power. I call these "linguistic opiates"—specific words, meters, syntax, story lines, and sentence structures that scientists say set off feel-good chemical reactions. They have the power to transfix an audience and are the secrets that timeless novels, blockbuster movies, electrifying speeches, hit songs, and even mesmerizing poems like those of Dr. Seuss or the classic holiday poem *The Night Before Christmas* have in common.

As it turns out, two growing bodies of science—neuroaesthetics and neuroacoustics—show that all human activity adheres to specific biological processes; this includes activities like listening to music, looking at a painting, or listening to a speech. The drawings that cavemen found appealing evoke the same biological reactions as the qualities of a Monet painting or a sculpture by Leonardo da Vinci. Martin Luther King's "I have a dream" speech elicits the same reactions in our brains as does Dr. Seuss's *The Cat in the Hat*. Anthropologists say these so-called laws of being human clearly demonstrate a link between our biological rhythms and the type of music, poetry, art, movies, and songs that move us on a chemical level as well as a deep emotional level.

THE BIOLOGY OF WORDS AND LYRICS

When you took biology class in high school, the coursework didn't include a discussion about art. But maybe it should have. Art affects our biology. How much we enjoy art directly relates to how well the art aligns with our biological nature. That's the conclusion of intense research over the past decade in biology, brain chemistry, perceptual psychology, evolution, and ethology (the study of animal behavior patterns in natural environments). According to this science, opioid peptides such as enkephalin (the endorphins) are produced in the human brain when we hear certain words, listen to speeches delivered in a certain meter, or read a poem with a specific structure. There literally are novels, songs, and movies that move us—or at least move our neurons and endorphins around. But not all art moves us: Only art that adheres to specific biological and primal secrets has the power to move us.

So what are the secrets? What, specifically, is it that makes some novels, poems, paintings, speeches, and songs so irresistible and unforgettable to the human mind? There are actually 13 secrets: 13 characteristics of human cortical information processing that are universal across cultures. So when you tap into these natural information-processing mechanisms, you become appealing, and your messages (or work of art) become appealing with mass audiences because they are actually in tune with our biological processes. But it's more than just being appealing; works of art and entertainment that align with these universal-processing traits have the power to become addictive, as you'll learn in this chapter when I talk about *Harry Potter and the Deathly Hallows*, the Beatles, movies like *Shrek*, and Agatha Christie novels.

Although I won't go into all 13 of these universal biological and brain processes here (that could be a separate book in itself), I will talk about the ones that occur most often in best-selling books, hit songs, highly rated TV shows, and mesmerizing speeches. I will also limit this chapter to the relationship between our biology and opiate-producing words and story lines; I'll discuss the relationship between our biology and melodies in chapter 7 and our biology and visual patterns in chapter 8. So let's look at specifics of the biology-art-literature connection that make successful movies, TV shows, books, and songs so irresistible.

Just how, exactly, does this art/biology connection work? Our bodies are literal boogying machines. Every human activity has a corresponding biological rhythm. Our muscle fibers vibrate 20 times per second and our cortical cell activity runs at a rate of around 40 cycles per second. Our hearts beat 72 times every minute. We breathe at a rate of 16 cycles per minute. Even human speech patterns have set rhythms that can be found across cultures. For instance, we enunciate phonemes at a rate of 14 per second. (Phonemes are the smallest sound unit in a language that distinguishes among meanings of words. One example: The /r/ and /l/ in *rip* and *lip* are phonemes.) Humans speak at a rate of six syllables per second. (The breath pulse of the thorax needed to produce a syllable adheres to the same rhythmic pattern.)

But what does all of this have to do with novels or songs or your ability to develop your own instant appeal? Everything. British neurologist Semir Zeki is at the forefront of neuroaesthetics—a term he coined—and he contends that all art, including literature, has a biological basis and that popular art obeys these laws of the brain and biology.[1] One way to increase the power of your writing (or your speech or your novel or the lyrics of your song) is to structure sentences in a way so that they align with our natural biological preferences for rhythm in linguistic communication, and to use words that trigger our brains to produce chemicals that create a mental high. In other words, if certain words align with our biological preferences, they'll trigger a release of endorphins in our brains, and we'll feel really good when we listen to your speech or song or read your novel. And if the meter of a story matches the rhythms of our biology, we'll feel "in sync" with the material.

To give you some examples of how this works, let's start by looking at opiate-inducing words and lyrics.

THIS IS YOUR BRAIN ON THE BEATLES
Words That Rock Our World

April 4, 1964, was a milestone in rock and roll history. On that day the Beatles accomplished what no other band had achieved before or since: All top five spots on the *Billboard* charts were held by Beatles songs. What was the secret to the success of the men with the mop tops? Partly it was the melodies of the songs. Partly it was the charisma of John, Paul, George, and Ringo. But the allure of their songs was also due in part—a large part, as it turns out—to the lyrics and the way they used melodies to highlight those words, causing an opiate-like high (without the use of any drugs!).

This was discovered when researchers Dr. Beth Logan and Ruth Dhanaraj at Hewlett-Packard's Research Science Institute in Cambridge, Massachusetts, set out to see if there were specific words that could increase a song's chances of becoming a hit. The pair converted 1,700 hit songs from eight different genres into two separate databases: acoustical and lyric. For each genre, they came up with a list of words that occurred most often in #1 hits, and many of these lyrics occurred across several types of music—from country and love songs to new age and pop and rap. It turns out the most frequently occurring words in #1 love songs are, in order: *yeah, oh, girl, hey, she's,* and *baby.* For *Billboard*-topping pop songs, the lyrics found most are *love, don't, oh, you're, baby,* and *say.*[2] As you can see, there's some crossover between genres: *baby* is a key word in hits for both love and pop songs. The word *don't* occurs in #1 hits in four separate genres.

"We found that lyric-based features were slightly more effective at predicting hits than acoustic-based features," Dr. Logan told me in a phone interview. "What's really interesting to look at is whether the melody in a song is used to reinforce, or highlight, the preferred words."[3] If the melody emphasized the preferred lyric, then the song has a greater chance of becoming a hit.

That's exactly what the Beatles did in their #1 hit "She Loves You." Remember that the word *yeah* is the most frequently found word in hit love songs. It occurs 29 times in "She Loves You" lyrics. And the mop tops used the melody and another element of addictive speech—a slight pause before and after the opiate-inducing word—to highlight the *yeah.* A cursory analysis of the other Beatles hits from April 1964 ("Can't Buy Me Love"; "Twist and Shout"; "I Want to Hold Your Hand"; and "Please, Please, Me") shows that each song contains no fewer than half of the most addictive lyrics for the specific genre; and the addictive words are often repeated several times throughout those songs.

In 1967 the Buckinghams also used melody to put additional emphasis on addictive lyrics. In a mere 121 seconds—just over two minutes—they sang mood-altering words 37 times in "Kind of a Drag," which spent two weeks at the top of the *Billboard* 100. When you listen to the song, you find out just how cleverly they used the melody to emphasize those hypnotic words (*baby, don't, love, oh, cause, girl, say*), thereby triggering a feel-good chemical reaction in your brain. In comparing many #1 Top 40 hits from several decades to Dr. Logan's list of genres and the most frequently occurring words from hits in each of those genres, I found that the most successful artists have used words in their songs that are appealing across genres; they don't just use addictive words from the genre of the particular songs they are crafting.

Dr. Logan also found that the *absence* of specific lyrics is equally— and in some genres more—important as a predictor of a hit than the presence of addictive words. She maintains songs that do *not* include the words *blood, children, war, dance, he's, away, day, eyes, there's, I've,* and *gone* are more likely to be hits than songs that contain those lyrics. Heavy metal and new age tunes often contain these nonaddictive words and, perhaps not surprisingly, they have created the fewest number of #1 hits. "If you want to write a hit song, it's probably best to stay away from heavy metal and new age music; those genres had by far the fewest hit songs of all that we studied," according to Dr. Logan.

The Beatles and Buckinghams aren't the only musicians to make use of "linguistic opiates" in their songs. In February 2002, a then-relatively unknown singer burst onto the music scene with a #1 album that sold 20 million copies—making it the best-selling album of the decade so far, and the second-best-selling album overall, just behind the Beatles.[4] *Come Away With Me* won a Grammy as well as the hearts of millions of music lovers around the globe. The single "Don't Know Why" from that album hit #1 on the *Billboard* Top 40 Adults Recurrents list in 2003. The singer was Norah Jones and she had two secret weapons in her arsenal for musical success: addictive lyrics and melodies that scientists say adhere to an "optimal mathematic pattern" for hit songs.[5] (I'll talk more about the optimal mathematical patterns for melody in chapter 7.)

"Don't Know Why" used the linguistic opiate *don't* from Dr. Logan's study seven times in a three-minute-and-six-second song. But more important than how many times the word occurred in the song was the placement of the word: at the beginning and end of the tune. Several separate scientific studies show that our brains are wired to pay more attention to the first 30 seconds and the last 30 seconds of a speech, song, or performance than the middle section. In "Don't Know Why," *don't* occurs an average of every 11.6 seconds in the first 35 seconds of the song and an average of every 12.75 seconds in the last 51 seconds of the song. Norah Jones instinctively weighted the two most "appealing" parts of a song (the beginning and the end) with one of the most appealing words for hit songs (*don't*). The Beatles did the same thing when they structured "She Loves You" to have the addictive *yeah* occur ten times in the first nine seconds of the song and seven times in the last eight seconds of the hit.

WHY AGATHA IS SO ADDICTIVE

If you want your writing to have instant appeal with large audiences, you may want to examine some Agatha Christie novels. Her works were filled with linguistic opiates. Neurolinguists at three leading universities in London, Birmingham, and Warwick say that Agatha Christie novels sold two-billion copies worldwide largely because she peppered her prose with words and phrases that raise brain levels of serotonin and endorphins—the chemical messengers of the brain that induce pleasure and satisfaction.

Christie is listed in the *Guinness Book of World Records* as the best-selling author of all time. After studying 80 of her novels, researchers found the specific words in Christie novels that stimulate the pleasure-inducing side of the brain include *she, yes, girl, kind, smiled,* and *suddenly.*[6] (Notice that *she* and *girl* are also included in the list of feel-good lyrics from Dr. Logan's study.) Dr. Roland Kapferer, who co-originated the study, says Christie's language patterns "stimulated higher than usual activity in the brain"[7] and caused a pleasure response that make her work "unputdownable."[8]

Addictive phrases in Christie's novels include "can you keep an eye on this," "more or less," "a day or two," and "something like that." These phrases have also been proved, according to the researchers, to cause chemical reactions in the brain that induce a feel-good high. Kapferer adds that Christie used virtually the same words and phrases over and over again in all of her novels.

Why is it that a handful of words or a few catch phrases can have the power to propel songs to the top of the *Billboard* charts or novels to the top of the best-seller lists? What do these words have that others don't? And why don't we find the repeated use of the same words and phrases over and over redundant and boring? Neurolinguists say it has to do with how words, phrases, and combinations of words affect our psychological and physiological states. Not only do words affect our thoughts, feelings, and emotions; they also can change our biology. Our bodies react to words in several ways: neurologically and biologically—by responding to the frequency vibrations produced by certain vowel-and-consonant combinations—and psychologically through the emotions and mental states created by the meanings behind the words.[9] "Word opiates" light up the insular cortex (the limbic part of the brain associated with pleasure).

Agatha Christie's writing isn't just pleasing to our brains; cavemen would also have craved Christie. Now, I know cave dwellers weren't exactly well read. And it's true that our brains are more developed than Neanderthal man's. Still, new genetic research findings show that Neanderthals might have spoken just like we do today.

Well, okay maybe not *just* like we do. But DNA samples collected from Neanderthal bones from a cave in Spain show that they did more than grunt and groan; scientists say the DNA of cave people contained the only known gene to play a part in speech and language.[10] Apparently Neanderthal talk good.

Even though caveman (or cavewoman) could apparently speak, researchers say he (or she) kept it simple. That's because of something called neural system fatigue. Within three to five minutes of any sustained activity—whether it's the caveman swinging his club or modern man listening to a speech or reading a novel—our neurons become less responsive and need a rest. (This isn't unlike the rest your muscles need when you lift weights.) Our brains simultaneously seek both novelty and simplicity. If we don't get those, then we tune out.

Scientists tell us we listen to information in a speech or read words in a novel in four-minute cycles before mentally checking out for about another four minutes before we return for another round of

rhythms—the patterns in which all humans speak. All humans are biologically programmed to speak and process information at a rate of six syllables per second, which aligns with the universal breath pulse of our thorax (which has a six-cycle-per-second frequency).[14] Linguistic anthropologists have also found that in all cultures—including Greek, English, Chinese, Japanese, French, and German—people will pause a few milliseconds every three seconds when they speak. During that brief pause, they will decide the words and meanings they'll use in the next three seconds. Guess what? Listeners also take a break after every three seconds of a speech to integrate and make sense of what was just said. Unfortunately, the speaker and listener aren't necessarily "in sync" in their pauses.

Did you notice any commonalities about all of those numbers in the previous paragraph? If you look at them again, you'll see that our biological processes and our speaking rates are based on either a three-unit cycle or a multiple of a three-unit cycle. Most popular literature across cultures also aligns directly with a three-unit cycle or a multiple of that.

For example, when linguists looked at lines of poetry from several different cultures, they found that the lines are universally divided into two- to four-second units, with three-second units by far being the most common across all languages.[15] A unit can be identified by punctuation marks in writing or by pauses in speaking. In addition, these units have a syllable emphasis placed at between 2.5 and 3.5 seconds (which is an average of three seconds). Even Greek and Latin epic dactylic hexameters—such as Homer's *Iliad* and *The Odyssey*—where the unit is between four and six seconds long, is clearly divided by a caesura (pause) resulting in two units of two to three seconds each. (A dactylic hexameter is a poetic meter where each line has six units, and each of those units has one stressed and two unstressed syllables. An example is Longfellow's *Evangeline*: "This is the / FOR est prim / E val. The / MUR mur ing / PINES and the / HEM locks.")

Dr. Seuss used this "power of three" in just about all of his writing. He adhered to a strict anapestic tetrameter in all of his poems up until very late in his life. Anapestic tetrameter is a traditional rhythm for comic verse that has four units per line, and each unit has two unstressed syllables followed by one stressed syllable. That means each *unit* has three syllables, and each complete *line* has 12 syllables. When you read a poem written in this meter out loud, it takes you about three seconds to say each 12-syllable line. The classic holiday poem *The Night Before Christmas* is written in this pattern. So is Dr. Seuss's *The Cat in the Hat*. No wonder these time-honored and much-repeated tales are so mesmerizing to the masses! The three-syllable unit and three-second line are powerful literary opiates because they complement the breath pulse of the thorax—which you'll remember is a six-second pulse. And because humans naturally speak at a rate of six syllables per second, the anapestic tetrameter—with it's three-second, 12 syllable lines—is a naturally comfortable meter.

You may be thinking, "Well, that's a bunch of nice information, but we don't speak like poets write." True enough. But you can still apply the same concepts. Some of the most charismatic speakers in history have.

John F. Kennedy, Ronald Reagan, and Martin Luther King often spoke in rhythms very close to the mesmerizing three-second unit. JFK paused, on average, every 2.4 seconds in his speeches; Martin Luther King and Ronald Reagan each spoke, on average, in units of 3.1 and 3.9 seconds, respectively (although Reagan occasionally did sometimes go up to six seconds—which is still a multiple of three).[16] All of these speakers were within the two- to four-second (note that the average is three seconds) biological preference for a speaking cadence. Of course their speaking rate isn't the only reason these orators mesmerized audiences, but it was a big part of it. They spoke in a rhythm that mirrored our biological beat.

THE LINK BETWEEN TALKING ON A CELL PHONE IN PUBLIC AND ONE ELEMENT OF HIT SONGS

Talk on a mobile phone in a public place like on a commuter train or bus, and you're apt to get angry scowls from your fellow passengers. Yet if you're chatting it up with someone seated next to you, other passengers won't even give you a second glance. Or, if you're on the phone in your home or office, the other people in the room could care less that you're on the phone.

What gives?

There is something about hearing only half of a conversation that gets most of us all hot and huffy. And it's always half a conversation by a stranger. Linguistic anthropologist Robin Eve says that's mainly because hearing half a conversation upsets our rhythmic balance. We humans have a need for what's known as "reciprocal oscillation" (some call it "back-channel speech")—the back-and-forth chatter between two people in a conversation that syncs with our natural biological rhythms.[17] She maintains that our need for this backchannel speech is so strong that when we hear half a conversation, our inner harmony is upset. This is especially true if the half-conversation is taking place in an environment where we have no control, such as in public places. We can ask our officemates to lower their voices, or we can ask our spouses to take calls in another room, but we can't insist that strangers put their cell phones "somewhere else."

Musicians who have achieved pop-chart success have tapped into this universal need for a "back-channel" rhythm in their songs (in addition to having the hypnotic lyrics I talked about earlier). Many Beatles songs—including "Please, Please, Me," "Twist and Shout," "She Loves You," "A Little Help from My Friends," and "Help"—had a reciprocal rhythmic oscillation between the lead singer (John, Paul, or John and Paul, depending on the song) and the rest of the band. The lead would sing a line, and the other band members either echoed the line, a thought, or a response to that line. This simulated the same back-and-forth interaction we get in conversation, and it syncs with our natural biological rhythms. Sometimes an instrument (such as the harmonica in "Love Me Do") can simulate the rhythm of reciprocal oscillation—even if no lyrics are sung. The Buckinghams used these same conversational rhythms in "Kind of a Drag." So did Frankie Valli and The Four Seasons in most of their hit songs ("Sherry," "Big Girls Don't Cry"). The point is, we need this back-and-forth rhythm to feel good about any human communication—whether it's a speech, a song, or a novel.

Many talented speakers are well aware of the human need for back-channel rhythms and will structure their presentations with regular audience participation breaks. Listen carefully to top motivational speakers, and they'll interject quick questions such as "Are you with me? Say 'yes,'" or "If you agree, say 'yes,'" that elicit a short response. James Arthur Ray—one of the motivational speakers featured in *The Secret*—uses this reciprocal oscillation technique more frequently than any other speaker I have heard recently. He doesn't just sprinkle his speech with these, he *floods* his speeches with back-channel communication! This instantly makes us subconsciously buy into him and his message because the way he presents it syncs with our biological rhythms.

Other ways to interject the feel of back-channel communication into your speech is to do regular, short question-and-answer sessions throughout your talk or have several speakers switch off presenting. The human need for reciprocal oscillation is why—if you're giving a speech where you are trying to build rapport with the audience—it's best to take questions as they come up and not ask the audience to "hold questions until the end." When a speaker delivers a monologue, not only is it mentally boring for the audience, but it also ignores our need for back-channel communication and upsets our biological rhythms and, therefore, our sense of well-being.

TRUTH OR VAGUENESS?
For a Speech with Instant Appeal, Use Both!

So far I've talked a lot about how the sound-wave patterns and beats of certain words and phrases affect our biology and make some literary works or speeches more appealing than others. You may think the meaning of the words has little effect. But that's not true. How we react to words and phrases is influenced, in part, by our psychological reactions to the meanings society has attached to those words.

Connotative associations help explain why causes such as global warming were slow to gain widespread support. Forgetting about sound-wave patterns for the moment, the term *global warming* doesn't sound all that threatening or urgent. The meaning we attach to *warming* isn't a bad one—especially for those of us who suffer through cold climes and subzero wind chills in the winter. In February, global warming sounds like a pretty cozy concept to us Northerners! Had we called the result of greenhouse gas emissions "planet contamination" or "global incineration," it may have generated a greater sense of urgency and earlier broad support for the cause.

There's a particular type of word phrase that carries especially strong connotative and persuasive powers in human communication. In all cultures, aphorisms—also known as "truisms," or sayings that societies believe carry a certain truth—have universal persuasive power. Any time an authoritarian suggestion is made, the subconscious mind is like a rebellious teenager: It wants to prove you wrong. The human mind will not accept facts, figures, and logic as true unless the data ring true deep inside us. So when we hear a fact or statement, our subconscious immediately goes to work to see if the statement "feels right." The subconscious mind—the real driver of decision making—responds to aphorisms. The fact that most people often unconsciously accept aphorisms as truth—whether these sayings are based in fact or handed down through fiction and folklore—makes them especially effective.

The late Johnnie Cochran used a variation of the "if the shoe fits" aphorism when he said, "If it doesn't fit, you must acquit" in the O.J. Simpson criminal trial. The subconscious minds of the jurors had already accepted the "truth" of the "if the shoe fits" aphorism. Because they accepted the aphorism as true, the evidence that the glove allegedly didn't fit reinforced the "truth" that being a criminal didn't "fit."

I've seen aphorisms work wonders in the trials on which I have consulted. Here are a few that I suggested to attorneys, and the types of successful cases to which they were applied:

- A miss is as good as a mile (medical malpractice suit).

- All that we learn from history is that we learn nothing from

history (negligence claim against a company with several prior
violations that had been acquitted in all prior instances).

- As you sow, so shall you reap (applied to several different
  cases).

- A man is known by the company he keeps (and its variation:
  if you sleep with dogs you wake up with fleas; both used in a
  gang-related robbery case).

- Possession is nine-tenths of the law (drug possession case
  where the accused claimed he was framed).

- Rats desert a sinking ship (corporate espionage case).

Of course, we've all seen aphorisms used in political campaigns.
Here are a few I have used with candidates as I helped prepare them
for debates and press conferences:

- Even a broken clock is right twice a day.

- Doubt is the beginning, not the end, of wisdom.

- Don't change horses in midstream. (The movie *Wag the Dog*,
  which was a comedic look at the manipulation of mass media
  and public opinion, also prominently featured this aphorism
  in ads for the president's reelection bid.)

- Give him an inch and he'll take a mile.

- A bad penny always turns up.

- Don't kill the goose that lays the golden egg.

The subconscious mind also can be persuaded by another factor:
vagueness (or openness). You'll remember that Agatha Christie kept
details of her stories vague so that our brains wouldn't be distracted
by too much detail. This is where most corporate speakers really fall
down: They beat an issue to death with facts, figures, and data, but
all that does is cue the subconscious mind to rebel and try to prove

you wrong. When you limit facts in a presentation (thereby keeping it more vague) and rely instead on "adjunct suggestions"—or suggestions that you attach to a truism—you have a greater chance of persuading people to your point of view. Whenever you attach a suggestion to a statement that is universally viewed as true, it makes it more likely to be accepted by the intellectual brain, the part of the brain that's seeking out connections and logic. That's not to say you shouldn't have some meat in your presentations or back up your assertions with data. But too many speakers have far too many facts cluttering up what would be an otherwise compelling oratory.

You can find some of the most blatant examples of adjunct suggestions on late-night infomercials. The pitch people will often say something such as, "You can't predict the future" or "you have no control when you are working for someone else," and then immediately attach it to a present-tense suggestion. (For example: "When you dial the phone right now you are making a step to secure your financial future and take control of your life.")

Throughout the 2008 presidential primaries, I heard many candidates delicately attach adjunct suggestions to truisms in the debates. These are often so subtle that they pass us by, which is exactly why they work to persuade the subconscious mind and, ultimately, the conscious mind. Remember the instant appeal power of truisms the next time you write a speech.

THE PERSUASIVE COMMUNICATION LESSONS OF SOAP OPERAS AND THE iPOD SHUFFLE

Do you write your speeches in the "tell-them-what-you're-going-to-tell-them, tell-them, tell-them-what-you-told-them" (or "TTT") organizational format? If so, your speech will do one of two things: fall on deaf ears or activate the "fight" response and get people all riled up to want to prove you wrong.

Researchers in both anthropology and cognitive science tell us that if you want to motivate or persuade, the old-school "TTT" format is the least effective way to organize your content. You see, the brain of every member of your audience will focus on finding flaws in your facts if you use this tired method. Whenever you fire up the PowerPoint and start to rattle off facts and figures to support your position, the brains of audience members begin to argue with you.

We all have a perceptual bias—a set of our own beliefs, facts, and figures that our subconscious has accepted as absolute truth—and the brain doesn't like anything that challenges those beliefs. When those attitudes are challenged, warning bells go off in our brains that tell us we're being threatened—or at least that our beliefs are being threatened. The primal brain craves security, and when our deeply ingrained ideals are accosted, we immediately look for reasons why the challenging information is off base.

The other problem with the "tell-them-what-you're-going-to-tell-them" approach is that you are trying to convince someone on only an intellectual level by engaging the cortex. But real persuasion happens in the reptilian and limbic brains—the primal and emotional centers. Tapping into those two areas requires a completely different approach to speechwriting (or writing of any kind). To get the brain to relax and buy into what you are saying, you have to short-circuit the cortex by overloading it. Once the cortex is effectively "shut down," your message can bypass the logic of the brain and tap into the real motivational center in our noggins, which is the limbic system. In all of the jury trials I have consulted on, there is one constant: People are not motivated by logic and reason alone. Sure, you have to know what you are talking about, and I'm not saying you shouldn't support your message with facts. But people will always make emotional decisions first and then use logic to *reinforce* the emotional decisions they have *already made*.

Most people assume that if they tell a story or two, then they have engaged our emotions. Not true. That's because most people tell stories in a linear way, with a clear beginning, middle, and end. But when you do that, you're still activating primarily the logical part of the brain, not the emotional. And it's our emotions that persuade us first, not logic.

So, if the old method of speechwriting and storytelling doesn't work, what does? How can you tap into the limbic (emotional) brain? For the answer to that, we need to look at an old standard in the broadcast industry, as well as a new standard in music.

According to the Museum of Broadcast Communications, soap operas are the most enduring, most popular, and most appealing genre of television drama in the history of world broadcasting.[18] No other form of television fiction has attracted more viewers across more demographics in more countries over a longer period. Teens watch soaps. Women 18 to 49 years old do. Men over 50 tune in.[19] And these people, from all across the world, tune in again and again. The United States, Britain, Australia, and Latin America all have soaps that have been running for a quarter of a century! (Most producers would kill to have that kind of longevity and cross-demographic appeal in television!) There's a reason for the addictive qualities of the soaps, and it's in the way these simple productions structure their stories. In short, they shut down the "thinking brain" and activate the "emotional brain."

How do these addictive television dramas do it? First, they have several plots going on at the same time. They will start one story line, and then start another, and another without wrapping up the first one. This method of storytelling aligns perfectly with the brain's preference to not have loose ends. Our cognitive system likes to have things all wrapped up. It wants to hear your facts, access its own internal database of related facts, accept the parts of your message that match its own database, and refute the parts of your message that contradict it. So no matter how strongly your facts support your theories, it'll be a very tough sell if your facts don't fit with the perceptual bias of the listener.

This thought process only works, though, when stories and ideas are presented in logical, linear ways (as it is with the "tell-them-what-you're-going-to-tell-them" method). But the soap opera format has several unresolved plots going on at the same time. So when we see or hear one story, our brains immediately start to look for a completion to it; but while it waits for that closure, another line of thought (another story) is introduced and then another and so on, up to the point that about five subplots are going on at the same time. This causes an overload because the brain can't keep track of all of those open-ended story lines. The mind goes into what's called a trance-derivational search as it desperately tries to close the open story lines.[20]

Eventually, it loses track of all of the stories and just gives up. If you use this approach in your speech-writing, this is the point where the mind is in a semihypnotic state and is open to suggestion. This is the point where a specific message can be implanted into the brain without being obvious, because the brain's defenses are down. In this state, the brain of a listener isn't looking for holes in your theory (or facts) as it naturally would with the "tell-them-what-you're-going-to-tell-them" method. Rather, it is a bit dazed by all of the open story lines. This disorientation allows the "thinking" brain (the neocortex) to relax, and it readily accepts any statements or suggestions you make. But you have to make those suggestions at the right time.

I've just described what neurolinguistic programming (NLP) practitioners call the "nested loops" method of story telling. It is a powerfully persuasive method of motivating people to action, rallying people to a cause, or convincing someone to your point of view. I personally have used this with my clients in fund-raising to increase donations to their cause, with politicians to garner greater support, and with lawyers in closing arguments to win over juries to their point of view. Nested loops are one of the most powerful instant appeal factors in speechwriting and storytelling.

In the past four or five years, I have noticed that young audiences, especially, prefer speakers who use the nested loops method of story-telling. At first, I couldn't figure out the reason for this generational preference for stories that were out of order. But then I read some research by lecturer Michael Bull, called the "world's leading expert on the social impact of personal stereo devices" by the *New York Times*.[21] Bull says the random-shuffle feature of the iPod has become one of the key new listening habits. In a *Wired* magazine article, Bull described the appeal of the random-shuffle mode, as told by one of his interview subjects: "As it's on shuffle I don't know what's coming up next, and it often surprises me . . . I like the sensation though."[22]

When you put your iPod on shuffle mode, it's a completely different cognitive experience from when it's on regular mode. Instead of knowing which song will come up next while listening to an album—as you do in regular mode—your brain is thrown a surprise after every song. This relates back to the brain's need for novelty to remain engaged. While Agatha Christie satisfied that need by moving our minds along faster with the generous use of dashes throughout her stories, speeches and soap operas can satisfy that need by using the nested-loop method of storytelling. Both the iPod shuffle mode and nested loops short-circuit our "thinking" brain, and allow our "feeling" brain to enjoy the experience.

So how can you use this "nested loops" method in your speeches? First, abandon the fact-based approach to persuasion and use stories instead. Five stories to be specific. Next, begin the first story related to your topic, then begin a second story, then a third, a fourth, and a fifth. After you have "opened" the fifth story (but have not concluded it), you then state your call to action, or the main thing you want your audience to do or believe. (Remember: This is the point when the subconscious is most open to suggestion.) Once you have done that, you then close the stories in reverse order, starting with the fifth story, then the fourth, and so on. For some reason five stories is the most effective for sufficiently confusing and overloading the mind so that it's receptive to your suggestions. And because you have been telling stories with protagonists who battle multiple antagonists and who eventually reach a turning point and a resolution (stories about real life, in other words), you have activated the emotional center of the brain in a powerful way.

I've seen this format get outstanding results in several arenas. It is a bit tricky until you get used to it, and you do have to understand how to time each loop—otherwise you'll come off as rambling. But once you master those techniques, you will have a persuasive speech format that can't be beat! Internationally acclaimed peak-performance coach Tony Robbins frequently uses nested loops in his presentations.

SPELLBINDING STORY LINES
Why Potter *Is Just as Addictive as Pot*

Academy Award–nominated screenwriting guru Terry Rossio—along with his partner Ted Elliott—has written some of the most successful American films of the past 15 years, including *Aladdin*; *Pirates of the Caribbean: The Curse of the Black Pearl*; and *Shrek*. Rossio is, no doubt, a creative genius. But he also realizes that creativity alone won't win the hearts and minds of audiences. Something else is needed for a movie to have instant appeal, and that "something else" is what is known as "literary universals" or "narrative universals": stories and discourses (ways of telling the story) that strike a biological, cognitive, or psychological chord in humans across cultures.

Literary universals are features (such as narrative themes and story structures) that recur across cultures and are genetically unrelated and distinct in their traditions. For example, Greek and Chinese traditions are genetically unrelated; Greek and Latin traditions are not. A literary trait is also considered universal if it occurs in cultures that are vernacularly different; in other words, in societies that have not influenced one another in their language traditions.

Terry Rossio used narrative (literary) universals to help him create Academy Award–winning masterpieces. To understand how and why those themes are universally appealing, we have to first look at how the brain works when it hears or sees a story.

Cognitive researchers tell us that the big clump of gray matter in our heads is basically a self-rewarding system; that is, it sends off pleasure-inducing chemicals every time it experiences something that is good for, or advances, its innate adaptive and survival abilities.[23] So when, for example, we watch a movie or read a novel where the good guy beats out the bad guy, a whole bunch of little receptors in the brain get all fired up and begin producing a lot of feel-good chemicals such as endorphins and other pleasure-associated neurohormones like the catecholamines.[24] The good guy wins, we feel good.

But why does the brain get so excited about good prevailing over evil? Part of the reason is because we are hard-wired that way. When we see a physical, moral, or social virtue triumph over a negative force, the subconscious breathes a sigh of relief, knowing that our security is preserved. (Remember the reptilian comfort universal to protect our kin from chapter 4?) The same thing happens when we watch movies that relate to the myriad other human universals; that which engages us is often intrinsic.

That's a pretty simplistic explanation and not all universals are biologically innate. Some are social, and some are emotional. But scientists believe that it's this autonomous and reflexive cognitive reward system that primordially drives what humans across cultures think is right, beautiful, truthful, good, and good for us. Universal narrative themes in literature align with this cognitive reward system.

The *Harry Potter* series tapped into two literary universals— individual advancement and good versus evil—so powerfully that many readers showed withdrawal symptoms after finishing *Harry Potter and the Deathly Hallows*, the last book in the *Harry Potter* series. Muhlenberg College psychology professor Dr. Jeff Rudski conducted a survey to find out just how addictive *Harry Potter* novels are. He and his team used craving scales originally designed for smoking addiction and applied them to *Deathly Hallows.*

As it turns out, *Potter* is just as addictive as pot. Ten percent of the 4,000 *Harry Potter* fans polled by Rudski and his team showed signs of addiction; the addiction rate for marijuana users runs between 5 percent and 10 percent. When I talked with Dr. Rudski about the study, he said many fans experienced withdrawal symptoms such as sleep disruption, loss of appetite, a lower sense of well-being, and higher irritability at the end of *Hallows*. (These are the same withdrawal symptoms experienced by marijuana users, according to the National Institute on Drug Abuse.[25]) He added that one woman in the study said finishing *Hallows* was depressing because, "(My) growth followed Harry's growth and now that it's over, it's settled, and I feel as if there's no place to go."[26]

J. K. Rowling had masterfully triggered the reward system of the brain with the literary universal of personal growth. Fans read about Harry Potter's development, and they liked it because it paralleled what they were going through. That lit up the opiate circuit of the brain and activated feel-good endorphins. And because readers liked it so much, they craved more *Harry Potter*, which activated the dopamine receptors in the brain. So there was this craving-and-pleasure cycle set up in many *Harry Potter* readers. They simply couldn't get enough.

Rudski says what he calls "core" *Potter* fans—those who centered on the plot elements of the books—had higher levels of withdrawal than fans who were more focused on ancillary elements (such as the online communities created around the *Harry Potter* series or the actors involved in the movies). And this makes sense, because by getting involved in the plot, core fans were getting more involved with the literary universals that have proved to be a strong pull to people across all cultures. What's interesting is that the fans who demonstrated the least amount of withdrawal, or no withdrawal at all, were those who found a way to perpetuate in their own lives the human universal of individual growth that was sparked by the *Potter* novels. Rudski's 15-year-old daughter, for example, took up the guitar to form a wizard rock band. She also started studying Latin because she wants to understand Rowling's choices for the names of her characters. She found a way to take Harry's growth, through which she lived vicariously while reading the books, and turn it into her own growth.

The literary universal of growth is also why self-help books seem to have instant and unending popularity with readers; they play right into our primordial programming to do better and to be better. Self-help books that also create ancillary activities—such as online communities related to the books—also tend to do better because, just like the online *Harry Potter* fans, the addiction can be perpetuated.

In his book *The Mind and Its Stories: Narrative Universals and Human Emotion*, University of Connecticut English professor Patrick Colm Hogan outlines three universal narrative structures: the heroic tragi-comedy (where the good guy or gal—either with our without supporters—defends against domination by a negative force), the romantic tragi-comedy (about romantic union), and the sacrificial tragi-comedy (where the hero sacrifices for a cause or a person).[27] Hogan maintains that each of these is tied to attaining happiness— either social happiness (heroic tragi-comedy), individual happiness (romantic tragi-comedy), or spiritual happiness/enlightenment (sacrificial tragi-comedy). Notice that the *Harry Potter* series touched on all three of these.

Throughout his book, Hogan details the cross-cultural universal emotional patterns that are woven into our most enduring and endearing stories. You'll find many of those patterns in box office successes (as well as mesmerizing speeches used by savvy CEOs and politicians).

If we look more deeply into the reasons why these three categories of narrative are so popular, it once again gets back to how we're wired; it seems that these stories speak to both our psychological needs, as outlined by Maslow's hierarchy of needs and our primal conditioning. The heroic tragi-comedy relates to both our esteem needs (to be respected) and our self-preservation instinct (to avoid domination). The romantic tragi-comedy speaks to our need for intimacy, love, and belonging, as well as our primal urge to perpetuate the species. (If the guy gets the girl, then the next logical assumption is that reproduction will be involved or, at the very least, the union of two people will make them a stronger "unit" than either would be individually.) And the sacrificial tragi-comedy hits on both our self-actualization emotional need and our morality.

Hogan clearly demonstrates in his book that these three narrative universals show up in all kinds of literature—from screenplays to novels and poetry. After studying thousands of literary works, he found that the organization and structure of his three types of narrative universals is surprisingly similar not only in their theme, but also in their organization and development.

Now back to Terry Rossio—the screenwriter extraordinaire who has several blockbuster films to his credit. Rossio says whenever he got stuck on a story line while writing *Shrek*, he'd consult a list of 36 dramatic situations that French writer Georges Polti claims are the basis of all commercially successful films. Not surprisingly, all of Polti's situations can be placed into one or more of Hogan's three literary universals. Using these literary universals apparently worked for Rossio: *Shrek*, in addition to being a box office smash hit, is listed as third on Bravo's "100 Funniest Movies" list. The film had such widespread appeal and commercial success that it's now on its third sequel.

The human universals for narratives show up in all literary art from novels and poems to historic speeches, movies, and hit songs. A Barcelona-based company that uses artificial intelligence to predict hit songs relies on Polti's work as part of its prediction process. Even seemingly silly, nonsensical poems like Dr. Seuss's *Green Eggs and Ham* can be linked to the dramatic universals of Polti or Hogan. (Sam's unnamed pal was domineering and unwavering in his desire to try the delicacy until after a train wreck that caused an abrupt change in his personality. Remember that the primary basis for heroic tragi-comedy is achieving social happiness, and prior to the train wreck Sam's friend was morose, irritable, and just wanted to be left alone.) *Green Eggs and Ham* is the fourth-best-selling children's book of all time,[28] which once again speaks to the mass appeal of literature that adheres to one of the universal themes.

In his analysis of mythology, Franz Boaz found universally appealing statements in many popular works as well. He discovered that phrases such as "If I were," "If I could," and "If this had not happened," appear with a much greater frequency across cultures than could happen by chance.[29] Commonalities in character-trait development also exist in literature in many different civilizations. There's apparently more to art than the creative process. It also seems to involve an awareness of our biology and our innate preferences for certain words, structures, syntax, and story lines.

But using opiate-inducing words and phrases, or developing primordially pleasing story lines, isn't enough to persuade and engage an audience. We also have to look at how we put all of those individual elements together. In his book on narrative universals and emotion, Hogan noted that various story elements—including character types and location—are just as important in engaging emotions as the themes.

A British company that one London newspaper called the "Flopbusters" claims to be able to predict whether a movie will be a hit or miss with audiences based on the specific way those elements of a story are presented.[30] The company—called Epagogix—has fed script, location, cast, and costume information from all movies since the 1970s into a computer and used artificial neural networks to look for emotionally engaging patterns of blockbuster hits. According to a *New Yorker* article penned by Malcolm Gladwell, the company's team of hit predictors outlined four story elements that are prone to pay off at the box office: a love interest, an interesting location, a woman in peril, and the consummation or possibility of consummation of the love relationship.[31]

But the Epagogix team goes on to say that even these main elements have to have specific qualities to reap box office gold. One of those that has shown up in Epagogix's data is a black/white combination in the lead cast members—such as Julia Roberts and Denzel Washington in *The Pelican Brief*, Tommy Lee Jones and Will Smith in *Men in Black*, or Mel Gibson and Danny Glover in *Lethal Weapon*. That's really no surprise when you look at Hogan's universals for literature, or remember that in chapter 5 I mentioned that duality is a human universal—humans need opposition to make sense of things. Our brains are programmed to think in terms of black or white, right or wrong, left or right, up or down, friends and enemies. We are drawn to stories that contain those elements because they are more comfortable for our brains to process.

As far as the elements of location, Epagogix claims desert islands and prison settings tend to be among the best for bringing in big box office money. Why is that? Again, look to human universals. Humans are social animals. We live in interactive groups. We have a social instinct. And putting someone on a deserted island or in a prison is counter to our social instincts. When we watch a movie where someone is stranded on a desert island or in a prison, our reptilian security system sends off alarms and our emotions go into overdrive. Social isolation or solitary confinement is not only punishment—it can literally make people crazy.

Dr. Stuart Grassian is a psychiatrist and an expert in the effects of isolation and sensory deprivation on human behavior. He believes that long-term social isolation can cause permanent biochemical changes.[32] Grassian lists nine such permanent psychological effects caused by these biochemical changes, including seven of the most common: difficulty thinking and concentrating, difficulty with memory, perceptual disorders, hallucinations, panic attacks, increased aggression, and problems with impulse control.[33] What's really interesting, though, is that Grassian says even short-term isolation can cause varying degrees of psychological problems.

You don't have to be in a prison or on a deserted island to suffer ill effects of social seclusion. He says psychological and biochemical effects have been seen in Arctic and Antarctic explorers, patients confined to the intensive care unit of a hospital, patients immobilized long term in a hospital (such as in those in spinal traction), pilots during solo jet flights, and even people with some sort of sensory deprivation, such as reduced vision or hearing.[34] These would, no doubt, also make compelling settings for potential hit movies, given that they would evoke an intense emotional response in the audience.

In chapter 8 I talk about something called mirror neurons that make audiences literally feel the pain of the people they see on the screen. Basically, the brain can't tell the difference between *watching* someone else in prison, for example, and *being* in prison. (That means when you watch a show where an actor is in prison, you unconsciously believe you are, at least temporarily, in prison yourself.) When you couple the mirror neuron factor with the human universal factor, it's no surprise why a deserted island or a prison scene would get us emotionally charged.

PRACTICAL APPLICATION
Spellbinding Speeches

When we look into cognitive science and anthropology research, we can understand why some movies, stories, poems, and speeches move us and others don't. Based on my eleven years of research into various sciences (psychology, anthropology, biocommunication, neurosemantics, neurology, and biology), I've found that the most persuasive writing and delivery techniques align naturally with our cognitive and biological processes, as well as our anthropological conditioning. Here are some ways to structure and deliver a speech—or a story within a speech—that align with those processes.

Write to Confuse the Brain

Soap operas and the "shuffle" feature on the iPod are appealing to the brain because they confuse the brain; our noggins don't know what to expect next, and that short-circuits, in a way, the part of the brain that is looking to shoot holes in a theory. If you write to confuse the brain by using nested loops, you'll have an easier time persuading people to your point of view.

Write—and Speak—to Our Natural Biological Rhythms

Remember that humans both speak and listen in three-second chunks. You may be thinking that if our natural cognitive processing unit is in three-second units, then we should prepare speeches where all sentences adhere to that rhythm. But that wouldn't be effective. Or practical. Audiences would tune you out. The key isn't to have all of your sentences in three-second beats; rather, it is to use this cadence when making critical points that you want readers (or listeners) to remember, to buy into, or to feel good about. A tactic that has been observed in speeches and poetry across cultures is that a short line (three seconds) is used to deal with light subjects, and a long line (six to twelve seconds) details tragic matters.[35]

Having said that, it is a good practice to speak in some sort of regular rhythmic pattern so the audience can "feel your beat." One of my clients naturally speaks in five-second units, followed by three two-second units. (Ronald Reagan, incidentally, also had this pattern in some of his speeches.) Even though this doesn't adhere to the universally preferred three-second speaking rhythm, it does set up a strong pattern that audiences can tap into. Most executives whom I hear have no strong rhythm to their speaking; they're merely spewing words out of their mouths in no particular meter or pattern. Unfortunately, such speakers unwittingly forfeit audience allegiance.

You should also try to write so that the number of syllables per line adheres to what is universally preferred across cultures. While anthropologists have found that lines can contain between four and twenty syllables and still be appealing to our brains, most languages that don't use fixed lexical tones (such as English) contain between seven and seventeen syllables per second.[36] In tonal languages (such as Chinese, in which the metrical syllables take about twice as long to articulate), the rhythm preferred by the brain is four to eight syllables per second.[37]

Include Content That Aligns with Human Universals

As I've mentioned, the reptilian, or primal, brain is the driver of our decisions. Human universals are so deeply ingrained in our anthropological roots that they have particular persuasive appeal. These ideas and situations are preferred across cultures. Refer to Hogan and Polti's universals, which I've outlined in this chapter, for a good starting point for crafting speeches and stories.

Write to Increase Feel-Good Endorphins in Your Listeners

Three tips you've learned in this chapter that can help you increase the feel-good endorphins in your listeners are:

1. Include back-channel communication (reciprocal oscillation) in your presentations.
2. Use aphorisms, because the primal brain has already accepted these as universal truths.
3. Include words and phrases that raise the levels of seratonin and endorphins and create a feel-good high in your audience.

Write for Neanderthals

Keep it short. Just as the cavemen spoke in short, simple phrases, listeners today also prefer conciseness. This may seem contradictory to the first recommendation, which was to write to confuse the brain. But you confuse the brain by the way you structure the stories—in nested loops—not by the complexity of the story lines or the details.

Remember that Agatha Christie never gave her readers too much detail; she kept a lot of information vague, allowing the readers to fill in the blanks. That approach aligns directly with what the brain prefers—gaps and openness. You want to keep the plots (themes) simple to avoid neural system fatigue and sustain interest in the topic; you want to overload the cognitive processing system by shutting down the logical part of the brain (using nested loops) to shut down biases so people can be open to your point of view.

As you've seen in this chapter, literary works that have mass appeal—and that includes speeches, TV shows, songs, and novels—use words, phrases, rhythms, and meters that mesh with our biological beats and our brain-wave patterns.

We've now covered six of the eight primal triggers that create instant and widespread appeal:

1. The conspicuous flaw factor
2. The visual preprogramming factor (does it look like a duck?)
3. The reptilian comfort factor
4. The sacred cow factor
5. The jackass factor
6. The language/biology factor

In chapter 7, we'll see how sound-wave vibrations affect our health, our behaviors, and even our attitudes.

CHAPTER 7

Good Vibrations

— THE BIOTUNING FACTOR FOR CAREER SUCCESS

Cells in our body have their own musical language. Stanford University musician Jonathan Berger says our cells give off different sounds when we're swinging a golf club correctly than when we take a wild swing that sends the golf ball into the sand trap. According to Berger, when you swing a golf club incorrectly, the cells in your body make a horrible sound. (He compares that sound to the screeching sounds made by a child who is learning to play the cello but hasn't quite mastered the instrument.) But when you swing the club perfectly, all of your muscles and joints are working the way they should and the cells in your body make what Berger calls a "pure sound."

Berger has captured these sounds and is using them to help golfers improve their game through a process called sonification. By listening to the muscle-and-joint musical that the body makes during a golf swing, and comparing that to the sounds made during a perfect swing, he can identify new patterns and information about a person's swing. In short, he "sonifies" a golfer's body by putting it to music. If he hears a symphony, the golfer is pretty close to a perfect swing. If the sounds are "off key," then the swing is off. The greater the sound distortion, the more work the golfer has to do on his or her swing. When the sounds are played back to the golfers, they can hear the difference between their swing and a perfect swing, and they can make adjustments in their body movements until they hear the perfect golf symphony.

Berger says healthy cells—those with voltages between 70 and 90 millivolts, according to some scientists—also give off different sounds than diseased cells (which have voltages below 15 millivolts). He has been working with cancer researchers and mathematicians to detect cancer by assigning different sounds to different data points— creating a symphony of sounds based on the information contained in our cells. He says our ears can tell the difference between the low-pulsating beat of a benign "cell symphony" and the tinnier sounds of a "malignant symphony."[1]

It makes sense that if our cells naturally send off certain sound-wave and frequency vibrations when we take a perfect golf swing or when we're in good health, then the reverse would also be true: We could also use sounds to manually "tune" our bodies to have a perfect golf swing, achieve optimum health, or improve the way others react to us by "tuning" their emotions. In fact, we can.

Scientists have been using something called "biotuning" for some time now to do everything from helping people improve learning and memory to reaching peak performance and enhancing creativity. But what is relatively new is using biotuning in a different way: to help you be more persuasive, change the way people react to you, and even improve stock performance and increase company profits. That's what this chapter is all about: helping you use the concepts of biotuning to send off a good vibe and get great results.

THE SOUND EFFECTS OF SUCCESS

Aaron Naparstek is, according to information from his blog, a well-informed, intelligent man who's active in his community and abreast of local political issues. He's a journalist who has written for publications such as *New York* magazine, is a published book author, is a community organizer for urban environmental issues in New York City, and is a founder of the Park Slope Neighbors community group.[2] Yet, Aaron confesses in his blog that on election day, he "pretty much *always* finds (himself) standing in the voting booth with absolutely no idea who the judicial candidates are at the bottom of the ballot."[3] So how does he decide whom to vote for? In his blog he says, "I either end up picking a couple of names that *sound* [emphasis added] honest or I just don't vote for anyone."[4]

Sound can bias the brain to a mental state. And, as Aaron has demonstrated, the sound of your name can bias people to rally to you or rebel against you—even if they know nothing else about you or what you stand for. But these judgments go beyond whether you look like your name, as I discussed in chapter 3; the collective sound imprint sent off by the vowel-and-consonant vibrations of your name affects how people react to you. Just as our DNA reacts differently to rock and roll than it does to classical music, it also reacts differently to different names. Scientists call this the "name-letter" effect, and they argue that it is influential enough to encourage us to seek out names that resemble the career outcomes we desire.

For years, I've been following the research showing the impact that sound vibrations have on our biological reactions, emotions, and DNA. Neurological research that uses technology such as positron emission tomography (PET) and functional magnetic resonance imaging (fMRI) have helped scientists identify exactly which parts of the brain are involved in processing emotions, sensations, and memory. Other research into biocommunications, psychoacoustics, and psychophysics (which, among other things, seeks to map sound frequencies onto the psychological perception of pitch) has demonstrated that very specific sound-wave frequencies and rhythms can trigger a whole array of specific emotions and memories.[5]

The name you choose to call yourself has a large bearing on how others will react to you and how successful you will be in your given profession. The name John Smith, for example, has a different sound-wave pattern than Jonathan Smith, which, in turn, sends off a different sound-wave vibration than either John William Smith or J. W. Smith. Even slight changes in a sound-wave pattern can activate different parts of the brain. The unique vowel-and-consonant vibrations created by these different names send out sound waves that activate different parts of the brain and different emotions, which subsequently make us respond differently to a John than we do to a Jonathan.

So, for example, if you're a social worker, you'll have an easier time attracting clients if your name is John William Smith rather than John Smith, which would be a good choice if you're the head of a multinational corporation and want to attract powerful people. If you want to be perceived as a thought leader with cutting-edge visionary insights, then use Jonathan Smith. And if you're a chief marketing officer or head of an ad agency, then use J. W. Smith.

How do I know this? At my company we have a proprietary software program that capitalizes on research in the biocommunications and psychoacoustics fields. It allows us to input a name (or a song title or a book title) and use algorithms to analyze the sound-wave patterns formed by the vowels in a name, the consonants in the name, the combination of vowels and consonants, as well as the cadence—or beat—produced by pronouncing the word or phrase. We match the resultant combined sound wave and cadence pattern against a database of sound-wave patterns and beats that have been proved, through fMRI brain scans, to trigger specific emotions by activating specific parts of the brain.

In short, we analyze the frequency vibration and rhythm created by that name and then identify the impact the sound vibration has on our brain waves. What part of the brain is lit up by "Andy" versus "Andrew" or "Sue" versus "Susan"? In tests we've done with politicians, pen names for authors, book titles for publishers, and stage names for newscasters and actors, we've found the program has been an accurate predictor of the type of reaction a name will get from people—and the likelihood of someone or something with that name being positively received in a certain industry or situation.

The editors at *Pregnancy and Newborn* magazine had heard about those successes from our program, and they contacted my company to help three couples come up with names for their babies that would align with the life goals and desires the parents had for their children.[6] (Some may object to this: What if the child grows up to have goals different from the parents' goals for the child? Fair enough, but remember this: Newborns don't name themselves anyway, so why not choose a name that will be more appealing to larger groups of people? When the child gets older, he or she can then choose a name or variation of a name that suits him or her.)

Your name clearly not only affects how others respond to you, but it also affects how *you* respond to certain situations. After all, you hear your own name perhaps more than anyone else, and your own brain-wave patterns are changed every time someone says your name. Certainly more factors than just the sound of your name come into play in determining someone's success. But several mainstream scientific studies have also proved a strong and direct link between a person's name and his or her success. Let's take a look at a couple of these studies.

WHAT I DID LAST SUNDAY

Suppose I told you that a group of experienced elementary school teachers was given eight separate paragraphs written by tenth graders on the subject "What I Did Last Sunday," where the students had written accounts of their escapades on the weekend day. Each paragraph had the name of the student author attached to it. The students were Adelle, Bertha, David, Elmer, Hubert, Karen, Lisa, and Michael. Not knowing anything about the quality of the written paragraphs, which four students do you think wrote the better essays?

You probably already guessed that papers attached to the more common names—David, Karen, Lisa, and Michael—were perceived as the better essays. This widely quoted study from the *Journal of Educational Psychology* found that a student's name has a direct correlation with how teachers grade the student. Even though the paragraphs were all average in quality and the names were attached to the papers at random (for example, one paper might have the name Adelle attached to it one time and another time have the name Karen or Lisa attached to it), teachers handed out significantly higher grades to the papers with desirable names attached to them. Teachers apparently expect students with popular names to be smarter because they got a better "vibe" from those names. When I ran two of the names—Bertha and Lisa—through my company's sound wave–pattern analyzer, the results matched the reaction of the teachers. "Bertha" sends off a brain wave and rhythm pattern that triggers a part of the brain associated with emotions; "Lisa" lights up the logic and reasoning centers of the brain. Subconsciously we apparently make the assumption, whether right or wrong, that a Bertha is more emotional and a Lisa is more intelligent.

"INITIAL" SUCCESS—AND FAILURE

In another study, Leif Nelson at the University of California, San Diego, and his colleague—Joseph Simmons from Yale University—found a strong link between an individual's initials and his or her accomplishments.[7] They did two studies that looked at the relationship between a person's initials and negative performance labels.

In the first project, they analyzed the performance of major league baseball players over a span of 93 years. They found that players whose names began with K struck out at a higher rate than other batters. Why? Nelson and Simmons claim it's because in baseball, strikeouts are recorded with a K, and that fact subconsciously has a negative impact on the player's batting performance.

In the second study, the pair examined 15 years of grade point averages (GPAs) for students graduating from a large private American university with master's degrees in business administration (MBAs). They discovered that students whose names begin with C or D earned lower GPAs than students whose names began with A or B. They confirmed their results in the laboratory with anagrams.

The scientists contend that the reason baseball players with a K initial and students with a C or D initial performed lower was that people have an unconscious fondness for their own names, and that makes them slightly less successful at achieving their goals if that letter also happens to represent a negative outcome.

While I agree with their findings, I disagree with their explanation. I maintain there's a different reason for the link between initials and performance—especially considering that their study also found students with names that started with A or B didn't perform any better than students whose names started with letters other than C or D.

In running the letter K through our sound analyzer, we found that the sound-wave vibrations sent out by that letter are lower and subsequently produce a "lower" brain-wave vibration. Specifically, K sends off a vibe that makes us feel less confident, less aggressive, and somewhat fearful. When we ran C through our software program, we found that it sends off a higher-frequency vibration and triggers cheerful, outgoing, and happy-go-lucky feelings. Perhaps C-named people are more interested in being social butterflies than in cracking the books. D sounds tend to reduce vibrations in the part of the brain that relates to creativity and ingenuity, which could account for the lower grades. A vibrations induce the "fight" response of competitiveness and confidence—typical "type-A" traits. Although B vibrations activate the part of the brain that triggers fear and low self-confidence, they also cause the medial insula—the part of the brain associated with "gut" feelings—to light up. It could be that B people can get a better "gut feeling" about the right answer on exams than people with other initials.

GETTING A GOOD VIBE: WHAT'S REALLY IN A NAME

Whenever I consult with political candidates, authors, or CEOs who want to launch a national personal-branding campaign, I always evaluate the vibrational and rhythmic qualities of myriad adaptations of the person's name. When you change your name, you change both the sound waves that are sent off when someone says your name, as well as the beat of your name.

Name modifications are often easier to do for women because they can choose to use either their married or maiden names. But changing your name really can change your fortunes if you align it with the brain-wave patterns that cause you—and others—to react in a way consistent with your desired outcomes. What do I mean by that? As mentioned earlier, the vowel-and-consonant vibrations sent off by the sound of a person's name can literally change our brain-wave patterns and cause us to respond differently to different names.

To help explain how this can work, let's look at a few examples. Which name would be best for Hillary to use if she decides to run for president again someday? Hillary Clinton? Hillary Rodham? Or, what about Hillary Rodham Clinton? Well, to decide that, we have to take into account a couple of things. First, we need to examine the vibrational and rhythmic quality of each name. And, as you'll remember from chapter 3, we also have to make sure the impressions sent off by the name align with the subconscious visual messages sent off by Hillary's facial features.

The name Hillary Clinton produces a higher-pitched, higher-frequency vibration. It borders on eliciting a nervous energy response. The frequency patterns also show that this name stimulates the logical and information-processing parts of our brains (the frontal lobe), which would make us unconsciously feel that she is intelligent and has good mental reflexes. Hearing the name Hillary Clinton triggers another part of the brain—the part that lights up when we are engaged in competitive activities. (It would also stimulate competitive instincts in *her* mind as well.)

Hillary Rodham would be a good name if she wanted to be a teacher, counselor, social worker, or religious leader, because it emits a frequency that stimulates emotions of compassion, warmth, and comfort. When this name was fed into our analyzer, it demonstrated that waveform patterns were created that would cause the release of endorphins that produce feelings of tranquility, reduced anxiety, and comfort. It also seemed to activate the amygdala—considered to be the emotional center of the brain—which has direct and extensive connections with all the sensory systems of the brain. Again, although we want our teachers and spiritual leaders to be warm and fuzzy, we may not want that in our politicians.

Finally, the name Hillary Rodham Clinton created the weakest wave pattern of any of the three name variations; in other words, it's sort of a "bland" name that really doesn't trigger any strong emotions or reactions one way or the other. Like "Hillary Rodham," the dual last name has a warm, fuzzy feeling to it but lacks the punch (the added energy) of the stand-alone Clinton last name. That would make "Hillary Rodham Clinton" a poor choice for someone who wanted to be successful in either a helping profession or in a power position like the presidency. Additionally, the rhythmic quality of "Hillary Rodham Clinton" doesn't align with any of our natural biological beats.

So, because Hillary Clinton is a strong (competitive-and-intelligence-inducing) name with literally a "good beat," and her facial features are more masculine than feminine, this would be the best name of the three for her as a presidential candidate since that office requires strength of character and mental acuity. But there is a danger that this name-and-face combination could be almost "too strong" in some cases and could make her seem cold and aloof. She can—and has—offset that potential negative by adjusting her speaking style to be more low-key and conversational. Earlier in her political career she confused volume with projection in her presentations, and that—coupled with her strong name and dominant facial features—made her come off as too domineering and emotionless. But now she speaks in lower tones and uses more projection and less volume. The cumulative effect is a speaker who is powerful and confident but also more human.

Now, if she really wanted to become a counselor and go into a helping profession, she could do that, too; success in that arena would be helped along with a name change and a change in hairstyle and wardrobe choice to make her masculine features appear softer.

Men can also change their names to suit their desired outcomes. Consider the name Donald Trump. In analyzing several variations of this name—Don Trump, Donny Trump, and, of course, Donald Trump—we found something rare: a perfect score for one of these names for someone wanting to be a business leader. "Don Trump" has the same problem that "Hillary Rodham Clinton" has: The wave patterns sent off by the vowels in that name trigger completely different reactions than the consonant vibrations of the name. In other words, they cancel each other out; the name is pretty bland and doesn't really set off any strong feelings. Donny Trump would be a good name if he wanted to be a lawyer or a religious leader. But "Donald Trump" came back with a perfect score of 15 in our program for acceptance as a business leader: The vowels in his name trigger feelings of strength and determination; the consonant vibrations add a feeling of safety, grounding, and stability; and the "beat" of his name evokes feelings of optimism.

THE LOVABLE LOSERS

Being a Chicagoan for the past 16 years and a lifelong Cubs fan, I have to address this one: What does the Cubs name inspire? When we put *Cubs* through our wave pattern analyzer, we found that it produces a very scattered energy pattern; the parts of the brain associated with intense focus and concentration would barely light up at all when this name was said. It also triggers feelings of strong love and releases those endorphins that cause us to feel tranquil and happy.

Interestingly, the name also activates areas of the brain with a high concentration of receptors for dopamine (the ventral tegmental area). This could help explain why—despite having not won a World Series title for almost a century (at least at the writing of this book)—the Cubs remain the "Lovable Losers" with loyal fans around the globe. Much like the C-named student who is charismatic and fun-loving but who can't seem to buckle down, the Cubs are the pleasure-inducing life-of-the-party team of Major League Baseball that can't seem to focus and get the job done. (Hmmm, maybe now we can blame the Cubs' century-long World Series dry spell on the brain reactions caused in both fans and players!)

And for the South Side fans, consider this: Sox is a stronger name than White Sox because the latter triggers emotions of weakness and fear, while the former triggers the exact opposite—feelings of strength and even rigidity. Additionally, when you say "the Sox," the part of

words had on the fermentation process of whole-meal rice.[9] Thirty grams of rice were put into each of three separate glass containers: one labeled "thank you," a second labeled "idiots," and a third that wasn't labeled. For three weeks, participants daily said "thank you" in a melodious tone to the rice in the first container and said "idiots" to the rice in the second container. The rice in the third, unmarked container was ignored for the entire exercise. At the end of the experiment, the container that received daily statements of appreciation was bubbly, had a pleasant smell, and the water was clean; there was only a thin layer of mold on top. The rice that was called "idiots" on a daily basis was rotten, had a foul odor, the water was dark, and there was a heavy layer of mold on top. But the rice that fared worst of all was in the container that was ignored: a thick layer of mold had grown, the smell was hideous, and the water was turbid. It seems as if being ignored is worse than being ridiculed! Even negative sound-wave patterns are better than no sound energy at all.

A second, similar experiment was carried out in which the same verbal treatment was given to seeds of wheat in four separate germinators. Two of the germinators received daily verbal doses of "thank you" or "you beauties," while the other two groups of seeds were subjected to being called "idiots" or "you ugly ones." The seeds in all four containers were all subjected to the same environmental conditions regarding light, temperature, water, and so on. The results mirrored the first experiment: Wheat in both the "thank you" and the "you beauties" germinators grew quickly and was larger and healthier than the wheat that was called "idiots" or "uglies."

But the series of experiments got interesting when Dr. Cornelia Guja of the Ecological University of Bucharest decided to test if plants reacted *immediately* to sound stimuli. In her experiment, she hooked up a fern and a geranium to an electrograph—a machine that uses electrodes to measure cell activity and impulses sent off by the subject. (This device is normally used in biomedicine in Romania.) After attaching electrodes to the plant, Dr. Guja played Mozart and heavy metal CDs. The electrograph—which produces a printout that documents the cell activity of the subject being tested—showed that the plants emitted a stronger energetic field (increased cell activity) when classical music was played than when the plants were "listening" to heavy metal.

A fourth experiment was conducted where the plants were hooked up to a polygraph machine and placed in water (to raise the plants' electric conductibility). When hateful words were spoken to the plants, the polygraph needle oscillated violently; when kind words were uttered to the plants, the needle went back to a "normal" readout.

Japanese scientist Dr. Masaru Emoto wanted to push the what-effect-do-sound-wave-vibrations-have-on-living-systems envelope even further.[10] Dr. Emoto is a water guy. His life is devoted to studying water. At one point, he wondered if water could produce crystals at room temperature. He bounced the idea off of his scientific colleagues and they all agreed that it could not. But, after several months of experimentation, he was able to get a photograph of a water crystal. That's when he decided to see if sound vibrations would influence the shape of water crystals.

He placed a glass of water between two speakers and played three selections: one by Mozart, one by Beethoven, and the third from Chopin. Even though the water did create beautiful crystals in all three cases, the structure of the crystals was different for each composer. When Dr. Emoto tried this same experiment with heavy metal music, he found that the results were not crystalline, but rather asymmetrical, incomplete, dull-looking patterns.

What do these experiments mean for humans? They seem to suggest that changes in sound-wave vibrations not only affect brain waves in mammals, but also cells and molecular structures of all organisms. In humans, the impact is noticed most prominently in the brain, but we can be assured that our body processes are altered as well by changed cellular activity from sound waves.

I often coach my presentation-skills clients on how to select and arrange specific words in a sentence in order to elicit a specific "vibrational change" in the bodies and brains of audience members (that is, a change in their brain-wave patterns). What most people aren't aware of, but what the field of psychophysics has found, is that the order of certain sounds is just as important as the actual sounds because even a slight change in word order can change the way someone reacts. For example, saying, "Our profits are up 12 percent this year," sends off a different sound vibration and causes a different reaction than saying, "This year our profits are up 12 percent." What's also important is the length of the pause between the words, because those pauses affect how the brain processes and stores the information.

You can send off a "good vibe" in another way, and that is with the sound of your voice.

SETTING THE TONE
The Impact of Your Voice on Human DNA and Emotions

Most of us feel sleepy earlier in the evening during the winter months than we do during the summer. It gets darker earlier, so our bodies tell us it's time to go to bed earlier. Scientists call this "biological sympathetic oscillation." What that means is that your body looks to the external environment and "sets" itself according to the most powerful external stimuli, or cycle, that it can find. Researchers now tell us that our brain waves and emotional reactions are also "set" to match the most powerful beats, sound vibrations, and pitches that we hear in our immediate environment. That means a persuasive voice is one that not only appeals to the emotions of mass audiences, but also changes the brain waves of listeners. You can literally "tune" the emotions of your audience by the way you manipulate the pitch, cadence, volume, and vibrato of your voice.

Peter Cetera, formerly of the group Chicago, was one singer who had what musicologists call "emotional vibrato"; that is, his voice evoked emotions deep within the core of people across many cultures. Part of the reason his voice was so appealing to audiences was because it was distinctive: You could pick Cetera's voice out of a police lineup. And audiences like a distinctive voice. But more importantly, audiences want to feel emotions—specifically emotions of vulnerability. Cetera's voice seemed made for sad and endearing love songs because it makes us feel his pain and experience his emotions—more than even the lyrics do. This has less to do with being a good singer and more to do with the fact that his tenor vocals were so distinct and literally changed the brain-wave patterns of listeners. When Jerry Scheff replaced Peter Cetera as the lead tenor in Chicago, the band never had quite the same panache. Although Scheff is a gifted singer, nothing about his vocals make those "emotional sounds" stand out; there's no desperation, no fire in his voice, as there was in Cetera's.

Cetera also often sang with a falsetto voice—a singing technique that produces a pitch higher than the singer's normal range. Frankie Valli of The Four Seasons used a falsetto voice, too, in blockbuster songs like "Sherry" and "Big Girls Don't Cry"; so did Barry Gibb in many of the Bee Gees' songs. These musicians enjoyed top-of-the-charts international success largely because of our anthropological conditioning to be drawn to higher-pitched male singing voices. Specifically, it's our fight-or-flight response that favors a "head" or "falsetto" male voice.

A lower voice is associated with doom, strength, and foreboding; high voices are associated with vulnerability. To put it another way, traditionally, high voices have been considered the good guys. Take opera, for example; it's always the villain who is the bass or baritone, and the tenor is always the hero. The high-pitched falsetto or head voice makes us feel safe, happy, and "light." A lower-pitched bass tone in a singer, while pleasing to the ears, isn't quite so pleasing to our psyches and our primal conditioning. Just as we are drawn to the vulnerability of average and even unattractive people, so, too, are we drawn to voices that project vulnerability. That's not to say a beautiful baritone voice isn't pleasing to listen to. It certainly is. But when we hear a bass voice we sense the singer is superior and powerful, and we are a bit wary; when we hear the vulnerability of a higher-pitched voice, we feel the pain of the singer and want to rally to him.

Concertgoers often rate someone with an "emotional" voice as having a better-quality voice—even if that's clearly not the case. In one study at the University of Sydney, audiences listened to waveform recordings from 11 internationally famous opera singers. The listeners were asked to rate, in order, which singers they liked the best and to identify the emotions expressed in the cadenza of the singer. They were also asked to judge the vibrato quality of the singer's voice.

You guessed it: The results showed that the singers audiences liked the best were those who could evoke the most intense emotions—and they often rated these singers as having better vibrato, even though that often wasn't true![11] What these singers did have, however, were voices that evoked pleasing emotions—and in many cases these voices were higher pitched. It seems as if the more emotion a singer's voice can evoke, the better he or she is liked by audiences.

Audiences are also especially drawn to singers who have a wide range, as well as fantastic vibrato. Just as we prefer speakers who vary tone and pitch, we like singers who can do the same. A big part of Elvis Presley's appeal was his impressive vocal range. He could belt out full-voiced Gs and As in ballads that many opera baritones have a hard time matching.[12] The King could communicate so intimately with his audience because he had the triple threat: an "emotional" vibrato that resonates with the limbic brain, a wide range that further activated the limbic system, and versatility (he could sing rock, ballads, country, and blues). Our emotional brains were going full tilt whenever we heard Elvis.

Speakers as well as singers elicit certain emotional reactions from audiences based on the pitch and tone of their voices. If your voice can trigger positive emotions, you'll be a popular speaker and get positive results; if your voice makes listeners feel tense, insecure, fearful, or suspicious, you will have people tuning out. But unlike singers, speakers with high-pitched voices are *not* preferred. Why is this?

Well, first, we have to realize the difference between speaking and singing voices. Think of a popular song—even something like "Row, Row, Row Your Boat." Speak the first sentence, and then sing the second. What changes do you notice? If you're like most people, you'll find that you elongate vowel sounds when you sing. If you were able to get the song's melody out of your mind when you spoke the first sentence, you also probably noticed that prosody (the rhythmic and intonational aspect of language) and tempo were not as pronounced in your speaking voice. And finally but most importantly, most people sing in a higher-frequency pitch than they speak. We are biologically built to naturally sing in higher pitches and speak in lower tones. (The pitch range of a speaking voice is also much more limited than that of the singing voice.) Therefore, to the subconscious mind, a high speaking voice or a low singing voice seems out of sync with our natural programming. Although we may tolerate a high-pitched speaking voice or feel soothed by a low singing voice, something doesn't seem quite right to our subconscious.

A study by the Center for Voice and Swallowing Disorders of Wake Forest University Baptist Medical Center polled Americans on the best and worst speaking voices. Their findings reflect our primal preferences for lower-toned speaking voices. The "best" voices were, in order, the voices of James Earl Jones, Sean Connery, Julia Roberts, Katie Couric, Barbra Streisand, Sam Donaldson, Mel Gibson, Meg Ryan, and Anthony Hopkins. The voices that were rated as "Worst Overall" in the study were, in order: Fran Drescher, Roseanne Barr, Gilbert Gottfried, Bobcat Goldthwait, Joan Rivers, Howard Stern, Rosie O'Donnell, Howard Cosell, Dick Vitale, and Mike Tyson.[13]

What, specifically, is it that makes the "best voices" most preferred and the "worst voices" the ones audiences want to run from or tune out? And why wasn't someone like Oprah—who is wildly popular and has a lower vocal tone—on the "best voices" list? Whether you have a voice that others like depends upon three things: the frequency range (pitch) that your voice falls into, the vibrato of your speaking voice, and your vocal physiology—or how you either over- or underutilize your respiratory, phonatory, articulatory, and resonatory systems to produce sound when you speak.

Pitch is the first—and usually main—factor people use when deciding whether a voice is pleasant or obnoxious. The Wake Forest University researchers found that the most pleasing speaking range is between 110 Hz and 130 Hz for men and 200 Hz and 230 Hz for women. British and Irish accents consistently fall into these ranges. Of course there are exceptions, but more often than not people from those regions will have a pitch within the frequency vibration range considered most pleasing by most humans.

Jackson Gandour is a linguistics professor at Purdue University who has spent the last thirty years researching neurophonetics—a branch of neuroscience that studies how we perceive, produce, and react to speech. In February 2008, Dr. Gandour and his colleagues released a study that shows pitch plays a much larger role in cognitive processing than originally thought. He and his team looked at blood flow in the cerebral cortex during changes in pitch during speech. What they found is that the melody of speech doesn't just activate the brain areas associated with language, it also interacts with more general sensory-motor and cognitive processes. Gandour says both the right and left brain hemispheres are involved in processing pitch: The left hemisphere processes the linguistic information, while the right hemisphere engages neural mechanisms. So when you're speaking, your pitch not only affects the meaning of the words you say, but also the entire neurology of the listener.[14]

Even slight manipulations in our vocal physiology can evoke drastically different emotions in audiences. And remember, if we want to have audiences raving about our voices, then we need to make our voices "emotional" voices.

CREATING YOUR VOCAL FINGERPRINT

If you take a fork and strike the side of a wine glass, you'll get a much different sound than if you take the same fork and tap the side of a teacup. You know just by the sound that the two objects are very different. The sound an object makes is its acoustic fingerprint: it's unique to the specific object and can tell you a lot about its nature.

Your voice is the same way. How it sounds says a lot about your personality, your intelligence, your work ethic, how trustworthy you are, and even your health. People literally make decisions—albeit unconscious decisions—about whether they'll trust you, whether they think you're smart or a little dull-witted, or how good a team player you'll be based on the sound of your voice. And if they are listening to you over the phone, where they can't see you, they are also making decisions about your appearance—including your weight, height, and even your age.[15] The good news is that you can change your voice to suit your personality and your goals—and to increase your instant appeal quotient.

VOCAL PHYSIOLOGY
Creating a Voice That Audiences Are Drawn To

British speakers, Peter Cetera, James Earl Jones, and Julia Roberts all have vocal qualities that send off—in different ways—primordial sounds that cause a pleasure response in our bodies. We, too, can literally use the sound of our voices to "biotune" listeners and awaken the innate organic intelligence that causes people to rally behind us.

Even if you have a voice that sounds like nails on a chalkboard, you can make changes in your voice to change the reaction you get from people. Just as you have to work your abs or biceps to get the physical look you want, you also have to work the right parts of your voice to get the "right" sound for your intended purpose. By manipulating the location of your pharynx, you can control the length of the sound waves sent out when you speak and that, in turn, will determine if people perceive you as in charge and confident or immature and insecure. When you finesse the amount of air that flows through your vocal cords and nasal cavity when you speak, you can affect whether people view you as intelligent or dull-witted, trustworthy or suspect. When you manage the location and movement of your tongue and lips when giving a speech, you can mold an impression that you are someone who knows his or her facts, or someone who is talking off the top of his or her head. Finally, depending upon how sound resonates through your mouth when you talk, you can come off as lazy or pushy, or as having just the right amount of authority for the situation.

To give you an idea of how this works, let's take a few examples. You may remember Alberto Gonzales's testimony before the Senate Judiciary Committee. He was grilled on allegations ranging from illegal wire tappings to a string of suspicious U.S. Attorney firings. Most pundits said his testimony was completely unbelievable. Part of that had to do with the fact that he said, "I don't recall" 74 times during his testimony.[16]

But it was more than Gonzales's choice of words that made him unbelievable. He also has what most of us would call a whiney voice: high-pitched and nasal. That's a double-whammy for destroying credibility. First, a thin voice (high-pitched) sent off the impression that he was unsure of himself and also scared. (Think about when you are frightened; your voice usually goes up a few notches in pitch.) More troublesome, however, was his nasal resonance; too much air was passing through his nose when he spoke. This made him seem less authoritative and less professional, not to mention annoying.

The opposite of a nasal tone—called a "hyponasal tone"—is just as bad. Think about when you have a cold; if not enough air passes through your nose when you speak, then you sound ill. That's a hyponasal tone. It makes you come off as a bit slow-witted.

Correcting a nasal or hyponasal tone can be accomplished by manipulating the placement of your tongue and jaw, as well as by opening your mouth more widely when you speak.

Bill Clinton has a voice that makes most people *like* him but not *trust* him. He has a so-called breathy voice, which means that too much air passes through the vocal cords both before and during speech. For an exaggerated example of a breathy voice, think Marilyn Monroe. A breathy voice sounds soft and inviting, but it also triggers our suspicions and we don't quite trust the person as much as someone who doesn't have a breathy voice.

Exit polls during the 1996 presidential election showed that voters didn't like Bob Dole, but they did like Bill Clinton.[17] (Dole had a flat voice quality—a deep, low voice that gave the impression that he was in charge but also sent the impression that he was rather boring and bland.) According to those polls, voters chose Clinton—even though they admitted they didn't believe him, trust him, or find him credible! These feelings can in large part be traced back to the emotions evoked by his breathy voice quality. On the other hand, although voters were initially drawn to Dole's soothing, flat voice, he couldn't keep their interest.

If you often find that people don't quite trust your facts in a presentation, you may want to see if you have a breathy voice. One way to do this is to hold your hand in front of your face while you either say a line from a nursery rhyme or count to five. If you feel a lot of air hitting your hand when you speak, then you most likely have a breathy voice. To correct it, make sure you are breathing from your diaphragm when you speak, and not from your chest. Simply place your hand on your diaphragm when you talk; if your hand moves up and down, then you're breathing from your diaphragm; if it doesn't, you're most likely breathing from your chest. That means you have a breathy voice and you're unwittingly sending off the vibe that you are likeable but perhaps not fully trustworthy.

Oprah—like Bob Dole—has a voice that is deep, flat, low, resonant, soft, and inviting. When we hear Oprah's voice, the part of the brain that makes us feel safe and allows us to trust her is activated. When we first hear people with a "flat" vocal quality, like Oprah or Bob Dole, other very specific emotions are activated. First, we perceive them as being an "in charge" type of personality. We also initially consider them to be altruistic people and we are drawn to them. But someone with a flat voice will also cause listener fatigue very quickly because we find the vocal tone not stimulating enough to listen to for more than a few minutes.

Oprah also occasionally has a slightly throaty voice quality, which would normally cause us to tune her out even faster. But, fortunately, the talk show format is perfect for someone with Oprah's vocal qualities: Her soothing, "flat" voice draws us in, but because of the conversational nature of talk TV, we don't get bored with her voice. The variation in tone and pitch between Oprah and her guests keeps us interested and attentive. The combined qualities of her voice do, though, help explain why she wasn't listed as one of America's favorite female voices: The fatigue factor is too strong if we listen to her in a monologue for too long. (She was, however, among a list of 13 people who received an honorable mention. Her pleasing low tone is initially alluring; it's just difficult to keep our attention when that tone isn't varied enough.)

What can someone with a flat voice do to keep audiences interested? The easiest approach is to change volume, projection, and speaking tempo often. Oprah tends to talk at pretty much the same consistent rate most of the time, and also with pretty close to the same volume, projection, and cadence.

Another approach—which I wouldn't recommend without consulting a speech coach because you could cause damage to your voice if you do this improperly—is to change the size of your pharynx (which acts as a resonating cavity for sound) when you speak. (The pharynx is the tube-like cavity that connects the mouth and nasal passages with the esophagus. We use the pharynx to eat and breathe, as well as to speak.) If you ever had a slide whistle as a kid, you'll understand how the pharynx works. When you "open" the slide and increase the length of the resonating chamber (the tube of the slide whistle), the pitch is low. When you "close" the slide and shorten the resonating chamber, the sound goes up several octaves.

Your pharynx works the same way. When you lower your vocal folds (or vocal cords), your pharynx becomes larger and the sound is lower. Similarly, when you raise your vocal folds, the pharynx becomes smaller and the sound pitch higher. Frequently changing the placement of the vocal folds when you speak can help overcome the blandness of a flat voice tone. (Just a note of clarification: A lower-pitched speaking voice is always associated with higher credibility and authority, so I'm not saying someone with a low pitch should raise it. What is important is that if you have a low pitch, you must raise it occasionally throughout your presentation; otherwise, you will lull your audiences half to sleep.)

Vocal folds also play a part in how intelligent you sound when you speak. The vocal folds are working at their most efficient level when they don't open too widely and don't waste energy (and airflow) when you speak. That's called a "tense" voice. A lot of people confuse a tense voice with a high-pitched voice, but that's not accurate. A tense voice can be either high- or low-pitched. The advantage to a tense voice is it makes the speaker seem more intelligent than someone who is speaking with a breathier voice. Julia Roberts, Sam Donaldson, and Katie Couric all have tense voices. It's no surprise that they landed on the list of best voices.

Your articulation—in addition to your breath control—also contri-

thighs. Considering the sexual nature of much of rock and rap, this isn't surprising. Midrange sounds, on the other hand, are felt in the stomach and the chest. So depending upon what reaction you want to get from people, you can change the tone of your voice to suit what part of the body will literally "resonate" with your message.

For example, if you're telling a story and you want people to really feel it in their hearts, try to put your voice into a midlevel pitch so the sound will resonate in the chests of the audience members. Spiritual topics are best spoken about in a higher-range pitch because high-frequency vibrations are associated with a "higher power" by most people, so you will want the sound to resonate high in their bodies. (Ever notice how most church organs are tuned to a high frequency—so high, in fact, that it's often difficult for most people to sing at that level?) Our "human instrument" responds to the frequency range of other instruments—including your voice.

A higher resonance is also good for topics that require clear thinking or clear action. Think about this scenario: Your child is in the middle of the street, chasing after a ball. An oncoming car is heading right for your child. You'd most likely yell in a loud and high-pitched voice to get the child to move. Because you wanted to communicate clearly, your instincts kicked in, and you used a higher-pitched voice that would resonate in the head and not the chest.

Here's another scenario: If you want to get people's attention at a railway station or airline terminal, which do you think would be the better voice—a male or female voice? Dr. Michael Hunter, of the Department of Psychiatry and Division of Genomic Medicine at the University of Sheffield, and coauthor of a study on male and female voices, says it's the female voice. "Most people at a railway station say female announcers are clearer," he says.[20]

Part of this could be because when females speak, they tend to pronounce sounds more toward the front of the mouth, rather than the back as men do. This frontal articulation is clearer and more precise. Hunter offers another possible reason. He says women's voices are often higher pitched and more melodic than men's voices— meaning there is more variation in pitch and volume during speech. Because the brain is trying to decipher the modulation in the typical woman's voice, Hunter maintains a female voice can communicate more information per sentence than a male voice. When we hear a woman's voice, the sound is resonating more in our heads than in other parts of our bodies and we are literally hearing an entire symphony of speech, with all the changes in pitch, volume, and tempo.

When men listen to a man's voice, on the other hand, they are "seeing" more than they are hearing, according to Hunter. He says the male voice activates the brain's visual region (as opposed to the thought center of the brain), and when men hear another man's voice, they are trying to visualize what he looks like—and not focusing as much on the content of what is said. Hunter says the visual centers of the brain are so strongly activated by a man's voice that the male voice is most often associated with hallucinations.

What does this mean for speakers? My suggestion is that men should use more visual descriptions of their topics when speaking, and women would do well to use more auditory explanations to align their words with how the brain is reacting to the sounds. Even simple changes in phrases such as, "look at the outcome" or "listen to the results" can help align the parts of the brain activated by a male or female voice with the content of the message.

Rhythm is another way we can change the physiology of our audiences. Speakers who talk at a faster rate can actually increase the heart rates of the people in their audience. This, again, is because of the biological sympathetic oscillation factor. Our bodies will adapt to whatever is the dominant sound in our environment. When you're the speaker, you're the dominant sound in the environment. You have, to a large extent, control of the heart and respiration rates, as well as the feelings and emotions of your listeners by the cadence, pitch, volume, and tone that you use. Every sound that your voice makes has a corresponding biological reaction in listeners.

TAPPING INTO ANTHROPOLOGY TO PREDICT HIT SONGS

Music, according to some researchers, is the art of thinking in sounds.[21] It's also the art of spending by sounds.

Music—and sounds in general—can change our attitudes, our buying behavior, our productivity, and our politics. To get a certain response from a listener, you just need to look at what part of the brain is responsible for that behavior or emotion and then find out what type of sound excites that part of the brain. That's what my company's name-analyzer software is based on. We suggest name changes that will produce specific-frequency sound-wave vibrations that will activate different parts of the brain to achieve a desired emotion or attitude. Ideally, you want a name that will make you feel good.

Music operates on the same principle. Even though music has been around for over 45,000 years, new research proves that our anthropological conditioning makes us prefer the same sounds and same music that our ancestors did thousands of years ago.

This brings me back to my discussion of the Beatles from chapter 6. Remember that songs by the British mop-tops contained words that produced feel-good chemicals in the brain? As it turns out, the melodies and rhythms of their songs also cause a reaction not completely unlike that of taking an opiate. Their music simply makes us feel good. But it's not that the music of the Beatles has influenced our DNA; rather, it's that our DNA has us programmed to like music that contains the same elements as that of the Beatles, Beethoven, Elvis, and other enduring artists. Neurologists, psychologists, and musicologists alike say we pretty much prefer the same types of musical elements that our Neanderthal ancestors did when they played notes of today's diatonic scale (think "do-re-mi-fa-so-la-ti-do . . .") on their bone flutes. According to Dan Levitin, a former music producer and currently a professor of psychology at Montreal's McGill University, mutations and adaptations take about 500 centuries to be encoded into our DNA.[22] So our brains still prefer musical elements that were in songs 45,000 years ago.

So does that mean that hit songs can be predicted? It appears so. Identifying and mapping those preferred, anthropologically embedded musical preferences is the work of musician Mike McCready. He founded a small New York start-up company called Platinum Blue Music Intelligence, which uses a computer program to predict the hit potential of a song. The company claims hit songs conform to a limited number of mathematical patterns that cannot be heard by the ear. How it works is that the program uses algorithms to compare songs to a database of top *Billboard* songs from the past five years.

McCready and his team have analyzed more than 50 years of music (a database of over one million songs!) for more than 70 different so-called sonic characteristics—such as tempo, cadence, melody, chord progression, and pitch. Musicologists say these characteristics produce the strongest reactions in terms of human perception. Once it identifies the sonic characteristics of a song, the software creates a chart that matches the universe of songs against those that became *Billboard* hits. Songs with mathematical similarities end up very close to one another on a chart. So when Platinum Blue experts get a new song from an artist, they plot the attributes of the new tune against the universe of successful songs; if it plots close to hit songs, it most likely will be a hit. If the song lands in a cluster away from the mathematical equivalent of a hit song, then it's back to the drawing board for the artist.

In 2005, Gnarls Barkley was about to release their first single, "Crazy." They went to McCready, and his algorithm predicted it would be a huge success. He was right. It became a top-ten hit throughout Europe, North America, and Oceania in the first half of 2006, reaching number-one on the single charts in the United Kingdom, Ireland, Denmark, Canada, New Zealand, and other countries.[23] "Crazy" made musical history when it became the first single to top the UK charts on download sales alone.[24]

The hit-song prediction technology also used mathematical algorithms to predict the success of independent artist Ben Novak's "Turn Your Car Around"—which was later recorded by Lee Ryan. That song hit the top 20 in several European territories, including peaking at #2 in Italy and #12 on the UK charts.[25]

Another relatively unknown artist submitted an album to McCready in 2002, when he was working with a similar version of the music-intelligence software at a Barcelona company he cofounded. Even though the tracks on the album had a vastly different sound from other hit songs of that year, the company's algorithm predicted that it would be a hit.[26] Not just a hit, but a *huge* hit.

The artist was Norah Jones and the album was *Come Away With Me*. The album sold 20 million copies worldwide and won several Grammy Awards in 2003, including Album of the Year, Best Pop Vocal Album, and Best Engineered Album.[27] One song on the album, "Don't Know Why," won Grammys for Record of the Year, and Song of the Year.[28] Norah Jones walked away with awards for Best New Artist and Best Female Pop Vocal Performance."[29]

How can a mathematical calculation be so accurate in predicting hit songs? Isn't musical preference subjective and individual? Not entirely. As Professor Levitin found, the brain is still programmed to prefer musical elements that our ancestors heard centuries ago. Platinum Blue's science works because it maps songs that have successfully tapped into the parts of the brain that are involved in processing complex emotions, sensations, and memory—all the parts of our noggins that are involved in listening to music and sounds. In a nutshell, you could say that the algorithms are extractions of all of the musical features that trigger the pleasure parts of the brain.

Two of those features that I've already talked about are emotional vibrato and back-channel communication, which you may remember from chapter 6. But there's another powerful component to appealing sounds: rhythm.

IN ONE EAR AND OUT THE POCKETBOOK
Biotuning for Profits and Productivity

Just as Hit Song Science can use our preprogrammed preferences for certain sounds to predict hit songs, we can also use that same science to predict what type of music will get people to open up their wallets. Depending upon what you're trying to sell, certain sounds can literally trigger parts of the brain that will get people ready to buy. For example, when you walk into a large computer store such as Circuit City, Best Buy, or Frys, what type of music is playing? It's usually up-tempo. There's a reason for that: Several independent research studies have found that items that require more thought—such as computers, cell phones, or health insurance—will sell more briskly if faster-tempo music is playing in the background. The faster tempo lights up the information-processing center of the brain and gets us to think more about the product.[30]

I put this to the test with a CPA client who was trying to switch from a typical event-driven practice (customers only came to him at tax time) to a membership fee–based practice where he would offer financial and tax advice throughout the year. He had originally hired me to tweak his sales presentation, but even after we crafted a compelling spiel detailing how the fee-based service would help his clients save and make more money, only a handful of clients (less than 12 percent of his client base) signed up for the new service. Every time I would go into his office, he would have soothing, slow-paced music playing in the background. When I suggested that he put on some peppier tunes, he resisted. (His exact words were, "You're nuts!") He said his clients were conservative and sophisticated, and they would object to upbeat music.

After a lot of arm-twisting he eventually agreed to let me replace his slower-paced musical selections with a combination of fast-paced classical music (such as Beethoven's Fifth) and up-tempo instrumental rock and blues. While all up-tempo music improved his sales, up-tempo music with fluid strong tones but not a strong beat (up-tempo classical) had the best results across all customer demographics. (His clients ranged in age from late 30s to late 60s.) After the musical switch to all up-tempo, strong-tone instrumentals, he was consistently converting upward of 48 percent of his clients to the new fee-based service—clients who had previously snubbed the offering!

Up-tempo music isn't appropriate for every sales setting. If you're selling emotional items—such as jewelry, food, cosmetics, sportswear, and even beer—slow music is better because it excites the emotional limbic brain. That's why you almost always hear slower-tempo music playing in grocery and jewelry stores. And one study found that medium-tempo music resulted in a threefold rise in drink purchases![31] That same study showed that if you want shoppers to purchase higher-priced items on the menu or higher-priced liquor, then Mozart is the music of choice.

Music doesn't just influence buying behavior; new research also finds that it determines how we perceive quality. According to a study published in the *Journal of Services Marketing*, slow pop (with a cadence of around 72 beats per minute) and fast classical selections make consumers think both service and merchandise quality are better than when other types of music are played.[32] A Japanese study gave an explanation for why we "feel better" about places that play music at the 72-beat-per-minute rate: That's the average resting heart rate of most healthy (but nonathlete) humans.

It's important for business owners not to confuse tempo with volume; background music is more effective at getting people to buy than foreground music. Foreground music will get people more involved in the song than the purchasing activity, whereas background music subtly activates either the emotional or information-processing parts of the brain without getting us into toe-tapping or humming mode. The goal of "persuasive music" is to activate specific parts of the brain to influence behavior and decision making—not to engage you in the song. That's also why regardless of whether the background music is up-tempo or slow, it's best if the melodies are unfamiliar.[33]

MUSIC TO INCREASE PRODUCTIVITY AND MAKE YOU SMARTER

Do you have a lot of "personality clashes" in your workplace? Are people highly productive—with the brain synapses firing—or are employees in more of a daydreaming state? The tunes and other sounds in the office can rev up productivity in much the same way that they spur consumer spending.

Imagine that your brain is a computer with two parallel processors—the right and left hemispheres. Most of us use either more of the left (logical) or more of the right (creative) brain hemisphere depending upon what task we're performing. But what if you could turn your brain into a supercomputer, using the full capacity of both the logical and creative parts?

You can. When the brain is exposed to a specific frequency

range—between 8 Hertz (Hz) and 12 Hz—the neocortex begins to synchronize the two hemispheres. When this happens, the nerve cells in the brain send out impulses at the highest possible rate. ("Hertz" is a unit of frequency equal to one cycle per second.) In short, you've just turned your brain into a supercomputer where both hemispheres are operating at maximum capacity and effectiveness.

This is part of relatively new technology called "audio-guidance" or "brain-wave entrainment": using specific sounds to induce brain states and improve brain functioning. The idea is to send different tones to each ear and have the two hemispheres of the brain "balance" the tones. When this happens, the brain "hears" a third signal, which is the difference between the two tones. Note that this third "sound" is not an actual sound at all, but rather an electrical signal that can only be perceived within the brain when both brain hemispheres work together.

This is how "audio guidance" tweaks the brain to maximum performance. It works because of something called a frequency-following response—the natural tendency of the brain to adapt its dominant electroencephalogram (EEG) frequency to match the frequency of the main sound heard in our environment.[34] The frequency-following response concept also helps explain why the classical music with varied tones played in the CPA's office resulted in more sales: The music forced the brains of clients to be more attentive and process information at a higher, more efficient level than when slower music was played. My client applied a specific audio stimulus to generate a specific brain-wave response. Even though he wasn't using specific brain-wave entrainment—where different tones are sent separately to each ear—he got pretty close to the same effect by playing music that "entrained" his clients' brains to the state he wanted.

If you want to boost the brainpower of employees and improve the productivity of your workforce, play sounds or music with a frequency between 7.82–8 Hz. This is the low end of the range that activates alpha brain waves. Why is that important? Because alpha brain waves induce peak performance. They improve problem-solving ability, enhance learning skills, increase creativity and positive thinking, decrease stress, and reduce anxiety.[35] When alpha brain waves are active, we are in a state of relaxed alertness and are able to think more clearly.

Unfortunately, few of us ever activate our alpha brain waves.

Think about the typical daily routine of an American worker. An alarm jars us out of a deep sleep, where delta brain waves were active. This causes our beta brain waves to kick in, causing stress and anxiety. (We're worried about traffic, being late, getting the kids off to school, or missing our commuter train.) Then we pour caffeine down our throats to force ourselves into a state of wakefulness (beta brain waves). All day we work under pressure; the boss gets on our case, we have tight project deadlines, and we have to deal with a series of annoyances and frustrations throughout the day. (The beta waves are dominant throughout this period.) Then we go home and collapse from exhaustion into a deep sleep (delta waves). So we've spent the entire day without activating the brain waves that can make us more productive (alpha).

Athletes know the power of alpha brain waves. Sports scientists have shown that alpha brain waves spike right before a show of peak performance. The alpha brain waves of an elite basketball player jump just before he or she makes that perfect free throw. The brain of an elite golfer will produce a burst of alpha waves right before taking his best stroke. Just before their best shots, elite marksmen and archers will experience a burst of alpha waves. Novice and intermediate athletes do not show this alpha brain-wave pattern.[36]

You may be wondering, "Okay. How do I find sounds that induce alpha brain waves?" Just do an Internet search for "brain-wave entrainment" and you'll find several vendors that sell music that can induce increased cognitive functioning, reduce stress, and increase creativity.

A lot of my clients ask me why I don't recommend one type of music for creative tasks like painting or writing and another for more logical and reasoning tasks, such as math or accounting. After all, the left brain hemisphere is used more in tasks that require logic and reason, while the right hemisphere is more dominant in artistic activities. My short answer is: Why settle for using only half a brain? When you merge both hemispheres of the brain and allow them to work together, you increase your overall mental fitness and enhance your cognitive functioning in general. Synchronizing both brain hemispheres gives the corpus callosum—the bridge between the right and left brain hemispheres—a good workout. If you work it enough, you can literally make this bridge physically larger and more capable of transmitting information back and forth between the hemispheres. It's sort of like having a faster computer processor: You can mentally process more information in the same amount of time, which enhances your overall mental performance.

SOUND
The Drug of Choice

A more radical use of sound to change both mental states and physiology is being pioneered by a piece of software called I-Doser. Basically it works like this: You purchase a "dose" of sound from a specialized audio player to get the feeling you want. The sounds emulate a broad range of drugs, from a cup of coffee to LSD. The audio file doses delete themselves after one play-through and are composed of binaural beats that sound like white noise to the ear. The company's website, I-doser.com, claims you can "synchronize your brain waves to the same state as the recreational dose" and that the audio drugs will "help the brain induce a state of mood lift, euphoria, sedation, or hallucination."[37]

Although it's not a good idea to have your employees on a simulated drug high, a strategic "dose" of a pick-me-up sound to get someone through that midafternoon slump may be helpful.

HEALTHY SOUNDS FOR HEALTHY PROFITS AND A HEALTHIER WORKFORCE

The house lights dim, the oboe sounds an A, and the orchestra tunes up. But the audience is sparse. Orchestras across the country have been having a hard time lately. Attendance has plummeted as audiences get older and there's just not as much interest in classical music anymore in popular culture.[38]

Could it be that the low attendance is somehow linked to that first A note played by the oboe? Some musicians think so. And the same vibration of that A note could help reduce the stress in your office, too.

If you're at the Metropolitan Opera, that A is played at a pitch of 440 cycles per second (or 440 Hz). If you're in Pittsburgh, the A pitch is 442; at the New York Philharmonic, it's 441.5; and in Berlin, the Bavarian Radio Symphony Orchestra tunes to an A at 446 Hz.[39] None of these, according to proponents of the so-called Verdi tuning method, are optimal for human listening. The Verdi method is based on the battle by Italian composer Giuseppe Verdi to stop the rising of the pitch to which orchestras are tuned. With Verdi tuning, all orchestra instruments would be tuned to an A note that vibrates at 432 Hz, as opposed to the common practice today of tuning to anywhere from 440 to the 450 + range.

What's so special about 432 Hz? Verdi claimed it has a scientific basis and it's a vibration rooted in nature. Although I won't get into a detailed technical monologue here, there is at least one solid example of an organic basis for 432 Hz: the movement of the sun. The note C, based on 432 Hz, can be reduced to a rate of one vibration per second. The measure of one second is based on the movement of the sun.[40] Other, in-depth studies show that planetary motions,[41] patterns found in nature,[42] and even the measurements of the Pyramids[43] and Stonehenge[44] are based on whole numbers that can be divided evenly into 432. Musical notes based on the other frequencies—such as 440 Hz—do not have mathematical correlations with rhythms and movements found in nature and astronomy. So there does seem to be some validity to the argument that 432 Hz is a vibration found most frequently in nature.

But what does that have to do with getting audiences to attend a classical concert? Well, when you think about what happens to singers when instruments are tuned to a higher frequency, you begin to understand how audiences can be affected. As instruments are tuned to higher frequencies, singers have to tense their voices (and their bodies) to hit the higher notes. The higher tension in the singers translates directly to higher tensions in audience members. A tense audience is not likely to return to the same venue. Audiences want their entertainment to relax them, not stress them out.

The 432 Hz "A" rate is also based in music history. The archaic Egyptian instruments that have been unearthed so far are largely tuned to 432 Hz, as were instruments in ancient Greece. Perhaps orchestras could see greater attendance—and greater profits—by lowering the pitch to which instruments are tuned; if audiences feel better when they listen to the music, they are more likely to want more of the same and return again and again to orchestras that perform with a 432 Hz "concert A."

So how does this discussion about tuning A to 432 Hz apply to the average person? Well, for starters, some notable experiments have been done on using sounds in this frequency range to offset stress in the typical office setting. Many companies are now coming out with "soundscapes" where the musical selections are based on the 432 Hz "frequency of nature." Although no formal studies have been done, several companies have reported dramatic drops in employee sick days when they play music based on this lower frequency. That would seem to point to at least anecdotal evidence of the healthful benefits of sounds based on the frequency vibrations found in nature. I have personally witnessed the benefits of so-called acoustic performance plans in companies—using melodies and tones to ease workplace tensions and improve employee focus. One was a call center and one was a health care organization. Both had high employee-turnover rates because of the high-stress environments they were in. And both saw employee-retention rates skyrocket after playing background music based on the 432 Hz vibrations.

RADICAL RAP GETS RADICAL VOTING RESULTS

Can music affect how we cast our votes?

You wouldn't think that music could affect political ideology. But that's just what Dolf Zillman and several of his colleagues at the University of Alabama found when they did a 1995 experiment where they studied the effect of political rap, mainstream rap, and rock and roll on the political attitudes of high-school students. The teens were divided into different groups, and each group was shown a different rock or rap music video. The students next voted in mock elections that featured candidates representing three separate ideologies: liberal, radical, or neutral. For each ideology, there was one black and one white candidate.

What happened next was surprising. After hearing political (militant) rap, the white students voted for the black liberal candidate or the black radical candidate, but *not* the white liberal candidate or white radical candidate. White teens who listened to radical rap were more receptive to movements that would empower African-Americans. But the same wasn't true for the African-American radical candidate, who *lost* the support of his black constituents after they were exposed to militant rap. Surprisingly, when whites were exposed to mainstream rap, they did not support the African-American candidates—they only did so after watching a *militant* rap video.[45]

What happened? Why would the white students who had been exposed to violent and anger-laden political rap videos that denounced whites overwhelmingly support African-American liberal and radical candidates and not white candidates with similar ideologies? You can attribute part of the answer to what happens in the brain when we listen to music: We often don't criticize what we hear, and there is a built-in "unconscious acceptance" associated with music. When white students watched the political rap that ripped white culture and called for black pride, the students subconsciously sympathized with the plight of the African-Americans. Music does, after all, engage the emotional parts of the brain. Why didn't the radical rap have the same positive effect for the African-American candidate with black voters? Most likely because the black voters were already well aware of their situations, and the political videos weren't engaging any new emotions.

The University of Alabama researchers say that exposing Caucasian high school students to radical rap can improve racial harmony in schools. The effects of music on personal and social attitudes, beliefs, and behavior are profound. And astute businesses can use this information to be more aware of the far-reaching effects their choices of background music have on their customers and employees.

THE NONMUSICAL EFFECTS OF MUSIC

People spend more money and time on music than on sex![46] We like music, and our anthropological conditioning even makes us crave it—no matter what culture we live in or what type of music we prefer. As a species, anthropologists say we humans have been listening to music for more than 45,000 years, since the first bone flute was used by ancient civilizations. Music is part of our evolution. And it continues to be a major part of our lives. As you've found in this chapter, music—and sounds of all sorts—can affect everything from how someone reacts to our name to what people buy and our political ideologies.

What you've read in this chapter about the influence of music on things like productivity, profits, and improved brain functioning clearly demonstrates how important music is to business. It's not just a nice entertainment diversion. Music—including tone, pitch, and beat—is integral to our health, success, and productivity. Yet music programs are often the first to be cut when schools face a budget crisis. If more businesses would study the impact of music, they would be more profitable and have happier employees with improved cognitive functioning, higher productivity, and increased problem-solving ability.

I firmly believe that courses in music should be a prerequisite for business classes. No, I'm not a musician, and I couldn't carry a note if it were in a brown paper bag. (My ill-conceived evenings of karaoke with friends have made that fact embarrassingly clear!) But I have seen firsthand in my consulting business the huge leaps forward companies make when they strategically integrate music not only into their marketing and point-of-sale plans, but also into their employee-development plans and office-space plans.

Science supports my observations. Researchers say that our reactions to specific types of music is universal: The structural components of sound—pitch contour, pitch interval, and beats—are encoded automatically in the auditory pathways of our brains and cause us to have specific biological and psychological reactions to specific music-related stimuli.[47] Scientists have found that babies react to different types of music in almost the same way that adults do, which is further evidence of just how ingrained our musical preferences are.

The message is clear: Playing a different tune can not only persuade people to your point of view, but can also positively influence corporate profits!

PRACTICAL APPLICATION
Using Biotuning to Increase Your Appeal

The research is clear and conclusive: Synchronizing sound-wave patterns with specific biological processes, sounds in nature, and our anthropological preferences can do everything from improve a golf swing or office productivity to motivate people to buy. As you learned in this chapter, there are many ways you can biotune elements in your environment to get others to respond more favorably to you or your products and services. Here is a recap of six of the most powerful biotuning activities.

1. *Biotune your name to activate the emotions and reactions you want from others.* This can be as simple as using a variation of your given name (for example choosing Sue, Suzy, or Suzanne; or Ken, Kenny, or Kenneth) or using an initial and your last name. The point is to understand the parts of the brain activated by the sound-wave vibrations created by the consonant-and-vowel combination of your name. The most accurate way to do this is by running your name through a sound analyzer that applies mathematical algorithms to your name and then compares those with similar sound-wave patterns that make

specific parts of the brain light up. At our company, we offer "name biotuning" for people, products, books, and song titles. This is not a focus-group test but rather a test of the specific parts of the brain that specific words and word phrases activate.

2. *Biotune your voice to send the right impression.* What is the "right" impression? That depends upon your desired goals and your personal brand image. You can use your voice to make others perceive you as more intelligent, friendlier, more creative, and even more successful. Or, in some cases, you may not want to come off as too smart or too successful. In this chapter, you learned some of the main ways to manipulate the physiology of your voice to create those specific impressions.

3. *Biotune your business to increase sales.* Whether you sell products over the Internet, have a storefront retail space, or a professional office, the types of music and sounds you have resonating through your business have a significant impact on how much people buy—as well as the perception of service quality. Although music on websites can be annoying, use the same rule that you would use in an office setting: Keep the volume low, and for purchases that require a lot of thought—such as professional services, technology, and insurance—up-tempo instrumental music that is higher in pitch will trigger more purchases. If you're selling jewelry, food, or luxury items, slower-paced instrumentals are more effective. And if you want to move people quickly (such as in a busy restaurant at dinner), play up-tempo music with a strong beat. I've also seen some websites that use nearly inaudible beats to biotune site visitors.

4. *Biotune your office for harmonious relationships.* As you learned from the section on rap music, certain types of music can improve social behavior and increase the level of social acceptance and tolerance.

5. *Biotune your office to improve employee productivity and increase employee retention.* Playing sound-wave frequencies that are closest to

nature (in the 432 Hz range) can increase employee feelings of well-being and reduce stress. A handful of companies have documented increased employee retention after infusing their offices with these "natural" sounds.

6. *Biotune for motivation.* The next time you plan a motivational session for your business, you may want to skip the motivational speakers and go right to motivational music. Just as specific sounds can induce brain-wave patterns in the brains of your customers to get them to buy, certain sounds can also motivate and mobilize your employees to action. And the sound recordings will be around long after the motivational speaker leaves the stage.

Sound isn't just some arbitrary element in our environment. Sound has the power to persuade, to soothe, and even to change our physiology, as it did with Jonathan Berger's sonification process to improve a golf swing. When we manage the sounds in our everyday world—whether it's the sound of our names or the sounds we play in the office—we can truly affect the way others feel about us and about our products and services. And when we do that, we strengthen the bond we have with colleagues, customers, and co-workers, and in the process create instant appeal.

CHAPTER 8

What Our Minds Really See

Reality TV shows have been all the rage for nearly a decade. We've had *Survivor, The Apprentice, Dancing with the Stars, American Idol,* and *America's Next Top Model,* just to name a few. There seems to be no end in sight for the popularity of these shows where seemingly anybody (with or without talent) can become a "somebody," at least for his or her fifteen minutes of fame. While the underdog concept— the idea of the average person being able to go from obscurity to fame and fortune—is part of the appeal of these shows, there's a bigger pull to their popularity, and it's something scientists consider a type of unconscious mind-reading device deep in the brain stem. I call it the mental real estate factor.

Mental real estate involves creating specific visuals that will trigger specific primal responses. The mind doesn't see just the objects or the action in front of it. For example, when you watch a football game, your mind doesn't just see a bunch of players on the field. It sees and, more important, makes you feel as if *you* are on the field playing right along with the football players.

Once you understand how this device works, you'll have a powerful tool that can help you gain popularity for your products, your cause, and even your executives. You'll understand why *Dancing with the Stars* is so popular. You'll know how to get the public on board with your charitable cause or environmental crusade. You'll know what specific product shapes and designs have the most mass appeal. When we harness the power of this one simple biological quirk, we open up a whole new world of persuasion, appeal, and even office productivity. To better understand what this device is and how it works, let's look at some examples of it in action.

MOVEMENTS, MOTION, AND MIND READING

Television ratings have consistently put the Super Bowl in the top ten of most viewed programs, regardless of which teams are squaring off. The average Super Bowl matchup will garner about a 40 rating and a 60 share—or around 44 million viewers— no matter if it's the Bears versus the Colts or the Rams against the Patriots.[1] Meanwhile, ratings for the Academy Awards show have been wildly inconsistent and heavily dependent upon who's hosting, who's up for an award, and the popularity of a specific movie.[2] The largest-grossing movie of all time, *Titanic*, brought in titanic Oscar ratings of about 55 million viewers. But when 116th-ranked *Chicago* was nominated, it fetched just 33 million viewers for the awards show.[3] Over the past several years, viewership for the Oscars has seen a steady decline, with only the occasional spike. What's the difference in appeal between these two events that makes one always a ratings hit and the other a hit-or-miss?

The political hot-potato issue of climate change has gone from Academy Awards–like inconsistent popularity to Super Bowl fanaticism in just the past few years. In 1989, polls showed that roughly one in three Americans worried a great deal about global warming; that number dipped to 24 percent in 1997, rebounded to 40 percent in 2000, then dropped again between 2001 and 2004.[4] Barely a politician uttered a word about global warming in the 2000 and 2004 national elections in the United States. Today, though, polls show that a whopping 63 percent of Americans—nearly two thirds of the population— are not only concerned about the environment, but they think global warming is the single biggest environmental threat facing the world.[5]

In fact, they think this danger is just as pressing as terrorism.[6] This time around, in the 2008 elections, all political candidates from the two major parties, as well as third-party candidates, concede that global warming is real and they have plans to address it. Political candidates in other countries are also talking about the issue.

Why are Academy Award ratings dependent upon the actors and hosts involved, yet Super Bowl ratings are unaffected by the teams participating? What has caused people to suddenly get red hot on global warming and make it a center-stage issue? A big part of the answer lies in the biological roots of the human psyche, in a collection of brain cells called mirror neurons. Mirror neurons are the mind-reading devices that scientists say cause us to be enamored by certain TV shows, movies, and even social causes.

Neuroscientist Giacomo Rizzolatti and his colleagues at the University of Parma recently discovered these mirror neurons accidentally while conducting motor experiments on monkeys.[7] The researchers were monitoring the motor cortex activity of the animals as they grasped a peanut. But one day the scientists didn't have the monkeys grab any food at all; the animals were just sitting around watching the researchers. To the scientists' surprise, the same neurons that were active when the macaques reached for food also started buzzing in the same way when they merely watched the scientists pick up a peanut. The monkeys mentally mirrored the action they observed, even though the animals didn't take any action.

The key finding was that the monkeys didn't just recognize an object, they also recognized action, emotion, and even intent. The Italian scientists who made the discovery say this phenomenon has never been found on a cellular level before and that its implications are far-reaching—possibly explaining why we feel empathy, how our language evolved, and even how productive we are in the office. These neurons also explain why most Americans prefer to watch *Dancing with the Stars* instead of a presidential debate, why we cry at sad movies, and why watching someone else work makes us less productive.

To understand how mirror neurons work, let's look at exactly what happens when you're sitting on the couch watching an episode of

Dancing. You stare at the TV screen as the dancers cha-cha across the floor. Photons—or units of light—hit the retinas of your eyes and send the image of the cha-cha-ing dancers and the steps they're performing to the visual centers of the brain, where the dance steps are analyzed and patterns in the movement are detected. Next, this information is zipped off to the mirror neurons, located on either side of the head near the ears, and these cells remap the pattern of dance steps onto the appropriate sequence of muscle twitches that help you produce an identical dance step—even while your butt is still firmly planted on the couch.

It doesn't matter if you've never danced a day in your life; your brain, at that moment, unconsciously *thinks* you actually *are* dancing as you watch the performers. Consequently, if the dancer trips, then your psyche says you're physically taking the same stumble and you feel the same embarrassment the dancer feels. Your brain literally goes through the motion of each step and the feeling of each emotion with the performer. This same thing happens when you watch a football game or witness people going through a tragedy: Your brain can't tell the difference between *seeing* someone else get trounced during a tackle or searching through the rubble of a home lost to a hurricane, and *experiencing* those things yourself.

If we begin to look beyond the research and apply the findings to everyday situations, you begin to understand how activating the mirror neurons can cause so many other reactions in us. For example, if you want to increase your productivity at work, you may want to close your office door. Canadian researchers say working alone speeds your progress because when we see someone else doing their work, our mirror neurons start to fire, and rather than picturing ourselves doing our own work, we picture ourselves doing the task that the other person is performing. This sets up a tug-of-war, of sorts, in our brains: We *see* ourselves doing *someone else's work*, while we mentally *try* to do our own. The mirror neurons will win out, though, and our bodies won't perform our tasks as well because our muscle patterns start to mimic those of the other person.[8]

You also experience the power of mirror neurons every time a charismatic speaker moves you emotionally. Engaging speakers can trigger your mirror neurons simply by unbuttoning a coat jacket, momentarily removing his glasses, nodding his head up and down while making a statement, taking a strategic stroll, giving a wave of the hand, or making a specific facial expression at just the right juncture in his presentation. Because our ability to speak arose from our ability to interpret the meanings behind complex facial expressions, gestures, and movements, we are able to automatically interpret the subtle meanings behind subtle gestures.

Remember the actor I told you about in chapter 1 who had the audience mesmerized during the live infomercial pitch? Her biggest persuasive appeal was the way she activated the mirror neurons of her audience when she said, "If you're willing to buy one packet of two *right now*, I've been factory authorized to give you another two-pack." She raised her hand at the exact moment she said "right now" and nodded her head while saying "another two-pack." Had she raised her hand or nodded her head while saying any other words in the pitch, her sales would have suffered; for her pitch to work, she had to coordinate specific words with exact movements. The savvy speaker who knows exactly the right type of facial expressions to use and exactly the right type of movement to make at exactly the right place in her presentation will have the audience virtually eating out of the palm of her hand.

I applied the power of mirror neurons to help an underdog U.S. Congressional candidate defeat a seasoned, polished politico in an election. The incumbent was a savvy, smooth talker with loads of experience and a large following. My candidate was a little rough around the edges when it came to his oratorical abilities. So I worked with him to use that roughness to make authentic, yet very specific gestures that would activate the mirror neurons in audience members at his rallies.

One such gesture was to unbutton his coat, open it widely, and walk out to the side of the podium at the exact moment he stated his stance on gun control: "My opponent is worried about people walking around with concealed weapons and wants more gun control. But honest, hard-working folks have nothing to hide, and that includes their weapons. Ranchers and hunters, for example, are responsible people who use weapons responsibly. They aren't sneaking around stalking people with their guns. They aren't criminals. They're citizens invoking their Second Amendment right."

This movement engaged the mirror neurons of the audience, and voters unconsciously gave a mental thumbs up to his message. The open-coat movement activated the comfort response: Because *he* opened his coat and seemed comfortable, *voters* felt physically and mentally comfortable themselves and transferred those feelings to him. (He had made the exact same statement in previous speeches and debates, sans the coat-and-side-step movement, but it always generated negative constituent and media response. This time, it got positive media play and positive polling results.) This is just one example of a subtle movement that can change and influence the mind-set of a mass audience if executed appropriately. It can't come off as staged or phony, or it's all over. It has to be performed naturally.

We crafted several of these specific gestures for each plank of his political platform and worked with him to make them natural and truly authentic to him. The result: The candidate, whom reporters said was a long shot, won his maiden 2004 election bid, as well as reelection in 2006. His chief of staff e-mailed me about midway through the congressman's first term to tell me that the candidate "has really become quite an effective speaker on the floor" by using many of the techniques that activate mirror neurons.[9]

In another case, I had a presentation-challenged CEO of a toy company casually begin playing with one of his company's products just as he outlined a new direction he thought the company should take in the upcoming year. (He had originally planned a series of data-laden PowerPoint slides to make his points during this annual-report speech.) Investors—usually a non-emotional bunch—commented for weeks afterward about how excited they were about the performance of the company and the CEO's leadership (despite the fact that his presentation clearly stated company profits had dipped drastically in the current year). The CEO had tapped into something universally appealing across cultures—the concept of play—and activated that universal pleasure by triggering the mirror neurons of the listeners. The result was an audience that left with a pleasurable experience and a good feeling—even though the company was in dire financial straits.

Why did these simple, barely noticeable movements have such a big impact? It's because *seeing* and *doing* are the same thing to the mirror neurons in the brain. When you watch someone perform an action or show an emotion, the mirror neurons can't tell the difference between what *you* are doing and feeling, and what *the person you are watching* is doing and feeling. Your brain puts you in the other person's shoes and you subconsciously do and feel everything that he or she does. This ability to instantaneously mimic the actions and emotions of others is a product of evolution and it came in handy for our early ancestors; they didn't have time to go take several training courses and complete a test on how to skin a bear and prepare a meal. They had to learn quickly by watching others. Mother Nature provided us with a built-in, expedited processing center to make sense of the physical motions we see in others so that we can replicate actions quickly and improve our chances of survival.

Mirror neurons also form the basis for much of our humanity because they allow us to experience true empathy, and it's that empathy that mobilizes us to action. It wasn't until we vicariously felt the utter devastation and hopelessness of Katrina victims that our mild concern for the environment shot into full-blown activism. For many years, global warming didn't light much of a fire under us. All the facts, figures, data, and pictures of melting ice caps that purported to support the theory of global warming made most of us yawn.

But when Katrina unleashed her fury on the Gulf coast in 2005, she gave us a front-row seat to the ravages of environmental change. We were forced to vicariously feel the effects of shifting global weather patterns, not just intellectualize them. We cried as we watched heartsick victims desperately search for missing loved ones, and our mirror neurons made us feel as if we were right there in New Orleans going through the same agonizing search. We became horrified and angry as we witnessed shaken and hungry survivors scrounge for food, water, and shelter, and once again our mirror neurons made us believe *we* were the ones desperately trying to survive.

If you lived in New York, Chicago, or Los Angeles—far removed from Katrina's ground zero—your mirror neurons still fired in empathy, reflecting and even simulating the actions and reactions of Katrina victims as you watched the events unfold on TV. We became, at that instant, as a nation, believers in global warming because we *felt it* even if we weren't in New Orleans. We had seen the plight of hurricane survivors and we reacted as if we were personally going through the ordeal firsthand. From that point on, any facts refuting global warming fell mostly on deaf ears. Because our mirror neurons caused us to literally feel the pain of the survivors, our primal survival programming kicked in to make us want to do whatever we could to protect our species from future assaults by Mother Nature, and we saw a war on global warming as a method of survival.

This kind of mirror empathy is often the pivotal force in winning court cases, too. Several people still scratch their heads and wonder how O. J. Simpson, with so much evidence against him, was found innocent in criminal court of the murders of Nicole Brown Simpson and Ron Goldman. Mirror neurons played a big role. As the jurors watched O. J. Simpson physically struggle to make a glove found at the murder scene fit his hand, it was as if they, too, were struggling to get the glove to fit. They could literally *feel* the glove getting tighter and tighter as they vicariously pulled the glove farther and farther onto their hands until it simply wouldn't move anymore and became stuck. That, coupled with Simpson defense attorney Johnnie Cochran's now-famous "If it doesn't fit, you must acquit" oratory, was a biological and emotional slam-dunk for the jurors. The physical empathy created by mirror neurons had played a significant part in convincing a jury to acquit O. J. Simpson.

Empathy is a powerful emotion and it is the main by-product when mirror neurons fire. But in order to fire, mirror neurons need an action to mimic. Many speakers try to create empathy in their audiences by retelling a story. But that's the problem; they *retell* the story, they don't *relive* it. This is a problem with a lot of campaign stump speeches. Candidates retell chronological and factual accounts of calamities that affected one or more of their constituents. This becomes the obligatory "human interest" story in their speeches. Although that approach appeals to the logical mind, it doesn't do much to engage our emotions, and it is our emotions—not our logic—that persuade. People make emotional decisions first then use logic to support their emotional decisions.

THE MIND-READING POWER OF MIRROR NEURONS

Here's the real interesting thing about mirror neurons: We mimic the *intent* of others as well as the action and emotions we see. According to scientists, mirror neurons are a type of mind-reading device that operate on an unconscious level. Even though their activity is reflexive and involuntary, when mirror neurons fire, they encode not just movements but the meaning behind the movements. For example, if I show you a video of my hand reaching for a half-empty glass of wine next to a plate of food, your mirror neurons would instinctively grasp that I intend to take a sip of the wine. But if I showed you the same video with the half-empty glass of wine next to an empty plate and crumpled napkin, your mirror neurons would know that I plan to clear the table.

How did you know that in the first video I wasn't planning to clear the table or that in the second video I didn't plan to drink that last sip of wine? The mirror neurons encoded the information gleaned from my facial expressions, gestures, and the environment to "read," in effect, what I was planning to do with the glass. This is similar to an experiment UCLA neurologist Marco Iacoboni did where the brains of 23 human volunteers lit up when the intent was to drink a cup of tea, but when the intent was to remove an empty teacup, their brains were not as active. Other experiments were conducted on infants, which showed they could tell the difference in intent when mom picked up a set of car keys to play, and when she picked up the keys to take a drive.[10] This proves that our mirror neurons are interpreting actions even before we learn the meaning of language.

Mirror neuron research has vast implications for the marketing industry, and it helps to explain why late-night infomercials and certain types of copywriting are more effective than others. Seeing the people on infomercials sit outside their ocean-front homes, drive their luxury cars, and have carefree, relaxed lifestyles, makes our mirror neurons fire as if *we* were sitting in front of the home or driving the luxury car. It makes it that much easier to pick up the phone and order the product-of-the-hour because our unconscious minds make us believe, if only temporarily, that we *are* that successful person and that we do the same things (such as use the product) that these successful people do.

Nike taps into the mirror neurons with the many videos on its website that show football players rushing on the field, runners jogging down city streets, and basketball players shooting hoops in dramatic slow motion. The mirror neurons of Nike's site visitors are firing at full force. Contrast that with the New Balance site, which has static photos of runners and joggers. The photos do nothing to engage our mirror neurons because there's no action for the mirror neurons to mimic. Mirror neurons need *movement* to move us into action—whether it's buying running shoes or voting for a congressional candidate.

Many researchers, including Vilayanur Ramachandran of the University of California at San Diego, believe mirror neurons have applications far beyond marketing and persuasion and will answer key questions about human evolution, learning, language, ingenuity, and culture. He claims that "mirror neurons will do for psychology what DNA did for biology: They will provide a unifying framework and help explain a host of mental abilities."[11] So in addition to explaining why we go gaga over sports or why our skin crawls at scary movies, mirror neurons may also explain such things as how our language evolved. And the more we understand that, the more we will be able to understand the depth of instant appeal.

WHAT YOU SEE ISN'T WHAT YOUR BRAIN GETS

You've just learned about one facet of mental real estate: mirror neurons. Now, let's explore two more that have to do with how the mind can create gaps in what we see.

As I mentioned in chapter 6, Ohio State researchers found that audiences only remember 3 percent of what they hear and see in a presentation. That's largely due to two conditions called inattentional blindness (not being able to see things that are actually there) and change blindness (being oblivious to major changes in a scene or environment). These two conditions also explain why some ads get our attention and others don't. Let's look at inattentional blindness first.

Daniel Simons of the University of Illinois at Urbana–Champaign and Christopher Chabris of Harvard University wanted to find out just how much we actually "see" in our environment. The pair of psychology researchers asked a group of undergrads to watch a short video where two groups of people—one where members wore white t-shirts and one where they wore black t-shirts—pass a basketball among themselves while standing in front of an elevator. Some of the passes were bounce passes; other passes were made by tossing the ball in the air. The undergrads were asked to either count the number of passes made between people wearing black or white shirts, or keep track of the bounce passes versus aerial passes.

But the psychologists added something to the series of videos that they made: a major distraction. In one video, a woman wearing light pastel colors and carrying an umbrella walked right through the middle of the ball-passing action. In another, a woman wearing a gorilla suit casually strolled through the middle of the frame. And in another, the woman wearing the gorilla suit walked into the center of the basketball action, stopped, turned toward the camera, pounded her chest, and then walked off.

After watching the video, the undergrads were asked if they noticed anything unusual taking place in the video. As it turns out, only about half noticed either the umbrella woman or the gorilla.[12] Simons and Chabris say this is because what we physically see versus what our brains perceive and what we remember is based on what we pay attention to. This explains why you might not notice when a co-worker gets a haircut or shaves his beard, or why you can't see your friends waving at you in a crowded restaurant if you're focused on finding an open table.

It's been a lament of creative directors at advertising agencies for years that the simplest, least creative commercials are the ones that get people to buy, whereas the humorous and highly creative commercials—although they make us laugh—don't prompt us to pull out our wallets. That's because all of that creativity distracts us from the product and the message. We are so focused on the entertainment that we miss the pitch. And if we miss it, we can't remember it. Recall of advertisements is, after all, a critical factor in how effective the commercial will be.

Scientists have discovered that how well we remember a commercial depends not only on the type of commercial, but also the type of show in which a commercial is placed. Brad Bushman is a University of Michigan researcher who set out to see if sex and violence really do sell in commercial advertising. Specifically, he wanted to see if people remembered sexual or violent ads more than neutral ads. He divided 324 undergraduate students (162 men and 162 women) into groups and assigned each to watch either a show with violent content, sexual content, or neutral content. Students were told the purpose of the experiment was to rate the television programs.

But after they finished rating the shows, they were given a surprise brand-recall test of the ads placed within the shows. Each show contained nine ads: three with violent content, three with sexual content, and three with neutral content. The nine products advertised were 1-800-COLLECT, Budweiser, Levi's, M&M's, Mountain Dew, Nike, Pepsi, Pringles, and Snickers, so they all had broad market appeal. There were three commercial breaks in each show, and each break contained one violent, one sexual, and one neutral ad. (Participants only saw one type of ad for each product. For example, if they saw a violent Mountain Dew ad, they did not see a sexual or neutral Mountain Dew ad.) The undergraduates were asked to recall the names of the nine brands in the ads in any order they wanted.

Violent ads were the least memorable of all; they were 20 percent less memorable than the sexual ads, which in turn were 18 percent less memorable than the neutral ads. But the type of shows that an ad was placed in also had an impact on how memorable it was to viewers. Bushman found that sexual and violent TV programs decreased recall for all forms of commercials—even those with neutral content. He concluded that "sexual and violent programming might impair commercial memory because they [*sic*] consume attention and limit the cognitive resources available for commercial processing."[13] In short, viewers are so engrossed in the show's content that they become "inattentionally blind" to the commercials.

The inattentional blindness phenomenon isn't just limited to commercials or TV shows. It rears its ugly head in corporate presentations, too.

While inattentional blindness happens because of *what* we pay attention to in our environment (we're hyperfocused on one element in the environment), change blindness is caused by *how* we observe the landscape around us.[14] We don't look at a scene in a steady way. Instead, our eyes dart around, looking at interesting parts of the environment, and that information is sent to our brains to build a mental map that corresponds to the scene. But if anything new is introduced to disrupt that eye movement, then we don't notice or remember that new element, even if we "see" it. This disruption can be caused by a flicker on a TV screen, scene changes in a movie, or even by mud splashes on a windshield when you're driving. In one experiment on change blindness, subjects didn't even notice when the heads of actors in a movie scene were switched!

Advertisers need to be especially aware of change blindness. For example, one of my clients—a health care organization—was running a public service announcement (PSA) about childhood obesity. Members of the marketing team said the campaign wasn't effective at getting the message to kids, so they called me in to get my take on the PSA. I asked what their objective was, and they said it was to get children to be more active and to realize that it was cool to be active. So I took a look at the 30-second spot and found the problem: The PSA was edited in such a way that it created massive change blindness.

The ad consisted of a series of quick cuts and dissolves and pans between inactive and active teens. The first scene was a girl chatting online, followed by a fast dissolve to a tight shot of a fast-moving bicycle wheel, which immediately zoomed out to reveal the same girl, along with four of her friends, racing around on their bikes. The second scene had a teenage boy playing video games, which cut to an action shot of someone skateboarding. (The camera was mounted on the helmet of the actor, so there was a lot of movement and motion to the second segment.) The third segment showed a girl watching TV, and then the camera panned to the window where a group of girls could be seen playing soccer outdoors. When teens in focus groups were asked what they remembered most about the commercial, they most often said seeing people playing video games and chatting online. Only 8 of the 37 teens remembered seeing the bike segment, 12 recalled the skateboarding, and 15 said they saw the soccer segment.

Why did the kids remember more of the sedentary segments than the action segments? Two things. First, because they were so intensely interested in video games and online chatting, they naturally focused on that more. When the new topic was introduced, they didn't even notice it, because they were still thinking about the preferred video games and chatting. (That's inattentional blindness.)

Second, the camera movements and transitions between the sedentary and action segments were just like a mud splash on a windshield; they interrupted the "view" of the action and caused the teens' eyes to miss much of the next action segment. (That's change blindness.) The solution I proposed was to re-edit the PSA and have the action segments longer than the sedentary segments in order to give the teens' eyes and minds a chance to readjust to the new scene and reduce the blindness. More important, I suggested eliminating any pans, zooms, and tight action shots during the transitions between the inactive and active segments to reduce the change blindness. The more movement that can be eliminated during a scene transition, the more people will remember what comes after the transition.

After the changes were made, another focus group was assembled with a separate group of 37 teens. This time, over 59 percent (22 of the 37) remembered the bike segment, 29 (78 percent) recalled the skateboard segment, and 26 (70 percent) remembered the soccer segment.

As with inattentional blindness, change blindness can also reduce the effectiveness of a speech.

THE LAWS OF VISUAL APPEAL

So far in this chapter I've talked about three components of mental real estate: mirror neurons, inattentional blindness, and change blindness. But our neurological reaction to art also plays a big part.

Ron Fisher says we have an innate desire for aesthetics. Fisher is assistant professor of radiology at Baylor College of Medicine in Houston, and he's been studying things like why we linger over some paintings in museums and not others, why we decorate our homes the way we do, or why we take the time to match our clothes in the morning. What he discovered, in short, is that we're really just like reptiles.

In his research, Fisher found that our response to art and aesthetics doesn't happen in the cortex—the region of the brain responsible for complex thought processes.[15] Instead, the only neural activity he found that was specific to enjoyment of paintings was in the midbrain and the ventral striatum. These two brain structures have been preserved through thousands of years of evolution and are even found in reptiles. And just as in chapter 6, where we found that there are certain words that create dopamine-reward pathways similar to those that occur with pot use or cocaine addiction, Fisher says our preference for certain types of art is a deep, primitive, reptilian pleasure response that creates those feel-good chemicals, too. As you'll see a little later in this chapter, successful companies use one specific "law of art" in product design that creates these same feel-good chemical reactions.

Fisher discovered this phenomenon by putting people in a functional magnetic resonance imaging (fMRI) scanner and showing them a series of 80 different paintings representing all styles of Western art from the eleventh century to the end of the twentieth century. The research subjects were asked which paintings they liked and which ones they didn't. When Fisher and his researchers compared brain activity that occurred when people looked at paintings they said they liked and ones they didn't, he found that our enjoyment of art begins with an unconscious primal pathway that activates a known reward system—the same thing that happens in reptiles. So the next time you paint your house, choose new carpet, or buy a new bedspread, you might want to remember that the Komodo dragon decorates her home as well!

Other researchers say they've found the common denominator of all appealing visual art—including product design. Vilayanur Ramachandran, director of the Center for Brain and Cognition at the University of San Diego, has proposed a new scientific theory of art that lists eight laws of artistic experience that "artists either consciously or unconsciously deploy to optimally titillate the visual areas of the brain."[16] One of these "laws of art" is the peak-shift effect, and it helps to explain why the comic strip will always be around, why the design of the Absolut bottle is so alluring, and why we can't resist the design of the iPod.

The peak-shift effect is well known in animal discrimination learning. Here's how it works: If a rat is taught to differentiate between a square and a rectangle (of, say, a 3:2 aspect ratio), and the rat is rewarded for choosing the rectangle, it's no dummy: The rodent will respond more frequently to the rectangle. But what's strange is that the rat will respond to an even greater degree to a rectangle that is longer and skinnier (with, for example, a 4:1 ratio) than the original rectangle. So the rat learns to respond not to a prototype but to a rule: rectangularity.

Humans are no different. We respond to rules of art just as the rat responded to the rule of rectangularity. And both responses—the rat's to a skinnier rectangle and humans' to specific art forms—are based on our preference for exaggeration.

Ramachandran has found that caricatures and comics, in particular, light up our primal aesthetic sense. (That helps to explain the enduring appeal of comic books.) Think about caricatures of politicians (since political caricatures are the most prevalent). What a caricature artist does is take the essence of someone and exaggerate one element of it. For example, a caricature of Hillary Clinton often exaggerates her high cheeks and large, toothy smile. Ramachandran says what the artist has done is unconsciously taken the average of all human faces, subtracted it from Hillary's (to get the difference between Hillary's face and all others), and then amplified the differences to create the caricature. What you end up with is a face that is more "Hillary" than Hillary's—not unlike the skinny rectangle that was more of a rectangle than the original prototype.

But why is this exaggeration so appealing? According to Ramachandran, the exaggeration of one characteristic amplifies our neural mechanisms far more powerfully than the original object; it creates a "superstimulus" to which specific brain circuits respond, and that, in turn, creates a powerful emotional connection to the art that has this exaggeration.

But this peak-shift effect doesn't apply only to form: It can be exploited in other dimensions as well. A Van Gogh or a Monet can be thought of as a caricature in "color space," according to Ramachandran.

The peak-shift effect can be applied to human appearances too. Differentiation—which is an exploitation or amplification of a specific trait or attribute—sells and is memorable. Popular personalities often use mental real estate to differentiate themselves from others. Elvis had his stage outfits. The Beatles had their haircuts (which created imitation "haircults"). Leonid Brezhnev had his unibrow. Elton John has his colored glasses. Companies create mental real estate through the peak-shift effect with their product designs as well: the Absolut bottle, the iPod, and the PT Cruiser all exploit design differences as part of their appeal.

HOW PRODUCT PACKAGING APPEALS TO OUR PRIMAL PROGRAMMING

Companies that regularly re-brand and re-package existing products often see sales spike immediately after the change. Now scientists have uncovered exactly why the change in a product's mental real estate can boost sales. And it is directly connected to our primal survival instincts.

Researchers in one study have identified a brain region that causes us to seek out adventure. It's activated whenever we take up a new activity, choose an unfamiliar option, or reach for a product that has just been re-packaged.[17]

The primal part of the brain—the same region where the dopamine reward pathways light up when we eat potato chips, look at a comic book, or hear addictive words and phrases—also gets excited when we try new things. As it turns out, our brains interpret new product packaging as an adventure of sorts. And adventure is a primordial urge.

In the study, volunteers played a game where they were shown several cards, each with an image that they had already seen before. Prizes were linked to each image, so participants clearly knew that choosing some cards over others would result in better prizes. When researchers showed the volunteers images that they had never seen before, blood flow to the ventral striatum (the same part of the brain that lit up in Fisher's peak-shift effect research) increased substantially. Most participants chose the unfamiliar image over the familiar one—even if it meant getting a smaller reward.

This may seem strange because the brain—through dopamine neurotransmitters—gives us an emotional high every time we do something that provides us with a reward. How can choosing a card that will give us a *less* valuable reward set off the dopamine pathways more than one associated with a *greater* reward?

Researcher Bianca Wittman of University College in London says the reason is that seeking new and unfamiliar experiences is a fundamental behavior tendency and is important for our survival.

In an article published in the online research portal *World Science*, Wittman gives the example of a monkey who decides to deviate from his banana diet and try some new cuisine, even if it means moving to an unfamiliar part of the forest.[18] The same part of the monkey's brain lights up when he ditches the bananas for some new chow as when humans choose a new product. Just as the monkey may find his diet enriched by trying a new type of food, we enrich our lives by trying new things. And the researchers found that we're hard-wired to choose new experiences over familiar, even arguably safer ones, if it may be good for us in the long run.

That's why so many manufacturers regularly change the composition and packaging of their products. Those words "new and improved" trigger the adventure-seeking part of the brain and make us reach for the new product—even over a long-time preferred product. So, the next time you find yourself wanting to try a "new and improved" version of a product, stop and think about whether it's the *product* you really want, or the new experience.

THE PRIMAL APPEAL OF CERTAIN PATTERNS

Babies fear certain patterns (such as those resembling a snake) and are drawn to others (such as the curving shape of a seashell, or the roundness of a ball). The visual shapes and patterns we find appealing as infants don't change as we grow into adolescence and adulthood. Shapes that draw us in—just like music or specific sounds that appeal to us—are rooted deep in our DNA. Primal conditioning tells a baby to instinctively fear the shape of a snake that could harm it, yet at the same time those instincts draw the baby in with spherical shapes that represent comfort and completeness.

The ancient Roman architect Marcus Vitruvius Pollio ("Vitruvius") spent a lot of time studying structure and form—not of buildings, but of the human body. He used his expertise in ratios and patterns to uncover some interesting correlations, such as the following: Your face equals one tenth of your total body height; the weight of your foot is one sixth of your total body weight; and the shape of your DNA under a microscope follows the exact same pattern as the corneas of your eyes.[19] Every part of the body follows these same predictable patterns. Because Vitruvius found these ratios to be remarkably precise and uniform in humans, he recommended that all buildings be built according to the ratios found in the human body. Some physicists and philosophers later found that the same ratio Vitruvius saw in the human body (1 to phi, or 1:1.618) can be found in every part of nature: from seashells and fish to planets and palm trees. (You may remember from chapter 2 that phi became known as the Golden Ratio.) Here are just a few examples of how, according to some experts, these same patterns and ratios come up again and again in our everyday life:

- Leaves, flowers, and seeds share the same spiral shape.
- The pattern of a snowflake is the same as the internal structure of our own cells.
- The motion of the tides in the ocean follows the same pattern as the swirl of a seashell.
- The movements of planets and the moon mimic the same spherical patterns.
- Stonehenge, megalithic tombs, and other ancient sites are situated along underground electromagnetic tracks; the energy grid formed by these tracks adheres to Vitrivius's ratio.
- The construction of the Great Pyramids at Giza aligns perfectly with Vitrivius's ratio of 1:1.61803, even though they were built centuries before the Golden Ratio was discovered.
- The path of a moth flying toward a light follows the same spiral pattern as that of a seashell.[20]

So what does all this design duplication mean for instant appeal? First, it means that some architectural designs are more soothing to our senses than others. One of the most pleasing is a rounded, theater-type design. It's no accident that sports stadiums and theaters are designed in a circular pattern. True, in theaters the rounded pattern assists the acoustics; but more than a few architectural studies have found that people are more comfortable, more at ease, and more receptive in rounded rooms and settings than square or rectangular ones.

A few years back, my company decided to test this theory to find out if room shape would have any impact on how well a speaker was received. I enlisted the help of one of my best corporate speakers for the experiment. We had him give a 10-minute motivational presentation to a group of 26 mid-level managers at a company (14 men and 12 women). In the first speech, he was in the company's presentation theater—a room designed in a semicircle, with graduated seating and a stage at the front. After his presentation, we had the managers rate the speaker on ten items, such as relevance of the material to their jobs, the speaker's style, and how likely they would be to want to hear this speaker again. The rating scale for each question was 1–10, with 10 being the best.

Next we had the same speaker give the same speech to another group of 26 middle managers at the same company (this time equally divided between men and women). This time he spoke in an adjacent room, which also had a small platform stage but no graduated seating, and the room was square.

The evaluations were surprising: The first group gave the speaker an average rating of 9. The second group gave our speaker an average rating of 7. We initially thought part of the reason could be that in the theater setting there were nice, comfy chairs, whereas in the square room the audience was seated on padded folding chairs. So we decided to redo the experiment in another company, using the same speaker in the same room, and changing only the seating pattern.

In this second test, we took one group of 19 middle managers (11 men and 8 women) and arranged folding chairs in a "classroom" style: in linear rows parallel to the stage. With the next group, we used the same room for the presentation and didn't change a thing in the room except for the arrangement of the chairs: This time we placed them in a semicircle facing the stage. (The second group of 19 managers contained 12 women and 7 men.) The result? Our same speaker giving the same speech garnered a 6 average rating from the group seated in the classroom-style setup and an 8 from the group seated in the semicircle.

Even though the speech content and the speaker remained the same, there seems to be at least some correlation between the seating pattern of an audience and how well attendees respond to a presenter. This may be something to keep in mind the next time you have to give a presentation where you're trying to pitch a product or persuade someone to your point of view. Since our little experiment, I have recommended that all of our political and CEO clients try to request a semicircle seating arrangement whenever they can. Whether it's a "placebo effect" or the real deal, most of my clients say they truly do seem to get a warmer response from audiences in the semicircle setup than the classroom configuration.

MARTHA AND DONALD
A Tale of Two Apprentice *Shows*

In 2005, Martha Stewart and Donald Trump had the same brilliant producer (Mark Burnett), the exact same reality-show setup (contestants completing weekly challenges to win an apprenticeship), and even the same "boardroom" setup. Yet "The Donald's" *Apprentice* was a smash success in the ratings, but Martha's fizzled and flopped. What happened?

Martha was simply on the wrong stage.

Donald Trump's personal brand is one of business tycoon: direct and decisive. The boardroom setup—with its rectangular (harsh-edged) table and dark décor—suited him perfectly. "The Donald" was in the element we associated with him.

Contrast that with Martha Stewart's personal brand. Sure, there have been stories circulating about her terse management style and short temper. But to most Americans she was known as the queen of all things domestic. Yet for her *Apprentice* show, she was placed on a stage that didn't fit with that brand. She, too, was in a sparse boardroom with an imposing rectangular table and cold décor. This was too much of a disconnect for viewers—and for Martha. She was out of her element and clearly was uncomfortable. So was the audience. A better approach for Martha Stewart's *Apprentice* show would have been to have all of her challenges related to cooking, interior design, and fabulous floral arrangements—the things she was known for by her audience. Additionally, her "boardroom" meetings would have been more "Martha" (and, therefore, more believable to the audience) had they been held around a kitchen table or in a cozy den. I suspect that kind of show would have been a hit.

Jay Leno also knows the importance of choosing the right stage to fit your personal style and personal brand. Leno came up through the comedy ranks by performing in intimate clubs where he was very close to the audience and on a small stage. When he landed *The Tonight Show* gig, he found the large stage uncomfortable and too far removed from his audience. He much preferred the intimacy with the audience that a smaller stage would bring. So, he had a smaller stage constructed on the set of *The Tonight Show* just for his monologue. He was more comfortable, and so was his audience.

The Chicago Cubs have perhaps the most powerful mental real estate created through the stage called Wrigley Field. Win or lose, the Cubs continue to fill "The Friendly Confines" to capacity at every home game. Many other teams have seen attendance tumble when they are on a losing streak. Not the Cubs!

A big part of the reason is the environment at Wrigley. There's nothing quite like sitting in the stands and seeing the ivy-covered brick wall, or watching an actual person sitting behind the scoreboard physically change the numbers after each inning. Or looking up into the media booth and seeing Cubs legend Ron Santo doing the play-by-play. Replace the rickety old human-powered scoreboard with a gigantic glaring Jumbotron, and you take away the bewitching character of the Wrigley ballpark. Remove the outfield ivy, and you lose some of the magic.

Jumbotrons, after all, don't align with our primordial preferences.

PRACTICAL APPLICATION
Applying Mental Real Estate to Personal Communications

In the following sections, we are going to learn just how to apply the various components of the mental real estate factor to our everyday lives.

Activating Mirror Neurons

The key here is to make people feel as if they are actually *experiencing* an event. You can accomplish this by triggering the mirror neurons of your audience through live demonstrations, action videos, or acting out stories or anecdotes related to your topic.

A more simple, straightforward way of mobilizing mirror neurons is to use specific facial expressions at strategic junctures in your message. Tony Robbins is one of the masters of activating mirror neurons in his audience through his animated, exuberant presentation style. But if you're more of a low-key speaker, you can accomplish the same thing by calmly reliving (not just retelling) stories by coordinating your gestures, talk, gaze, and walk with your verbal message.

Dr. Wayne Dyer, an internationally renowned self-development author and speaker, has mastered this technique perfectly. He literally gets the audience members to physically *feel* as if they are right there with him during the event he's revisiting. He does this by activating the mirror neurons of the audience members in several ways. For example, he walks attendees through each setting of the story he is reliving, and he moves to a different part of the stage each time he transitions to a new topic or describes a new environment. He uses his entire body to demonstrate the emotion he felt during the event he's describing. He even presents barefooted in a few of his presentations to get his audience to feel grounded and at ease.

Dr. Dyer also uses another mirror-neuron-activating technique to get you to buy more of his books after your hear him speak. At certain points during his presentation, he will often say something like, "Let me tell you a story." He'll then walk over to a table and pick up one of his books and read the story from the book. Now, he knows this story by heart. He's given the same presentation hundreds of times where he's told the same story. And he even wrote the story for his book. But when he picks up the book and reads from it, your mirror neurons fire and you unconsciously think that *you* are reading from the book. This triggers the "buy" response in your brain, and you most likely will end up leaving the seminar with one of his books. Just about every professional speaker I know uses this technique to boost "back of room" book sales.

Another mirror technique used by all successful speakers, salespeople, and even those home-shopping hosts is the head nod. When a speaker nods her head up and down as she is describing the feel-good benefits of her product or service, your mirror neurons fire to make you feel as if you are literally nodding your head, too. Subsequently you unconsciously say yes to what the salesperson is saying.

A final point on mirror neurons: PowerPoint numbs the mirror neurons. So do most charts and graphs or word slides of any sort. And yes, that includes even those zing-bang slides with dizzying animation. You see, our mirror neurons can't relate to movement made by an inanimate object. They can only relate to movements by other living, breathing beings. PowerPoint actually shuts down most of our emotional and neurological transmitters and pretty much renders a presentation ineffective.

In my company we've done brain-wave monitoring of audience members as they watch a presenter using PowerPoint—and as they watch the same presenter speaking without the slides. When the speakers spoke to a slide, brain-wave activity was nearly nil in audience members. But when slides were replaced with anecdotes that brought the data to life, brain-wave activity—especially in the regions of the brain associated with emotions, memory, and retention—was all abuzz. The brain activity was strongest during demonstrations where the speaker used a prop of some sort (such as a product, toy, or other physical object) to make a point.

Inattentional Blindness and Change Blindness

In this chapter you learned how inattentional blindness can affect whether we remember TV commercials. But one of the most prevalent events where inattentional blindness occurs is during PowerPoint presentations. Most speakers throw up a slide with myriad bullet points and begin rambling on about one of the points. But while the speaker is talking about point number one, one audience member may be looking at point number four and another at point number five because they may be more interested in those points.

Even if the speaker says, "If you look at bullet point number one," the audience members will still be distracted by the other information on the slide, and they'll be looking there and not fully listening to the speaker. You can overcome this by only having *one* item per slide, and eliminating all words from slides—and that includes titles, company logos, and agenda items. All of these are visual clutter, and distract attention from the main visual, graphic, or photo. All of those distractions create inattentional blindness that will cause listeners to miss your main message.

Inattentional blindness happens in speeches because most presentations are like TV or radio ads: We ignore most of them because they all sound the same and we've heard the same messages delivered in almost the same manner before. But when you activate mirror neurons through reliving a story *and* you send a clear signal to the listener about exactly what he or she should be paying attention to, you drastically decrease the effects of inattentional blindness.

Those swanky slides that have so much animation they require Dramamine to watch cause viewers to miss the key elements. If you must use slides (and I recommend you don't, because any slide has the potential to increase change blindness), then have no animation, no builds, and no transitions (such as dissolves, wipes, or fades). Why? Because when movement occurs in or between slides, the eyes of the viewers are moving with the activity. As I mentioned, when our eyeballs are in motion, we are literally "blind" to information that comes during or immediately after that movement. It takes several seconds for our eyes and brains to readjust from the motion.

Gestures and moving around on stage are generally good to keep interest in your presentation. But don't gesture or move or nod your head when you are making a critical point. Even your own movements can cause change blindness. When you have a *factual* point you want to be sure people remember, simply pause, look directly at the audience, and make your statement without gesturing or moving your body. During other times, such as when you are trying to make an *emotional* point by reliving a story, go ahead and gesture and move to keep the mirror neurons active—and to keep the audience emotionally engaged.

Peak-Shift Effect

The key learning point to the peak-shift effect is that amplified differences (such as those of caricatures) stick in the mind. You can amplify your own uniqueness and difference through your staging and personal dress.

Gerry Spence, the buckskin-fringe-jacket-wearing lawyer, has created a personal brand with an amplified difference by making his dress match his demeanor. Geek-in-Chief Bill Gates dresses the part, wearing a shirt, tie, and often a jacket during his formal presentations. King of Hip and Cool, Steve Jobs, who is in the same industry as Gates, also dresses to his individual part; he wears jeans, sneakers, and a black long-sleeved shirt—even during formal shareholder presentations.

Martin Moltz is an associate circuit court judge in Cook County, Illinois. He happens to have a passion for roller coasters and he travels around the country in his spare time just to ride roller coasters at different amusement parks. (He has some amusing stories to tell as well!) I have yet to see him at a business event or speaking in public when he isn't wearing a tie with some sort of roller coaster on it. People remember him. One of my clients even called me after an Illinois State Bar Association after-hours networking event and asked, "Hey, I need some legal help. Who was that guy at the reception the other night with the roller coaster tie? Is he a lawyer? I'd like to give him a call." Now, there were at least 150 other lawyers at that event, but my client wanted "the guy with the roller coaster tie." Differentiation sells. (Unfortunately because Martin is a judge, I couldn't refer my client to him for legal advice. Still, the fact that he was remembered in a room full of other attorneys is impressive!)

What is your peak-shift visual difference? Amplify it, and you could increase your business. Whether you're like Martin the roller coaster tie guy, Bill Gates, or Steve Jobs, find the dress image that matches the personal brand image you want to project—keeping in mind the peak-shift effect that says different is better.

Activate the Adventure-Seeking Part of the Brain

I've already talked about how product manufacturers change packaging to light up the part of the brain that seeks new experiences. But how can you apply this to a *person*?

One way is to sprinkle a presentation with words such as "new," "innovative," "unique," or "newfangled." These words alone will trigger an attraction response to your material. (Of course, you can't *say* you have new material if you're regurgitating the same old content! So be sure to do continual research to find relevant information that your audiences have not heard before. Pertinent current scientific journals are a great place to start.)

Another option is to position yourself as an innovator within your company. Be the one who is always coming up with new solutions to old problems. Find new (more efficient) ways of doing routine tasks. These are both ways to stimulate the adventure-seeking part of the reptilian brain—and will make you more appealing to management and co-workers alike.

Stage and Staging

Just as Jay Leno prefers a smaller, more intimate stage for his monologues, or Martha Stewart is more acceptable to viewers in a kitchen rather than a boardroom, try to find the stage that works best for you. Forget convention; find what resonates with you.

One of my clients was such a horribly nervous public speaker, yet when I spoke one-on-one with him while seated in a conference room, he was witty, charming, and convincing. What we found was that he simply wasn't comfortable speaking while standing in front of an audience and talking to slide content. So, we put a stool up on the stage and had him speak while casually perched on the stool. He used no slides and had no prepared data sheets. He simply vividly relived story after story that clearly demonstrated how changing from traditional marketing to online marketing would improve the company's business. At specific points in his speech, he would stand up, pick up the chair, and casually relocate to a different part of the stage where he would sit down and continue speaking. He (and his plan) was an instant hit! From that point forward, he always spoke while seated on a stool—and never while standing. He never gave data-dump presentations again. At the end of his presentations, he did hand out a written sheet with facts and data that supported his statements. But he kept the mind-numbing details out of his presentation. After all, if you're just going to give a data dump, you can send that in an e-mail. But to make a real connection and get real emotional buy-in with your presentation, you need the kind of mental real estate that gets the mirror neurons firing.

CHAPTER 9

The Lessons of Instant Appeal

⎯ HOW MORAL ENTREPRENEURS USE THE EIGHT PRIMAL FACTORS TO ENGINEER A CRISIS

For the U.S. war on drugs, the program's instant appeal began in the 1930s with the rise of Harry Anslinger to head of the newly formed Federal Bureau of Narcotics (FBN). Anslinger had been an outspoken opponent of illegal substances for many years, stemming from two traumatic experiences in his younger life. When he was 12, he heard the horrifying screams of his neighbor as she went through morphine withdrawal; later in his young adult life he witnessed violent outbursts among drug-abusing co-workers. By early adulthood, Harry Anslinger had his sacred cow: ridding America of the illicit drug trade. Later, his imposing physical presence and pit bull–like promotion of his cause would earn him the title, "Father of the Drug War." He set his sights on eradicating one drug in particular: marijuana.

Now he just had to convince the rest of the nation wiping out weed was a sacred cow in need of defending.

The FBN fell under the umbrella of the U.S. Treasury Department, which had a large interest in cracking down on the alcohol and drug trade: At that time illegal substances could not be taxed and were, therefore, considered a loss in revenue.[1] Although on the surface it seemed as if Anslinger was a conservative who truly believed cannabis and other drugs to be a threat to the future of American civilization, he also likely viewed the marijuana issue as a means for elevating himself to national prominence.[2] Whether he had a personal agenda or not, Anslinger was, no doubt, astute in the methods of using instant appeal to engineer a crisis and get public support. The crusade against drugs that he started in the 1930s went full force right on through the '90s. Even today, a less sensational "war on drugs" continues.

The first thing Anslinger realized was that he would need to create an "evil" that the "good people" of America could fight against. This meshed well with a reptilian comfort universal that is deeply ingrained in the primal brain: kinship protection. (You'll remember from chapter 4 that this includes duality—good versus evil—and the love of a common enemy to fight against.)

But to get our emotions fired up, the evil enemy needed a face and it needed mental real estate to go along with it. In the beginning, he found an easy target in the Mexican population. Anslinger initiated and then perpetuated the prejudice by submitting a letter to the House Hearings Committee that colorfully detailed how marijuana-smoking Mexicans acted like "sex-mad degenerates."[3] He enlisted the help of police departments, too, that claimed Mexicans were getting high on marijuana and going on assault, rape, theft, and murder rampages.[4] Our national fear had been ratcheted up quite a few notches. This despite data that refuted claims of mass Mexican drug abuse: from July 1 to September 30, 1930—the same time that Anslinger was making claims about widespread drug abuse rampages by Mexicans—the number of Mexicans arrested was just 6.61 percent of all drug-related cases.[5]

What Anslinger did in creating a face to personify the evil we were allegedly fighting against is the same thing that a lot of "moral entrepreneurs" do: target the different, the downtrodden, and the minorities. When the Mexican-menace tactic lost its teeth, he needed to find a new face that fit the crime. At that time, jazz musicians represented the counterculture. After all, most folks didn't like the content of jazz songs, which often promoted drug abuse.[6] Between 1943 and 1948, Anslinger ordered federal agents to keep a "Marijuana and Musicians File," which detailed the goings-on of jazz musicians.

The hope was that items in these files could be used against musicians at some point and lead to drug arrests.

So the war on weed had its mental real estate, its sacred cow, its "jackass" vocal leader, and the pull of powerful human universals. Now that the campaign had its anthropological footing by appealing to some powerful human universals, it needed an emotional footing to make it really stick. Anslinger did that by enlisting the support of several Hearst newspapers, which often ran stories using sensational language and graphic details of crimes, and they linked those crimes to marijuana use. Here is an example.

> *An entire family was murdered by a youthful addict in Florida. When officers arrived at the home, they found the youth staggering about in a human slaughterhouse. With an axe he had killed his father, mother, two brothers, and a sister.*[7]

Stories like this triggered the amygdala—the neurons in the brain that activate the fear response. When we fear something intensely, we will try to avoid it or eliminate it at all costs.

Don't get me wrong: I'm certainly not advocating recreational drug use of any kind, and I support efforts to crack down on all illegal drugs. But the way Anslinger devised his moral entrepreneurship campaign serves as a good case study of how someone can create a mass appeal campaign and get widespread public support for a problem that isn't nearly as rampant as the self-appointed moral leaders among us would have us believe.

For a social movement to become sticky, at least four of the eight instant appeal factors need to be firmly in place. (Appealing products and pop culture can often become mass icons with only one, such as Agatha Christie had with her hypnotic words and J. K. Rowling had with her addictive literary universals in the *Harry Potter* series.) The war on drugs had five instant appeal factors: (1) the appeal to the reptilian comfort universals, (2) mental real estate, (3) a tireless and dedicated "jackass," with (4) a sacred cow agenda, and (5) language that changed our biology. Anslinger was truly gifted at garnering mass appeal.

But a more recent example of mass allegiance had all eight of the instant appeal codes in place. Never before had such a perfect persuasive storm come together.

A PERFECT INSTANT APPEAL STORM
The War on Terror

U.S. President George W. Bush concocted the perfect instant appeal (and mass appeal!) campaign in his war against Iraq. All eight primal factors combined to garner the strongest allegiance capital we've seen any politician achieve in recent memory. He not only convinced the public that going to war was in America's best interest, he also accomplished a feat almost unheard of: He got the support of key members of both political parties and dozens of prominent interest groups and lobbyists. This one-two punch made him virtually immune to opposition either inside or outside of the government. His rally cry was *obliterate the "axis of evil"*—consisting of North Korea, Iran, and Iraq—because these countries were "arming to threaten the peace of the world" and "pose[d] a grave and growing danger."[8] Specifically, he claimed Saddam Hussein had weapons of mass destruction and had the power and the motive to do us in at any time.

As we learned later from a CIA report, Saddam Hussein did not possess stockpiles of illicit weapons at the time of the U.S. invasion in March 2003 and had not begun any program to produce them. Charles Duelfer, head of the Iraq Survey Group, authored the report. He testified at a Senate Armed Services Committee hearing that Iraq's weapons-of-mass-destruction (WMD) program was essentially destroyed in 1991 and that Saddam ended Iraq's nuclear program after the 1991 Gulf War.[9] But when George W. Bush went before the American public and made a speech about Saddam's weapons of mass destruction, a majority of Americans bought into it without question.

Why was it so easy for one person to persuade us to go to war on so little evidence? Why didn't more people question the allegations of WMD? Why did the media watchdogs play lapdog to Bush? To get the answer, we need to back up to September 11, 2001.

The day of the attack on the World Trade Centers and the Pentagon created an indelible image in our minds: The two airliners crashing into the Twin Towers, followed by horrifying video of people jumping from the towers to their deaths. Then, just a short time later, we witnessed another incomprehensible assault on our treasured icons: the collapse of the Twin Towers. This was as powerful as mental real estate can get. The media played it over and over again, and we watched in disbelief every time we saw those images. As we sat glued to our televisions and witnessed those images, our mirror neurons fired and had us reliving it as if we were right there on the scene. One instant appeal factor for mass allegiance—mental real estate—was firmly in place.

The events of 9/11 collectively pushed us as a nation into a state of anxiety and panic—bordering on post-traumatic stress disorder—where our primal fight *and* flight responses kicked in. The "flight" part came in our willingness to give up our rights, which many (mistakenly) believed would ensure our future protection. The "fight" part manifested in a near-universal support for the war. Collectively we didn't think (or at least we weren't thinking clearly); we just reacted according to our primordial programming to protect our kin.

Other mental real estate that played a strong role in cementing emotional support for the cause was the use of flags—flag pins, flag ties, flag bumper stickers, flags everywhere. You'll recall that kinship is a strong and binding human universal, and the constant presence of American flags ratcheted up our feeling of pride, patriotism, and purposefulness.

Next came the use of reptilian comfort universals and linguistic triggers to appeal to our primal instincts. President Bush repeatedly told us that it was our moral obligation to rid the world of the "evil ones." This verbiage played right into not only our anthropological conditioning to fight evil to protect our kin, but also the beliefs of the majority of the voting population—which was dominated by fundamentalist Christians. The sacred cow ideology was protecting our good, moral foundation and ridding the world of terror. And George Bush, right on cue, played the role we wanted him to play: the stubborn cowboy clinging to his sacred cow—the fight against terror—at all costs.

Perhaps we would not have been so quick to believe "Number 43's" claims or to back him so blindly had he been a more eloquent speaker. Because of his bumbling, Columbo-like delivery, we believed he was sincere and couldn't possibly have the capacity to dupe us. His conspicuous speaking flaw made him more convincing. His facial features fit the profile. (You'll remember from chapter 2 that his less-than-Golden-Ratio placement of facial features represents a face we can trust. In chapter 3 we learned that President Bush has facial features that we primordially associate with a warrior.) It was the perfect message from the perfect messenger. We were ready to throw our support behind him.

And what about the "good vibration" instant appeal primal factor? Well, Dubya had that, too. You'll remember from chapter 7 that I talked about my company's proprietary sound-wave analyzer that indicates what parts of the brain and corresponding emotions are triggered by someone's name. When we ran the name George W. Bush through our analyzer, the sound-wave patterns created by the vowels and consonants in his name suppresses the amygdala and its fear-processing networks. What that means is that people felt, to paraphrase the Allstate commercial, they were in good hands with George W.; they felt safe with him at the helm. In addition, the sound-wave patterns in the name "George W. Bush" are very close to those that we have found stimulate the production of the chemical oxytocin, which is the brain's natural hormone linked to bonding and trust. So not only did President Bush have a face we could trust and a demeanor we could trust on a primal level, but he also had a name that produced a biological impulse to trust. He had us hook, line, and sinker—or, more accurately, emotionally, anthropologically, and biologically.

And that's the lesson of *Instant Appeal*. Real allegiance, real buy-in, isn't all psychological. Rather, it's based on our primordial conditioning and our biological leanings that have created a centuries-old want/like reward system in the brain. We like ugliness, flaws, jackasses, hypnotic language, and good vibrations. We want places, products, books, and movies that align with the human universals, adhere to our sacred cows, and create compelling mental real estate.

We can use this information to become more persuasive and more powerful in our own lives. When we each find our "conspicuous flaw" and proudly promote it, we can create an impulse in others to trust us. We can manipulate our names and our voice tones to create "good vibrations" that trigger the release of endorphins in the brains of the people we come in contact with. We can write using appealing words and appealing literary universal themes. If we know our sacred cows and unabashedly advance them, we position ourselves as real leaders. And when we build a solid foundation of mental real estate, we create a living calling card with staying power.

But beyond self-improvement, one of the larger hopes of the secrets of *Instant Appeal* is that it will increase our awareness of how our everyday likes and wants—the music we prefer, whom we trust, the toys we like, the books we get addicted to, the new products we gravitate toward, or the social causes we buy into—are really made at an unconscious level by the reptilian brain's anthropological conditioning and changes to our biology. That doesn't mean we can't override those primordial and biological leanings. It's a tough fight, but with awareness we can do it.

The first step to preventing ourselves from being unwittingly duped by moral entrepreneurs who may not have our best interests at heart is to understand that persuasion is innate; our impulses are governed by our biological reactions to our environment and our anthropological conditioning. Thinking is not, contrary to popular belief, our dominant decision-making mechanism; engaging our intellect is not our first response to a new stimuli. Being aware of how most of our decisions are really made can help us understand what's *really* motivating us to throw our support behind a politician, a cause, or a social movement. Understanding instant appeal just might make some things—like social memes or moral entrepreneurs with personal agendas—less appealing and less effective.

The key is responsibility. The secrets of persuasion contained within *Instant Appeal* are tools that can be used responsibly, or abused. When used in a reputable manner, the eight primal factors of instant appeal truly can help you achieve blockbuster success without abusing the power they contain.

Notes

CHAPTER 1: AN INTRODUCTION TO INSTANT APPEAL

1. J. Martin and P. Lopez, "Are Fleeing 'Noisy' Lizards Signaling to Predators?" *Acta Ethologica* 3, no. 2 (April 2001): 95–100.
2. Robert Cialdini, Ph.D., *Influence: The Psychology of Persuasion*, Rev. ed. (New York: Collins Publishing, 1998), 4–5.
3. Michael Fumento, "Fuss and Feathers: Pandemic Panic over the Avian Flu," *The Weekly Standard* 11, no. 10 (November 21, 2005), http://www.weeklystandard.com/Content/Public/Articles/000/000/006/349zwhbe.asp (accessed June 30, 2008).
4. Ibid.
5. Pearl Wang. "Avian Flu: Inoculate Your Portfolio." *BusinessWeek* (October 10, 2005), http://www.businessweek.com/investor/content/oct2005/pi2005110_4988_pi015.htm (accessed February 20, 2008).
6. Centers for Disease Control and Prevention, "Avian Influenza: Current H5N1 Situation," http://www.cdc.gov/flu/avian/outbreaks/current.htm (accessed February 20, 2008).
7. Medical College of Wisconsin, "Putting Mad Cow Disease into Perspective: A Top Ten List of Things to Really Worry About," *Health Link* (January 30, 2004), http://healthlink.mcw.edu/article/1031002337.html (accessed February 20, 2008).
8. Neal D. Barnard, *Breaking the Food Seduction: The Hidden Reasons Behind Food Cravings—And 7 Steps to End Them Naturally* (New York: St. Martin's Press, 2003), 15–61.

CHAPTER 2: DUCKLINGS, DEFECTS, AND DEVOTION

1. Among the multitude of studies that have linked social benefits to attractiveness are: Alice H. Eagly, Richard D. Ashmore, Mona G. Makhijani, and Laura C. Longo, "What Is Beautiful Is Good, but . . . : A Meta-Analytic Review of Research on the Physical Attractiveness Stereotype," *Psychological Bulletin* 110 (1991): 109–112, and A. Feingold, "Good-Looking People Are Not What We Think," *Psychological Bulletin* 111 (1992): 304–341.

2. The following five research studies have drawn comparisons to attractiveness and career success: Robert L. Dipboye, Richard D. Arvey, and David E. Terpstra, "Sex and Physical Attractiveness of Raters and Applicants and Determinants of Resume Evaluations," *Journal of Applied Psychology* 62 (1997): 288–294; Irene H. Frieze, Josephine E. Olson, and Deborah C. Good, "Perceived and Actual Discrimination in the Salaries of Male and Female Managers," *Journal of Applied Social Psychology* 20 (1990): 46–67; M. Y. Quereshi & J. P. Kay, "Physical Attractiveness, Age, and Sex as Determinants of Reactions to Resumes," *Social Behavior and Personality* 14 (1986): 103–112; Susan M. Raza and Bruce N. Carpenter, "A Model of Hiring Decisions in Real Employment Interviews," *Journal of Applied Psychology* 72 (1987): 596–603; Debra Umberson and Michael Hughes, "The Impact of Physical Attractiveness on Achievement and Psychological Well-Being," *Social Psychology Quarterly* 50 (1987): 227–236.

3. For information on the advantage that less attractive candidates have in the job interview process, consult chapter 3, as well as these studies: Linda A. Jackson, "Gender, Physical Attractiveness, and Sex Role in Occupational Treatment Discrimination: The Influence of Trait and Role Assumptions," *Journal of Applied Psychology* 13 (1983): 443–458; Jerry Ross and Kenneth R. Ferris, "Interpersonal Attraction and Organization Outcomes: A Field Examination," *Administrative Science Quarterly* 26 (1981): 617–632.

4. For the research on attractiveness and performance evaluations: Thomas F. Cash, Barry Gillen, and D. Stephen Burns, "Sexism and Beautyism in Personnel Consultant Decision Making," *Journal of Applied Psychology* 62 (1977): 301–310.

5. For more information on how beauty is a detriment to job applicants: Madeline E. Heilman, "Information as a Deterrent Against Sex Discrimination: The Effects of Applicant Sex and Information Type on Preliminary Employment Decisions," *Organizational Behavior and Human Performance* 33 (1984): 174–186.

6. To read more about the effects of female attractiveness when applying for jobs in male-dominated fields, or for positions that have traditionally been held by men, read: Thomas F. Cash, "The Impact of Grooming Style on the Evaluation of Women in Management," in M. R. Solomon (ed.), *Psychology of Fashion* (Lexington, MA: Lexington Books, 1985), 343–355.

7. From a discussion on what makes CEOs successful: Richard St. John, in an

interview with the author on her Internet radio show, *Inside Out*, February 8, 2007.

8. For the study on average faces that were rated far more attractive than beautiful faces, see: Judith Langlois and Lori Roggman, "Attractive Faces Are Only Average," *Psychological Science* 1, no. 2 (March 1990): 115–121.

9. Theodosius Dobzhandsky outlined his findings in *Genetics of the Evolutionary Process* (New York: Columbia University Press, 1970), 65–94.

10. For a comprehensive discussion on the Golden Ratio and the work of Stephen Marquardt, see David Von Drehle, "Looking Good: Our Obsession with Physical Appearance May Not Be So Shallow, After All," *Washington Post* (November 12, 2006): W14.

11. Ibid.

12. Presentation Makers (now Vicki Kunkel International), "The Persuasive Power and Appeal of the Not So Pretty: A Comparison Study of Levels of Trust Between Beautiful People and the Less Attractive Among Us," March 12, 2004, p. 23.

13. The information about the specific types of physical flaws that we find comforting was gleaned from a March 2004 focus-group research study conducted by the author and her team for one of her political clients. The study is titled "The Persuasive Power and Appeal of the Not So Pretty: A Comparison Study of Levels of Trust Between Beautiful People and the Less Attractive Among Us."

14. Box Office Mojo, "E.T.: the Extra Terrestrial," http://www.boxofficemojo.com/movies/?id = et.htm (accessed March 2007).

15. Simplified Wiki, "E.T.: The Extra-Terrestrial," http://www.simplifiedwiki.com/index.php/E.T._the_Extra-Terrestrial (accessed March 2007).

16. Information on the appeal of Cabbage Patch Kids comes from Ann Wilhite, "Adopting Love," *Topic Magazine* 4 (Spring 2003), http://www.webdelsol.com/Topic/articles/04/wilhite.html

17. Ibid.

18. Ibid.

19. Information on Oprah's ratings come from: *Business Leader Profiles for Students. Vol. 2. Gale Group,* 2002; *George Mair, Oprah Winfrey: The Real Story* (New York: Birch Lane Press, 1994); Patricia Sellers, "The Business of Being Oprah: She Talked Her Way to the Top of Her Own Media Empire and Amassed a $1 Billion Fortune: Now She's Asking, 'What's Next?'" *Fortune*, April 1, 2002, pp. 50–64. It should be noted, however, that Oprah's official website says her show went to number one in only one month, not three as the other sources assert: http://www2.oprah.com/about/press/about_press_bio.jhtml

20. Many studies support our preference for "vulnerable" physical characteristics, and some even go so far as to say that what we find vulnerable is what we find cute. For a discussion on the visual vulnerability traits that we find cute (such as roundness, short, plump limbs), consult Natalie Angier's "The Cute Factor," *New York Times* (January 3, 2003): http://www

.nytimes.com/2006/01/03/science/03cute.html?_r = 1&oref = slogin (accessed November 15, 2007).

21. To learn more about the 200 identified human universals, consult Donald Brown's *Human Universals* (New York: McGraw-Hill, 1991), 1–256.

22. For a great analysis on the many ways Oprah has used her visual "ugliness" to garner worldwide adoration, see a reprint of Lee Siegel's *New Republic* article, "How Oprah Changed the World," at *History News Network*, http://hnn.us/roundup/entries/25978.html

23. Ibid.

24. For more on the detailed evolution of Mickey Mouse's appearance, see: Stephen Gould, *The Panda's Thumb: More Reflections in Natural History* (New York: W. W. Norton & Company, 1980), 95–107.

25. To learn more about the evolution of the teddy bear: Robert Hinde and L.A. Barden, "The Evolution of the Teddy Bear," *Animal Behavior* 33, no. 4 (1985): 1371–1373.

26. Ibid.

27. For a complete history of Barbie and society's reactions to her: Yona Zeldis McDonough (ed.), *The Barbie Chronicles: A Living Doll Turns Forty* (New York: Simon & Schuster, 1999).

28. If you want to read more about the extent to which girls abuse their Barbie dolls: CBC News, "Girls Often Torture Barbies, Researchers Say," (December 19, 2005), http://www.cbc.ca/story/world/national/2005/12/19/barbie -study-051219.html

29. For marketing and sales comparisons of Barbie and American Girl Place dolls, see: Doug Desjardins, "American Girl Place Struts into LA," *DNS Retailing Today* (June 27, 2005), http://findarticles.com/p/articles/ mi_m0FNP/is_12_44/ai_n14710700 (accessed January 26, 2008).

30. Worldwide Gross Sales tab of the Exhibits file located at http://www.share holder.com/mattel/earning.cfm

31. Phillip Wiggins, "Flat Profits Linked to Weak Economy," *New York Times*, February 2, 1987.

32. The hatred of beauty has become so prevalent in our society, that it has been referenced in much pop culture, including this fictional novel: Donna Tartt, *The Secret History* (New York: Ballantine Books, 1996).

33. More on the discussion of what constitutes vulnerable physical features and why we find them so alluring: Natalie Angier, "The Cute Factor," *New York Times* (January 3, 2006), http://www.nytimes.com/2006/01/03/science/ 03cute.html?_r = 1&oref = slogin (accessed November 15, 2007).

34. Barbara Card Atkinson, "The Doctor is Out (Of Touch)," MSN.com, http://tv.msn.com/tv/celebrityfeature/dr-phil/?GT1 = BUZZ3 (accessed May 1, 2008).

35. Ibid.

36. Ibid.

37. A May 1, 2008, search of lists of licensed psychologists in the California Board of Psychology's website (http://www.psychboard.ca.gov/), as well as a

search of the roster of licensees at the Texas Board of Examiners of Psychology site (http://www.tsbep.state.tx.us/roster_2007.html) found no evidence that Dr. Phil's license has been reinstated, thereby allegedly confirming the MSN story. An additional phone call to the Texas Board of Examiners on May 2, 2008, confirmed that Dr. Phil's license had not been reinstated in Texas. The author researched California licensed psychologists because Dr. Phil's show originates in California.

38. To learn more about the challenges Susan Lucci faced in her acting career: "An Emmy, Finally! After 18 Nominations, Susan Lucci Finally Wins," CBS News. (http://www.cbsnews.com/stories/1999/05/22/entertainment/main48087.shtml?source = search_story).

39. For the complete discussion on our rejection of beautiful celebrities: Catherine Donaldson-Evans, "Ducklings Preferred over Swans at Emmys," FoxNews.com (September 16, 2005), http://www.foxnews.com/story/0,2933,169510,00.html

40. Ibid.

41. October 2007 data from Compete (http://www.compete.com), a company that provides information on every site on the Internet, including site traffic history and competitive analytics.

42. Ibid.

43. Dale Kasler, "Craigslist to Charge for Some Job Ads," *Sacramento Bee* (October 5, 2007): D3.

44. Hitwise, an online competitive intelligence service, showed Google with 65 percent of the search engine market share as of December 2007: http://www.hitwise.com/press-center/hitwiseHS2004/searchengines200711us.php (accessed July 6, 2008). Also see Matt Asay's article, "Google's Market Share Tops 65%," c/net News, January 2, 2008, http://www.hitwise.com/press-center/hitwiseHS2004/searchengines200711us.php (accessed July 6, 2008).

45. A discussion on the many so-called "human universals" can be found in many journals and books, including: Franz Boas (ed.), *General Anthropology* (Boston, New York: D.C. Heath and Company, 1938), 609–668, from which the information about the universal valuation of ugly was taken.

46. Wallechinsky, Wallace, *The Book of Lists.*

47. Editors, "Show Time for Al Gore," *New York Times* (August 13, 2000), http://query.nytimes.com/gst/fullpage.html?res = 9E02E7DB123FF930A2575BC0A9669C8B63&sec = &spon = &pagewanted = 2 (accessed April 14, 2008).

48. For the editorial about why we couldn't get behind Al Gore: Gail Sheehy, "Flawless, But Never Quite Loved," *New York Times* (June 2, 2000), http://query.nytimes.com/gst/fullpage.html?res = 9B02EFD7133CF931A35755C0A9669C8B63&sec = &spon = &pagewanted = all (accessed April 14, 2008).

49. TV Ratings on *BroadcastingCable*, http://www.broadcastingcable.com (accessed June 2007).

50. *Studio 60 on the Sunset Strip* aired on NBC from August 5, 2006, to June 28, 2007, and received mixed reviews. Neilson ratings show that the pilot was seen by an average of 13.4 million total viewers in its initial airing on NBC, but the dropoff in viewership began in the show's second half-hour, and continued on from there. Ratings for the show's second episode were down 12 percent, by episode 5, the show lost 43 percent of its original audience and by the last episode, ratings were off by nearly 68 percent. Its last show achieved only a 2.7 rating and a 5 share.

51. IMDb (Internet Movie Database), "Trivia for Ugly Betty," http://www .imdb.com/title/tt0805669/trivia

52. Nadia Mustafa, "Who Are You Calling Ugly?" *Time*, December 6, 2006, http://www.time.com/time/magazine/article/0,9171,1566630–1,00.html (accessed July 6, 2008).

53. Jaclyn Giovis, "Cabbage Patch Comeback Kids," *South Florida Sun-Sentinel* (February 22, 2008), http://www.gazettetimes.com/articles/2008/ 03/05/lifestyles/family/fam06.txt (accessed July 6, 2008).

54. "Sam: Beloved Ugly. Owner of World's Ugliest Dog on What Makes Sam So Lovable," CBSnews.com, July 5, 2005, http://www.cbsnews.com/stories/ 2005/07/05/earlyshow/living/petplanet/main70 6245.shtml

55. CNN.com, "'Ugly dog' Sam dies at 14" (November 22, 2005), http://www .cnn.com/2005/US/11/22/ugly.dog.ap (accessed February 12, 2007).

56. Susie Lockhead, "Sam's Ugliest Dog," http://www.samugliestdog.com

57. Sheehy, "Flawless, but Never Quite Loved."

58. Danielle Sacks, "Crack This Code," *Fast Company* 104 (April 2006): 96.

59. Carlton Coon, *A Reader in General Anthropology* (New York: H. Holt, 1948), 349.

60. Padma Lakshmi's interview was part of a series on MSN.com titled, "Real Women, Real Beauty: Why Our Flaws Are Beautiful," http://lifestyle.msn .com (accessed October 21, 2007).

CHAPTER 3: DOES IT LOOK LIKE A DUCK?

1. Robin Thomas, Ph.D., University of Miami, in an e-mail interview with the author on September 27, 2007. All references to the University of Miami study came from this interview.

2. To learn more about how inferences drawn from facial features holds true across cultures, consult Ran Hassin and Yaacov Trope, "Facing Faces: Studies on the Cognitive Aspects of Physiognomy," *Journal of Personality and Social Psychology* 78, no. 5 (May 2000): 837–852.

3. For a complete discussion on how physiognomy affects our decision-making process, including everything from conclusions we draw about someone's personality to an individual's trustworthiness, read: Anthony Little, Robert Burriss, Benedict Jones, and Craig Roberts, "Facial Appearance Affects Voting Decisions," *Evolution and Human Behavior*, 28 (2007): 18–27.

4. Ibid.
5. Ibid.
6. On the issue of the personality and physical traits we look for in leaders, consult: Liisa Mynever Kyl-Heku and D. M. Buss, "Tactics as Units of Analysis in Personality Psychology: An Illustration Using Tactics of Hierarchy Negotiation," *Personality and Individual Differences*, 21 no. 4 (1996): 497–517.
7. For an in-depth discussion on personality terms and their social desirability, consult: Sarah. E. Hampson, Lewis. R. Goldberg, and Oliver P. John, "Category-Breadth and Social Desirability Values for 573 Personality Terms," *European Journal of Personality* 1 (1987): 241–258.
8. CBS Poll, "Obama Surges Ahead Nationally," http://www.cbsnews.com/stories/2008/02/25/opinion/polls/main3874915.shtml (accessed February 26, 2008).
9. Ibid.
10. Ibid.
11. On the issue of how we draw conclusions about candidates from the candidates' facial features, take a look at: Alexander Todorov, Anesu N. Mandisodza, Amir Goren, and Crystal C. Hall, "Inferences of Competence from Faces Predict Election Outcomes," *Science* 308, no. 5728 (June 10, 2005): 1623–1626.
12. Many studies have reduced the complexity of the human personality down to five characteristics. But when it comes to making decisions about the personalities of celebrities and politicians, audiences and voters consistently use only two or three of these factors. For a fascinating discussion on the main factors we evaluate when looking at celebrities and politicians, read: Gian Vittorio Caprara, Claudio Barbaranelli, and Philip G. Zimbardo, "Politicians' Uniquely Simple Personalities," *Nature* 385 (February 6, 1997): 493.
13. For the job candidate evaluation study, see: Madeline E. Heilman and L. Saruwatari, "When Beauty is Beastly: The Effects of Appearance and Sex on Evaluations and Job Applicants and Nonmanagerial Jobs," *Organizational Behavior and Human Performance* 23 (1979): 360–372.
14. For additional research studies that demonstrate a preference among hiring managers for less attractive women when it comes to managerial positions, see four additional studies: Stephen L. Cohen and Kerry A. Bunker, "Subtle Effects of Sex Role Stereotypes on Recruiters' Hiring Decisions," *Journal of Applied Psychology* 60, no. 5 (1975): 566–572; Robert L. Dipboye, Richard D. Arvey, and David E. Terpstra, "Sex and Physical Attractiveness of Raters and Applicants as Determinants of Resume Evaluations," *Journal of Applied Psychology* 62 (1997): 288–294; Robert L. Dipboye, Howard L. Fromkin, and Kent K. Wiback, "Relative Importance of Applicant Sex, Attractiveness, and Scholastic Standing in Evaluation of Job Applicant Resumes," *Journal of Applied Psychology* 60, no. 1 (1975): 39–43; and Virginia E. Shein, "Relationships Between Sex-Role Stereotypes and Requisite

Management Characteristics Among Female Managers," *Journal of Applied Psychology* 60, no. 3 (1975): 340–344.

15. For the West Point study, see: Allan Mazur, Julie Mazur, and Caroline Keating, "Military Rank Attainment of a West Point Class: Effects of Cadet's Physical Features," *American Journal of Sociology* 90, no. 1 (1984): 125–150.

16. Ibid.

17. For a discussion on the link between trust and facial features, among other conclusions we draw from facial attractiveness: David I. Perrett, et. al., "Effects of Sexual Dimorphism on Facial Attractiveness," *Nature* 394 (1998): 884–887.

18. Gerald J. Gorn, Yuwei Jiang, and Gita Venkataramani Johar, "Baby Faces, Trait Interferences, and Company Evaluations in a Public Crisis," *Journal of Consumer Research* 35, no. 1 (June 2008): 36–49.

19. Ibid.

20. For a complete list of the facial features we associate with a kind-hearted person, a mean person, a smart person, and a stupid person, see: Ran Hassin and Yaacov Trope, "Facing Faces: Studies on the Cognitive Aspects of Physiognomy," *Journal of Personality and Social Psychology* 78, no. 5 (2000): 837–852.

21. Ibid.

22. Robin Thomas, Ph.D., University of Miami, in an e-mail interview with the author on September 27, 2007. All references to the University of Miami study came from this interview.

CHAPTER 4: SMALL DOGS, BIG SUVs, AND THE FAILURE OF EPCOT

1. In-depth discussions on the principle of least effort can be found in several sources, such as: George Kingsley Zipf, *Human Behaviour and the Principle of Least Effort: An Introduction to Human Ecology* (New York: Hafner Publishing Co., 1949); Thomas Mann, *A Guide to Library Research Methods* (New York: Oxford University Press, 1987); and Zao Liu and Zeny Ye Yang, "Factors Influencing Distance-Education Graduate Students' Use of Information Sources: A User Study," *Journal of Academic Librarianship* 30, no. 1 (2004). Zipf was the first to discuss the theory, and the other two resources apply his findings to library design and electronic searches for information. Some also have used this theory to explain why we would rather see a generalist down the hall for information rather than go to a specialist who is across town.

2. "Conservation of energy" as a human universal was discussed as it relates to linguistic marking in Donald Brown, *Human Universals* (New York: McGraw-Hill, 1991), 98.

3. Ibid.

4. Jane Lampman, "'The Secret,' a Phenomenon, Is No Mystery to Many," *Christian Science Monitor* (March 28, 2007).

5. Reverend Vilius Dundzila, "Not Sold on The Secret," *The Advocate* (April 10, 2007), http://www.advocate.com/exclusive_detail_ektid44343.asp (accessed December 22, 2007).

6. Karin Klein, "Self-Help Gone Nutty," *Los Angeles Times* (February 13, 2007), http://articles.latimes.com/2007/feb/13/opinion/oe-klein13 (accessed December 18, 2007).

7. Jill Culora, "A 'Secret' Oprah Craze Hits New Yorkers," *New York Post* (March 4, 2007), http://www.nypost.com/seven/03042007/news/regional news/a_secret_oprah-craze_hits_new_yorkers_regionalnews_jill_culora .htm (accessed December 18, 2007).

8. Verne Kopytoff, "Instant Wealth Makes Employee Retention Google's Big Challenge," *San Francisco Chronicle* (January 7, 2007): A-9.

9. Ibid.

10. Information on Web stats was taken from Andy Greenberg's article, "The Privacy Paradox," *Forbes* (February 15, 2008), http://www.forbes.com/ebusi ness/2008/02/15/search-privacy-ask-tech-security-cx_ag_0215search.html ?feed = rss_technology_ebusiness (accessed February 19, 2008).

11. Ibid

12. Ibid.

13. "The Privacy Paradox," *Forbes.*

14. Saul Hansell, "Compressed Data; The Big Yahoo Privacy Storm That Wasn't," *New York Times* (May 13, 2002), http://query.nytimes .com/gst/fullpage.html?res = 9404E0DD1739F930A25756C0A9649C8B63 (accessed June 23, 2007).

15. Ibid.

16. Jeremy Crane, "January 2008 Search Market Share: Google Who?" http:// blog.compete.com/2008/02/08/search-market-share-january-yahoo-micro soft-google-ask-aol-msn-live/ (accessed February 19, 2008).

17. For a complete discussion of the AMP Agency's research on types of shoppers and their behavior, see: AMP Agency, "Unraveling Her Shopping DNA: AMP Agency Reveals Four Lifelong Shopping Mind-Sets," *Women Amplified*, available at http://www.ampagency.com/pdf/whatWeThink/ research/women_2007.pdf (accessed October 1, 2007).

18. For a detailed discussion on the success and appeal of movie franchises, see: Leah Hoffmann and Lacey Rose, "Most Lucrative Movie Franchises" *Forbes* (June 15, 2005), http://www.forbes.com (accessed June 12, 2007); also see BoxOfficeMojo.com

19. Ibid.

20. Ibid.

21. Eve Tahmincioglu, "Men Rule—At Least in Workplace Attitudes: Even Women Seem Skeptical of Female Bosses," *CareerBuilder.com*, http:// msn.careerbuilder.com/custom/msn/careeradvice/viewarticle.aspx?article id = 1285&SiteId = cbmsnbc41285&sc_extcmp = JS_1285_msnbc&GT1 =

10884&cbRecursionCnt = 2&cbsid = 34b9e62c428b4560939fbcff44a2dd52
-256063680-R0-4 (accessed January 30, 2008).

22. Ibid.

23. Jonathan Coulton website, "Archive for the "Thing A Week" Category,
    http://www.jonathancoulton.com/category/thing-a-week/page/11

24. T. D. Allman, "The Theme-Parking, Megachurching, Franchising, Exurb-
    ing, McMansioning of America: How Walt Disney Changed Everything,"
    National Geographic Interactive, http://ngm.nationalgeographic.com/ngm/
    0703/feature4/ (accessed June 16, 2008).

25. Mosley, Robert. "Disney's World: A Biography," *Scarborough House* (Janu-
    ary 2002): 275.

26. The discussion on the impact that repetitive motions has on our brain is
    based on information found in Barry Beyerstein's article, "Neuropathology
    and the Legacy of Spiritual Possession: Three Brain Syndromes—Epilepsy,
    Tourette's Syndrome, and Migraine—Probably Fomented Ancient Notions
    of Possession and Transcendence, *The Skeptical Inquirer* 12 (1988): 248–
    262, as well as Donald Brown's *Human Universals* (New York: McGraw-Hill,
    1991): 114.

27. Donald Brown, *Human Universals*.

28. *Time* magazine, "2002 Best Inventions," http://www.time.com/time/2002/
    inventions/tra_trikke.html (accessed January 14, 2008).

29. Ibid.

30. American Kennel Club, "Bulldog Muscles Its Way Into AKC's List of Top
    10 Most Popular Dogs in America," January 16, 2008, http://www.akc.org/
    news/index.cfm?article_id = 3408; and Jane Stancill, "Study: Hot Dogs Fol-
    low Fashion," Newsobserver.com, http://www.bio.indiana.edu/~hahnlab/
    MediaFiles/Dog%20Breeds/News-Observer.html

31. Liz Kim, "Tipping the Scale; Single Households Outnumber Marrieds, but
    Stereotypes Weigh Them Down," *Chicago Tribune* (January 18, 2007): 1.

32. Jerry Adler and Jeneen Interlandi, "Caution: Killing Germs May Be Hazard-
    ous to Your Health," *Newsweek* (October 29, 2007), http://www.newsweek
    .com/id/57368/page/2 (accessed October 30, 2007).

33. Ibid., p. 2.

34. John Cloud, "Why the SUV Is All the Rage," *Time* (February 16, 2003),
    time.com/time/2003/suvs (accessed November 13, 2007).

35. Ibid.

36. Jay Appleton, *The Experience of Landscape* (New York: John Wiley & Sons,
    1975), 69–73, 96–107, 119.

37. Carol Kaesuk Yoon, "Loyal to Its Roots," *New York Times*, June 10, 2008,
    http://www.nytimes.com/2008/06/10/science/10plant.html

38. Sheryl E. Kimes and Stephani K. A. Robson, "The Impact of Restaurant
    Table Characteristics on Meal Duration and Spending," *Cornell Hotel and
    Restaurant Administration Quarterly* 45, no. 4 (2004): 333–346.

39. One study that clearly shows a productivity increase and stress-reduction
    benefit of having a window view at work is: Phil Leather, Mike Pyrgas, and

Claire Lawrence, "Windows in the Workplace: Sunlight, View and Occupational Stress," *Environment and Behavior* 30, no. 6 (1998): 739–762.

40. Information on the profitability of restaurants and seating patterns that led the author to her conclusions was gleaned from several sources, including: Kimes and Robson, "The Impact of Restaurant Table Characteristics on Meal Duration and Spending"; Stephani K. Robson, "A Review of Psychological and Cultural Effects on Seating Behavior and Their Application to Foodservice Settings," *Journal of Foodservice Business Research* 5, no. 2 (2002): 89–107; Michael Silverstein and Neil Fiske, *Trading Up: The New American Luxury* (New York: Portfolio, 2003), 105–127; and Gerald Zaltman, *How Customers Think: Essential Insights into the Mind of the Market* (Boston: Harvard Business School Press, 2003), 47–165.

41. "Tie Marches On: Want a Blast from the Past? Open up Your Closet," *AARP Bulletin* 36, no. 4 (January/February 2007).

42. Ibid.

43. R. C. Bell, *Board and Table Games from Many Civilizations*, rev. sub edition (New York: Dover Publications, 1980), 90–97.

CHAPTER 5: GAINING POWER AND LOYALTY THROUGH ATTRACTION AND REPULSION

1. Talkers Magazine Online. "Latest Top Host Figures," *Talkers Magazine* (October 2005), http://www.talkers.com/talkhosts.htm (accessed June 21, 2006).

2. New York Times Best Seller Number Ones Listing, Non Fiction By Author, http://www.hawes.com/no1_nf_a.htm#L (accessed July 6, 2008).

3. Robin Toner, "Politics: On the Air; Radio Talk Show Host Fears for True Conservatism's Fate," *New York Times* (February 23, 1996), http://query.nytimes.com/gst/fullpage.html?res=9E02E2DB1039F930A15751C0A960958260&scp=1&sq=Politics%3A+On+the+Air%3B%3A+Radio+Talk+Show+Host+Fears+for+True+Conservatism%27s+Fate&st=nyt (accessed June 21, 1007).

4. *The Original Musings*, "Monopoly, Anyone?" (March 9, 2008), http://www.naebunny.net/~mommylemur/?p=256 (accessed June 15, 2008).

5. Talkers Magazine Online, "Latest Top Host Figures," *Talkers Magazine* (October 2005), http://www.talkers.com/talkhosts.htm (accessed June 21, 2006).

6. Ed Bark, "Stern's 'Private Parts' Tops Limbaugh's Mark," *The Wichita Eagle* (October 20, 1993): 4C. "Five Days After Its Publication, *Private Parts* had Become the Fastest Selling Book in the 70-Year History of Simon & Schuster."

7. Box Office Report, "Private Parts: Box Office Profile," Box Office Report, http://www.boxofficereport.com/byfilm/1997/privateparts.shtml (accessed June 21, 2007).

8. Ibid.

9. David Spade, "Howard Stern New King of Satellite," *Time* (April 30, 2006), http://www.time.com/time/magazine/article/0,9171,1187317,00.html (accessed July 6, 2008).

10. Lea Goldman and Kiri Blakeley, "Top 100 Most Powerful Celebrities," *Forbes* (June 15, 2006), http://www.forbes.com/2006/06/12/06celebrities_money-power-celebrities-list_land.html (accessed June 21, 2007).

11. Lillian Kwon, "Joel Osteen Resonates in a Society Where Damnation Messages Don't," *Christian Today* (October 20, 2007), http://www.christianto day.com/article/joel.osteen.resonates.in.society.where.damnation.messages .dont/14090.htm

12. Weather data for Washington, D.C., on January 13, 1982, was obtained from weather database Weather Warehouse, at http://weather-warehouse .com/index.html (accessed March 3, 2007).

13. National Transportation Safety Board, "Air Florida, Inc., Boeing 737–222, N62AF, Collision with 14th Street Bridge Near Washington National Airport, January 13, 1982," NTSB Number AAR-82/08, Government Accession Number PB82–910408 (August 10, 1982): 1–2.

14. National Transportation Safety Board, "Air Florida," 67.

15. Charlotte Linde's assessment of the Air Florida crash was taken from Deborah Tannen's article, "How to Give Orders Like a Man," *New York Times Magazine* (August 28, 1994), http://www9.georgetown.edu/faculty/tannend/ nyt082894.htm

16. National Transportation Safety Board, "Air Florida," 114–133.

17. National Transportation Safety Board, "Air Florida," 68.

18. Ibid.

19. For more on the pronoun study, read Laura Madson's and Jennifer Shoda'a article: "Alternating Between Masculine and Feminine Pronouns: Does Essay Topic Affect Readers' Perceptions?" *Sex Roles* 54, nos. 3–4 (February 2006): 275–284.

20. Interview with Laura Madson, November 30, 2007.

21. The impact of pronouns and children's cognitive processing can be found in an article by Lea Conkright, Dorothy Flannagan, and James Dykes, "Effects of Pronoun Type and Gender Role Consistency on Children's Recall and Interpretation of Stories," *Sex Roles* 43 (2000): 481–497.

22. Information about women using "we" more than men can be found in Deborah Tannen's article: "The Power of Talk: Who Gets Heard and Why," *Harvard Business Review* (September 1, 1995): 141.

23. Ibid.

24. "Unrepentent Ventura Deflects Furor Over Playboy," CNN.com (October 3, 1999), http://www.cnn.com/ALLPOLITICS/stories/1999/10/03/ven tura/ (accessed June 29, 2008).

25. Voter confidence ratings come from a poll commissioned by *Minnesota Public Radio* and *The Pioneer Press* and conducted by Mason-Dixon Political/Media Research, December 8, 1998, http://news.minnesota.pub licradio.org/features/199812/08_newsroom_poll/

26. "Jesse 'The Governor' Ventura," News Hour with Jim Lehrer, PBS, February 14, 2000, http://www.pbs.org/newshour/bb/politics/jan-june00/ventura_2-14.html (accessed June 29, 2008).

27. Patrick Condon, "Jesse Ventura Returns with a Book: Media Critic, 9/11 Conspiracy Believer, Potential President," *The Huffington Post* (January 5, 2008), http://www.huffingtonpost.com/2008/01/05/jesse-ventura-returns-wit_n_79925 .html (accessed February 12, 2008).

28. Larry King Live, April 1, 2008, http://transcripts.cnn.com/TRANSCRIPTS/0804/01/lkl.01.html (accessed June 29, 2008).

29. William Safire, "Shock and Awe: A Tactic, Not a Law Firm," *New York Times Magazine* (March 30, 2003), http://query.nytimes.com/gst/fullpage.html?res = 9A02E6D91230F933A05750C0A9659C8B63&sec = &spon = &pagewanted = 2 (accessed November 26, 2007).

30. Various news stories about the boycott of Dixie Chicks' music can be found, including this one: WCVB TV Boston, "Upset About Bush Remark, Radio Stations Dump Dixie Chicks" (March 14, 2003), http://www.thebostonchannel.com/entertainment/2040104/detail.html (accessed October 10, 2007).

31. Celestine Bohlen, "Think Tank; In New War on Terrorism, Words Are Weapons, Too," *New York Times* online archive (September 21, 2001), http://query.nytimes.com/gst/fullpage.html?res = 9B04EFDA163DF93AA1575AC0A9 679 C8B63 (accessed October 10, 2007).

32. Richard Siklos, "The Man Who Would Be Robbins, Covey, and Chopra," *Fortune* (April 8, 2008), http://money.cnn.com/2008/04/03/pf/siklos_James_Ray.fortune/index.htm

33. To learn more about Daw and Dougherty's study, see: David Biello, "Scientists Identify Brain Region Responsible for Risk and Reward," *Scientific American*, June 15, 2006, http://www.sciam.com/article.cfm?id = scientists-identify-brain; and Steven Kennerly, Mark Walton, Timothy Behrens, Mark Buckley, and Matthew Rushworth, "Optimal Decision Making and the Anterior Cingulate Cortex," *Nature Neuroscience* 9 (2006): 940–947.

34. Joe Bramhall, "McDonald's Corporation," *Hoovers.com* (retrieved November 27, 2007), and Joe Bramhall, "Yum! Brands, Inc.," *Hoovers.com* (retrieved November 27, 2007).

35. Joe Klein, *Politics Lost* (New York: Broadway Books, 2006), 20–22.

36. For a comprehensive analysis of six separate studies on risk aversion and gaming theory, consult Paul Glimcher and Aldo Rustichini's "Neuroeconomics: The Consilience of Brain and Decision," *Science* 306 (October 15, 2004): 447–452.

37. Klein, *Politics Lost*, 222.

38. Ibid.

39. John Eggerton, "Fox, CNN Most Trusted," *Broadcasting and Cable* (May 3, 2006), http://www.broadcastingcable.com/article/CA6331047.html?display = Breaking + News (accessed June 30, 2006).

40. Ibid.

41. Information on ratings for Bill O'Reilly's show was gleaned from various Nielsen Media Reports for the period 2000–2007.

42. TVNewser, "January Ratings: FNC Has Eight of Top Ten Programs," MediaBistro.com (February 1, 2008), http://www.mediabistro.com/tvnews er/ratings/january_ratings_fnc_has_8_of_top_10_programs_76427.asp

43. Project for Excellence in Journalism, "The State of the News Media 2006: An Annual Report on American Journalism," Journalism.org, http://www.sta teofthenewsmedia.org/2006/narrative_overview_intro.asp?cat = 1&media = 1

44. The Project for Excellence in Journalism, "The State of the News Media 2005: An Annual Report on American Journalism," Journalism.org, http:// stateofthemedia.com/2005/narrative_cabletv_intro.asp?cat = 1&media; eq5

45. TVNewser, "January Ratings."

46. The Project for Excellence in Journalism, "The State of the News Media 2007," Journalism.org, http://www.stateofthenewsmedia.org/2007/narrative_ cabletv_audience.asp?cat = 3&media = 6 (retrieved May 2, 2008).

47. The Project for Excellence in Journalism, "The State of the News Media 2004: An Annual Report on American Journalism," Journalism.org (2004), http://www.stateofthenewsmedia.org/2004/narrative_localtv_intro.asp?cat = 1&media = 6 (accessed February 19, 2008).

48. Perhaps the most famous study on familiarity and brand preferences is: Samuel M. McClure, Jian Li, Damon Tomlin, Kim S. Cypert, Latané M. Montague, and P. Read Montague: "Neural Correlates of Behavioral Prefer- ence for Culturally Familiar Drinks," Neuron 44, no. 2 (October 14, 2004): 379–387.

49. Harlan K. Ullman and James P. Wade, Shock and Awe: Achieving Rapid Dominance (Washington, D.C., Center for Advanced Concepts and Tech- nology, 1996). Accessed via project Gutenberg, E-book #7259 (January 2005), http://www.gutenberg.org/dirs/etext05/skawe10.txt (accessed De- cember 1, 2007).

50. TVNewser, "January Ratings."

51. Dahlia Lithwick, "Graceless: Did Nancy Grace Kill Melinda Duckett?" Slate (September 15, 2006), http://www.slate.com/id/2149686/ (accessed November 2, 2007).

CHAPTER 6: WORDS, NAMES, AND STORY LINES WITH ADDICTIVE APPEAL

1. Bill Werde, "The Nation; We've Got Algorithm, but How About Soul?" New York Times (March 21, 2004), http://www.nytimes.com/2004/03/21/ weekinreview/21werd.html (accessed December 21, 2007).

2. For the complete study on lyrics that occur most frequently in number-one hits, see: Beth Logan and Ruth Dhanaraj, "Automatic Prediction of Hit Songs," presented at the International Conference on Music Information

Retrieval, September 11, 2005. Available at http://www.hpl.hp.com/techre
ports/2005/HPL-2005-149.html

3. Dr. Beth Logan, in a telephone interview with the author, December 19,
2007.

4. David Dye, "Norah Jones: Sultry, Jazzy and Real," September 21, 2007,
http://www.npr.org/templates/story/story.php?storyId=14596005 (accessed June 30, 2008).

5. Hit Song Science is a company that has accurately predicted breakout
songs from musicians. The company claims to have identified specific
mathematical patterns that all hit songs adhere to. For more information,
visit http://www.hitsongscience.com

6. Richard Brooks, "Agatha Christie's Grey Cells Mystery," *The Sunday Times*
(December 18, 2005), http://www.timesonline.co.uk/tol/news/uk/article
767471.ece (accessed June 30, 2008.)

7. BBC News, "Linguists Study Christie's Appeal," BBC (December 18,
2005), http://news.bbc.co.uk/2/hi/entertainment/4539956.stm (accessed
June 16, 2007).

8. Ibid.

9. Much research exists on the relatively new fields in neuroacoustics and
neuroaesthetics. Some resources used for this chapter include: John-George
Smeaton, "The Future of Sound Design," University of Plymouth School
of Computing, Communications & Electronics (April 2007): 4–26; Robin
Eve, "Rhythm in Interaction," *Research Journal of the School of Environ-
mental Studies, Himeji Institute of Technology* (2004): 1–10; Robin Eve,
"Music as Representational Art: Parallels Between Linguistic and Musical
Structures," *Research Journal of the School of Environmental Studies,
Himeji Institute of Technology* 4 (2002): 119–131; Colwyn Trevarthen,
"Musicality and the Intrinsic Motive Pulse: Evidence from Human Psycho-
biology and Infant Communication," *Musicae Scientiae*, Special Issue
(1999): 155–215.

10. Charles Q. Choi, "Chatty Cavemen? Me Neanderthal, Talk Good," *Live
Science* (October 18, 2007), http://www.livescience.com/health/071018
-neanderthal-language.html (accessed January 9, 2008).

11. For information on the cycles and timing of our major biological processes,
consult Robin Eve's "Rhythm in Interaction," http://www.shse.u-hyo
go.ac.jp/robineve/AcaPub2004.htm (accessed December 21, 2007).

12. For a detailed discussion of how we learn and what we remember from
presentations, consult Esther Bagno, Bat-Sheva Eylon, and Uri Gamiel,
"From Fragmented Knowledge to a Knowledge Structure: Linking the
Domains of Mechanics and Electromagnetism," *American Journal of Physics* 68, no. 7 (2000): S16–S26.

13. For more on the language-biology connection, read: Grazyna Fosar and
Franz Bludorf, *Vernetzte Intelligenz* (Interlaced Intelligence), ISBN
3930243237. This book is only available in German, but there are various
translation services available that will translate entire books, such as Free
translation.com

14. For more on our biological preferences for speaking cadence, see: Eliot D. Chapple, "The Unbounded Reaches of Anthropology as a Research Science, and Some Working Hypothesis," *American Anthropologist* 82, no. 4 (1980): 741–758; and Frederick Turner and Ernst Poppel, "The Neural Lyre: Poetic Meter, the Brain and Time," *Poetry* 72 (October 17, 2001): 277–309. (Reprinted in Frederick Turner, *Natural Classicism: Essays on Literature and Science* (New York: Paragon House Publishers, 1985), 61–108.

15. Turner and Poppel, "The Neural Lyre," 61–108.

16. Vicki Kunkel, et al., "Rates of Speech of JFK, MLK and Ronald Reagan: A Metered Analysis of Five Presentations from Three of Our Country's Most Persuasive Speakers" (June 2000). This was a study conducted for one of the author's U.S. Senatorial clients in the 2000 election. The other authors of this research paper were part of the senator's campaign staff, and they insisted on anonymity in this book.

17. Robin Eve, "Rhythm in Interaction," 1–10.

18. For an in-depth review of the appeal of soap operas, read Robert C. Allen, "Soap Opera," Museum of Broadcast Communications, http://www.mu seum.tv/archives/etv/S/htmlS/soapopera/soapopera.htm (accessed December 18, 2007).

19. Ibid.

20. Shlomo Vaknin, C.Ht, "Talk to Influence: Nested Loops 2.0," *NLP Weekly Magazine*, http://www.nlpweekly.com/?p = 447 (accessed October 12, 2007).

21. Leander Kahney, "Music Magic Found in the Shuffle," *Wired* (April 16, 2004), http://www.wired.com/culture/lifestyle/news/2004/04/63068 (accessed June 10, 2006).

22. Ibid.

23. The explanation of the brain as a self-rewarding system was discussed by Turner and Poppel in "The Neural Lyre."

24. Ibid.

25. National Institutes of Health, *NIDA InfoFacts: Marijuana*, http://www .nida.nih.gov/infofacts/marijuana.html (accessed July 15, 2008).

26. Dr. Jeff Rudski, "*Harry Potter* and the End of the Road: Parallels with Addiction," in an interview with the author, February 26, 2008.

27. Professor Hogan's book is one of the best—and most reader-friendly— accounts of narrative universals in literature that I have found. He has written six other books on the subject, but for an easy-to-understand and thorough overview, read *The Mind and Its Stories: Narrative Universals and Human Emotion* (New York: Cambridge University Press, 2003).

28. Louis Menand, "Cat People: What Dr. Seuss Really Taught Us," *The New Yorker* 33 (December 23, 2002), http://www.newyorker.com/archive/2002/ 12/23/021223crat_atlarge (accessed June 30, 2008).

29. Franz Boaz, "Mythology and Folklore," *General Anthropology* (Boston: D.C. Heath and Company, 1938), 609–626.

30. Virginia Wheeler, "Flopbusters Aim for Box Office," *The Sun* (August 27,

2007), http://www.thesun.co.uk/sol/homepage/news/article266249.ece (accessed January 21, 2008).

31. Malcolm Gladwell, "The Formula: What If You Built a Machine to Predict Hit Movies?" *The New Yorker* (October 16, 2006), http://www.newyorker .com/archive/2006/10/16/061016fa_fact6?currentPage = 1 (accessed February 13, 2008).

32. Bruce Porter, "Is Solitary Confinement Driving Charlie Chase Crazy?" *New York Times* (November 8, 1998), http://query.nytimes.com/gst/full page.html?res = 940CE3DC113FF93BA35752C1A96E958260 (accessed June 30, 2008).

33. Stuart Grassian, "Psychiatric Effects of Solitary Confinement," Declaration submitted in *Madrid v. Gomez*, 889F, Supp. 1146 (September 1993).

34. Ibid.

35. To learn more about rhythms and beat universals in language across cultures, consult Turner and Poppel in "The Neural Lyre."

36. Turner and Poppel, "The Neutral Lyre."

37. Ibid.

CHAPTER 7: GOOD VIBRATIONS

1. To learn more about Jonathan Berger's studies on sonification, see Krissy Clark, "The Sound of Cancer, and Golf," *Weekend America*, American Public Media (January 12, 2008), http://weekendamerica.publicradio.org/pro grams/2008/01/12/staticTemplate.html (accessed January 12, 2008).

2. Information about Aaron Naparstek was taken from the blog "Streetsblog," where he is Editor-in-Chief. http://www.streetsblog.org/author/aaron/

3. To view Aaron Naparstek's blog and the entry about his voting habits, visit http://www.naparstek.com/2005_09_01_archive.php (accessed August 12, 2007).

4. Quote taken from Aaron Naparstek's blog, http://www.naparstek.com/ 2005_09_01_archive.php (accessed August 12, 2007).

5. For more information on PET scans and the parts of the brain associated with emotions, see Helen S. Mayberg, et al., "Reciprocal Limbic-Cortical Function and Negative Mood: Converging PET Findings in Depression and Normal Sadness," *American Journal of Psychiatry* 156, no. 5 (May 1999): 675–682. The best work I have found to date on how the brain processes emotion is Edmund T. Rolls, *The Brain and Emotion* (New York: Oxford University Press, 1999).

6. For the story on using our sound wave pattern software to help couples come up with names for their newborns, read Lacey Major's story, "Name that Baby," *Pregnancy and Newborn* (December 6, 2006): 83.

7. For the study on the impact of initials and performance, see Association for Psychological Science, "What's in a Name? Initials Linked to Success, Study Shows," *ScienceDaily* (November 15, 2007), http://www.sciencedaily .com/releases/2007/11/071114111138.htm (accessed December 26, 2007).

8. For a complete discussion of the research on stock performance and stock names, consult: Princeton University, "Stock Performance Tied To Ease of Pronouncing Company's Name," *ScienceDaily* (May 30, 2006), http://www.sciencedaily.com/releases/2006/05/060530083959.htm (accessed October 30, 2007).

9. To learn more about the experiments on the impact of sounds on plants, read Maria-Roxana Raceu and Andreea Telespan, "From the World of Those Who 'Talk' Without Words," International Environmental Project Olympid (2007), http://www.inepo.com/english/uplFiles_resim/Where%20are%20you%20sweet%20chil dhood.doc

10. To learn more about Dr. Emoto's experiments on the effect of sound wave vibrations on water crystals, see WellnessGoods.com, "Miraculous Messages from Water: How Water Reflects Our Consciousness," Life Enthusiast Co-Op, http://www.life-enthusiast.com/index/Articles/Emoto (accessed June 19, 2008).

11. Patricia Howes, et al., "Vibrato and Its Effect on Audience Perceptions of Emotion in Singing," National Voice Center, University of Sydney, Sydney, Australia (PAS-Conference, October 3–5, 2002), http://coo.med.rug.nl/pas/Poster%20abstracts/Howes_po_abst.htm (accessed January 15, 2008).

12. Henry Pleasants, *The Great American Popular Singers* (New York: Simon and Schuster, 1974), 274–275.

13. Wake Forest University Baptist Medical Center, "Americans Speak Out, Select the 'Best and Worst Voices in America' in Online Polling by the Center for Voice Disorders of Wake Forest University," press release, September 10, 2001, http://www.nrcdxas.org/articles/voices.html (accessed June 12, 2007).

14. Purdue University, "Linguist Tunes In to Pitch Processing in Brain," *ScienceDaily* (February 20, 2008), http://www.sciencedaily.com /releases/2008/02/080216114856.htm (accessed February 26, 2008).

15. David Epstein, "Men Hear Women's Melodies," *Discover* magazine (November 22, 2005); Diraj S. Sokhi, Michael D. Hunter, Iain D. Wilkinson, and Peter W. R. Woodruff, "Male and Female Voices Activate Distinct Regions in the Male Brain," *NeuroImage* 27, no. 3 (September 2005): 572–578.

16. Jason Ryan and Theresa Cook, "Gonzales Defends U.S. Attorney Firings, Resists Resignation: Embattled Attorney General Faces Tough Questions in Hearing That Could Decide Fate," *ABCNews.com* (April 19, 2007), http://abcnews.go.com/Politics/story?id=3057743&page=1 (accessed December 15, 2007).

17. Poll information for the 1996 election was found at: http://www.cnn.com/ALLPOLITICS/1996/elections/ (accessed July 15, 2007).

18. The Associated Press, "Doctor Says Voice on TV Caused Seizures," *New York Times* (July 11, 1991), http://query.nytimes.com/gst/fullpage.html?res=9D0CEED81030F932A25754C0A96 79 58260 (accessed January 22, 2008).

19. Steven Halpern, "Sound Healing, Music Therapy: Sound Health, Inner Peace and Beyond," *The Monthly Aspectarian*, http://www.lightworks.com/monthlyaspectarian/2003/September/halpern.htm (accessed January 23, 2008).

20. Epstein, "Men Hear Women's Melodies"; Sokhi et al., "Male and Female Voices Activate Distinct Regions in the Male Brain."

21. Jules Combarieu, *Music: Its Laws and Evolution (Authorized Translation)*. International Scientific Series, Vol. XCII (New York: Appleton, 1910).

22. Brad Evenson, "Why We Can't Get That Song out of Our Heads: With Rare Exceptions, the Brain Has a Deep Affinity for Music," *National Post* (July 7, 2003): A1.

23. Acharts.us, "Gnarls Barkley: Crazy," http://acharts.us/song/8190 (accessed July 6, 2008).

24. *BBC News*, "Crazy Song Makes Musical History," BBC (April 2, 2006), http://news.bbc.co.uk/1/hi/entertainment/4870150.stm (accessed May 4, 2008).

25. Ben Novack Biography, http://www.bennovak.com/biography.asp (accessed July 14, 2008).

26. Hit Song Science, http://www.hitsongscience.com (accessed January 24, 2008).

27. CD Universe, "Norah Jones Come Away with Me CD," http://www.cduniverse.com/search/xx/music/pid/2900523/a/Come + Away + With + Me.htm (accessed January 24, 2007).

28. Ibid.

29. Ibid.

30. Although five studies support the effect of music on shopping behavior, two that were used for this reference include: Julie Baker, A. Parasuraman, Dhruv Grewal, and Glenn Voss, "The Influence of Multiple Store Environment Cues on Perceived Merchandise Value and Patronage Interactions," *Journal of Marketing* 66, no. 2 (April 2002): 120–141; and Richard Yalch and Eric Spangenberg, "Effects of Store Music on Shopping Behavior," *Journal of Consumer Marketing* 7, no. 2 (1990): 55–63.

31. Paul King, "Mozart Exerts a Classical Pull on Diners' Wallets, Study Says—Side Dishes—Classical Music Played in a Restaurant Increases Spending," *Nation's Restaurant News* (October 20, 2003), http://findarticles.com/p/articles/mi_m3190/is_/ai_109271462 (accessed July 6, 2008 via FindArticles.com).

32. Jillian C. Sweeney and Fiona Wyber, "The Role of Cognitions and Emotions in the Music-Approach-Avoidance Behavior Relationship," *Journal of Services Marketing* 16 no. 1 (2002): 51–69.

33. Joseph Lanza, *Elevator Music: A Surreal History of Muzak, Easy-Listening, and Other Moodsong* (New York: St. Martin's Press, 1994), 17, 194–195.

34. For a complete description on how brain wave synchronization works, see Udo Will and Eric Berg, "Brainwave Synchronization and Entrainment to Periodic Acoustic Stimuli," *Neuroscience Letters* 424, Issue 1 (31 August

2007): 55–60 and Jeffrey Thompson, "Acoustic Brainwave Entrainment with Binaural Beats," http://www.therelaxationcompany.com/acbrenwibibe .html (accessed July 6, 2008).

35. Richard E. Madden, et al., "Low Intensity Electrostimulation Improves Human Learning of a Psychomotor Task," *American Journal of Electromedicine* 4, no. 2 (1987): 41–45.

36. Janet Young and Michelle D. Pain, *The Zone: Evidence of a Universal Phenomenon for Athletes Across Sports* (Melbourne, Australia: Monash University, 1999), http://www.athleticinsight.com/Vol1Iss3/Empirical_Zone.htm (accessed July 2, 2008).

37. I-Doser.com (accessed January 23, 2008).

38. The Associated Press, "Cincinnati Symphony Orchestra Attendance Plummets," Fox 19 WXIX TV (September 3, 2007), http://fox19.com/Global/story.asp?s = 6954499 (accessed December 21, 2007).

39. "The Pitch Game," *Time* (August 9, 1971), http://www.time.com/time/magazine/article/0,9171,903087,00.html (accessed January 22, 2008).

40. Patrick Thilmany, "Music and Your Health—The Relevance of Concert Pitch," *The Association of North American Waldorf Music Educators*, http://waldorfmusic.org/thilmany.html (accessed January 22, 2008).

41. Romila Thapar, "Cyclic and Linear Time in Early India," *Museum International* 57, no. 3 (2005): 19–31.

42. David Pratt, "Patterns in Nature" (January 2006), http://faculty.wlc.edu/buelow/MFL/Patterns%20in%20nature.pdf

43. Brian David Andersen, "The Keys, Locks and Doors of the Great Pyramids," Book-of-Thoth.com (August 18, 2006), http://www.book-of-thoth .com/article1600.html (accessed January 22, 2008).

44. Martin Doutre, "Understanding Stonehenge part 2: An Analysis of Stonehenge," De Danann Publishers, http://www.celticnz.co.nz/articles.html (accessed December 16, 2007).

45. Dolf Zillman, Charles F. Aust, Kathleen D. Hoffman, Curtis C. Love, Virginia L. Ordman, Janice T. Pope, Patrick D. Siegler, and Rhonda J. Gibson; "Radical Rap: Does It Further Ethnic Division?" *Basic and Applied Social Psychology* 16, nos. 1, 2 (February 1995): 1–25.

46. David Huron, "Is Music an Evolutionary Adaptation?" *Annals of the New York Academy of Sciences* 930, no. 1 (2001): 43–61.

47. Isabelle Peretz, Anne J. Blood, Virginia Penhune, and Robert Zatorre, "Cortical Deafness to Dissonance," *Brain* 124, no. 5 (May 2001): 928–940.

CHAPTER 8: WHAT OUR MINDS REALLY SEE

1. Wayne Friedman, "Superbowl vs. The Oscars: For TV Ratings, It Doesn't Matter Who's Playing," *TV Watch*, January 24, 2007, http://publications .mediapost.com/index.cfm?fuseaction = Articles.showArticle& art_aid = 54 423, (accessed July 2, 2008).

2. Ratings information for the Academy Awards was gleaned from Anita

Gates, "The Loser Is: Ratings for Awards," *New York Times* (February 24, 2005), http://www.nytimes.com/2005/02/24/arts/television/24awar .html (accessed July 2, 2008).

3. Wayne Friedman, "Superbowl vs. The Oscars: For TV Ratings, It Doesn't Matter Who's Playing," *TV Watch*, January 24, 2007, http://publications .mediapost.com/index.cfm?fuseaction = Articles.showArticle&art_aid = 5 4423 (accessed July 2, 2008).

4. For a detailed explanation of polls on environmental issues and global warming, check out: Environment News Service, "Polls: Water, Warming, Travel, Youth and Green Guilt," Environment News Service (April 23, 2007), http://www.ens-newswire.com/ens/apr2007/2007–04–23–03.asp (accessed August 25, 2007).

5. Statistics on the percentage of Americans who say global warming is a key issue was taken from a nationwide survey of 1,017 American adults that was conducted on behalf of the Yale Center for Environmental Law & Policy by Global Strategy Group, February 5–11, 2007. The results were published at: Yale Center for Environmental Law & Policy, "2007 Environment Survey—Key Findings" (March 5, 2007).

6. Ibid.

7. There are several excellent explanations of the mirror neuron research, including J. Madeline Nash, "The Gift of Mimicry," *Time* (January 19, 2007): 108–113; Robert Krulwich, "Monkey Do, Monkey See," *NOVA Science Now* (January 25, 2005), http://www.pbs.org/wgbh/nova/sciencenow/ 3204/01-monkey.html (accessed August 15, 2007); and "Mirror Neurons," *Nova Science Now*, http://www.pbs.org/wgbh/nova/sciencenow/3204/01.html (accessed August 15, 2007).

8. WGN-TV Chicago, "Working Alone," WGN 9 P.M. newscast (February 20, 2008).

9. Because the congressman I worked with is still in office, and also because of a confidentiality agreement I signed with his campaign not to disclose that I had worked with him, I am not able to give his name in this book.

10. "Mirror Neurons," *Nova Science Now*.

11. Madeline Nash, "The Gift of Mimicry," *Time* 110 (January 29, 2007), http://www.time.com/time/magazine/article/0,9171,1580423,00.html

12. The information on the inattentional blindness study comes from Daniel J. Simons and Christopher Chabris, "Gorillas in Our Midst: Sustained Inattentional Blindness for Dynamic Events," *Perception* 28 (1999): 1059–1074.

13. The study about effects of sex and violence on brand recall for TV ads was taken from Brad Bushman, "That Was a Great Commercial, but What Were They Selling? Effects of Violence and Sex on Memory for Violent and Sexual Ads," *Journal of Applied Social Psychology* 37 (2007): 1784–1796.

14. Information on change blindness was gleaned from M. F. Land, "Motion and Vision: Why Animals Move Their Eyes." *Journal of Comparative Physiology* 185 (1999): 341–352.

15. Details of Fisher's study on our primal need for aesthetics came from Kate

Ramsayer, "Images of a Social Brain," Baylor College of Medicine, http://www.bcm.edu/fromthelab/vol01/is3/02nov_n1.htm (accessed February 25, 2008).

16. Vilayanur S. Ramachandran and William Herstein, "The Science of Art: A Neurological Theory of Aesthetic Experience," *Journal of Consciousness Studies* 6, nos. 6, 7 (1999): 15–51.

17. Staff, Wellcome Trust and World Science, "Brain region for adventurousness reported found," June 25, 2008, http://www.world-science.net/other news/080625_adventure.htm (accessed July 1, 2008).

18. Ibid.

19. Jackie Craven, "Sacred Geometry," About.com, http://architecture.about.com/od/ideasapproaches/a/geometry.htm (accessed June 15, 2008).

20. For more information on Golden Ratio patterns found in our everyday lives, consult Bruce Rawles, "Sacred Geometry Home Page," Geometrycode.com, http://www.geometrycode.com/sg/index.shtml (accessed July 14, 2007).

CHAPTER 9: THE LESSONS OF INSTANT APPEAL

1. Larry Sloman, *Reefer Madness: The History of Marijuana in America* (New York: St. Martin's Griffin, 1998), 56, 65–83, 129, 130. Information on the taxing of marijuana can also be found at: Shaffer Library of Drug Policy, Transcripts of Congressional Hearings, "The Marijuana Tax Act of 1937: Additional Statement of H. J. Anslinger, Commissioner of Narcotics," http://www.druglibrary.org/schaffer/hemp/taxact/t10a.htm (accessed July 7, 2008).

2. This article and others penned by Anslinger are available from several sources, including: H J. Anslinger papers, 1835–1970 (bulk 1918–1963), Accession 1959–0006H, Historical Collections and Labor Archives, Special Collections Library, University Libraries, Pennsylvania State University, "Articles on Narcotics by Harry Anslinger, 1933–1961," Box 1, Folder 12; and Reefer Madness, "Excerpts from Marijuana: Assassination of Youth," http://www.reefermadness.org/propaganda/youth.html (accessed July 7, 2008.)

3. Armand L. Mauss, *Social Problems as Social Movements* (Philadelphia: J. B. Lippincott, 1975), 258.

4. Sloman, *Reefer Madness*, 29–31, 225, 231–33.

5. Data taken from John Helmer's *Drugs and Minority Oppression* (New York: Seabury Press), accessed via ANNALS *of the American Academy of Political and Social Science* 426, no. 1 (1976): 259–260.

6. Sloman, *Reefer Madness*.

7. This article and others penned by Anslinger are available from several sources, including: H J. Anslinger papers, 1835–1970 (bulk 1918–1963), Accession 1959–0006H, Historical Collections and Labor Archives, Special

Collections Library, University Libraries, Pennsylvania State University, "Articles on Narcotics by Harry Anslinger, 1933–1961," Box 1, Folder 12; and Reefer Madness, "Excerpts from Marijuana: Assassination of Youth," http://www.reefermadness.org/propaganda/youth.html (accessed July 7, 2008.)

8. George W. Bush, annual State of the Union Address (January 29, 2002).
9. CNN, "Report: No WMD Stockpiles in Iraq," (October 7, 2004), http://wwwy.cnn.com/2004/WORLD/meast/10/06/iraq.wmd.report/ (accessed February 26, 2008).

Acknowledgments

With apologies to Hillary Clinton, it practically takes a village to write a book.

Instant Appeal, like many books by first-time published authors, came about when someone said, "You really should write a book about this." That someone was a business colleague, Vickie Sullivan, who saw potential in the germ of an idea I had about what causes instantaneous and long-lasting appeal in people, products, and ideas. Before Vickie's declaration, I had simply been a voracious researcher who implemented and tested my theories with my clients. But she convinced me that my ideas were good enough to "bring the rest of the world in on the secret." Thank you, Ms. Sullivan! The book would have never come about without your shove, er, I mean, encouragement.

This book would also not have come about—at least not as quickly—had it not been for a serendipitous interview with business writer Gary Stern in New York City. Gary was interviewing me for a story he was working on when, just as the interview ended, he casually asked, "Do you have a book I could mention as part of your credentials in the story?" I told him I had a book *partially* written, but nothing complete. He asked if I had an agent. I didn't. And he graciously offered to send a summary of my book to his literary agent. Gary, I will never be able to thank you enough for your kind actions that led me to agent Linda Konner. (And I still owe you lunch and a latte next time I'm in New York!)

And to Linda, thank you for seeing the value in my original book proposal, and suggesting "tweaks" to make it more palatable to publishers. The many positive responses we received from various publishers are a testament to your expertise.

Speaking of publishers, I'd like to acknowledge the entire team at AMACOM, starting with Executive Editor Ellen Kadin, who immediately saw the value of *Instant Appeal*. Ellen was a tireless advocate of the book and was my most enthusiastic cheerleader throughout the publishing process. Thank you, Ellen. Many others at AMACOM also deserve thanks, including Erika Spelman, who brilliantly orchestrated the copyediting and proofreading processes; Lydia Lewis, whose diligence and hard work kept the book production on schedule under some very tight timeline pressures; Irene Majuk for a wonderful job at promotions; and Sabrina Bowers, who designed the look of the book's interior. The entire team put in many long hours on my behalf to make sure the book had just the right title, just the right feel, and just the right look in the overall design.

Special thanks to Senior Development Editor Barry Richardson and content editor Chris Murray, who clearly understood the message of *Instant Appeal* and suggested subtle yet monumentally important changes that made the book much better than it was originally. Michael Warrell of Design Solutions did a fabulous job on the cover design under some very tight time deadlines, and AMACOM Creative Director Cathleen Ouderkirk and her team were outstanding in identifying tweaks to make the cover design even better than it already was. Tina Orem is the most astute and conscientious editor I know. Tina, you are truly talented at what you do.

Suzy Farren was such a godsend for reading and critiquing my original and very rough-draft manuscript. Your quick mind and keen insights helped me to focus my message more clearly. The same goes for Mark Hughes, author of the best-selling book *Buzz Marketing*, who volunteered his expertise and offered brief but valuable editorial guidance after reviewing sample chapters.

Some people simply helped me keep my sanity through the whole process. Special thanks go to Michele Jochner, whom I could always count on when I needed to run an idea past someone or just needed to talk (or vent). Your friendship and support will never be forgotten. Then there was my British comic-relief pal, John Cromarty, who kept me in stitches with his "Britishisms" whenever I was having a stress meltdown. (His favorite was, "You bloody plonker! You're really off your trolley today, aren't you?" Somehow, that always made me laugh. As did his wry sense of humor. Thanks, John.)

Instant Appeal required a lot of research, and the folks at many local university research libraries deserve a special mention. Many thanks to the ever-helpful information assistants at the following colleges and universities: The University of Chicago, Northwestern University, Wheaton College, Benedictine University, Elmhurst College, Columbia College, and the University of Illinois.

But there's one group that warrants special recognition and thanks. In addition to gratitude, I would like to send out my heartfelt sympathy to the students, faculty, and staff at Northern Illinois University in DeKalb, Illinois. I often preferred to do my research sessions on your peaceful campus, in the laid-back and friendly setting. The placid backdrop was a welcome retreat and well worth the drive out of Chicago. I was deeply saddened by the tragedy of the deadly 2008 Valentine's Day shootings on your campus and moved by your strength in coping with the unthinkable. You are all a special group of people, and I am honored to have met some of you in the process of writing this book. Every person—students and library personnel alike—whom I encountered on your campus, without exception, was always so kind and helpful with my many (and I'm sure often annoying) requests. And many students had the patience of a saint, yet never complained, while I tied up the copy machines or microfiche. Thank you for being part of my life while I was researching *Instant Appeal*. Your strength, perseverance, and fortitude in the aftermath of tragedy are very appealing indeed!

Index